A Peacock or a Crow:

Stories, Interviews and Commentaries on Romanian Adoptions

Victor Groza, PhD

Daniela Ileana, MSSA

Ivor Irwin, MFA

Romanian Proverb: Nu umblati cu cioara vopsita (Do not tell me a crow is a peacock.)

Published by: *Williams Custom Publishing*, Div.

Lakeshore Communications

24100 Lakeshore Blvd.

Euclid, OH 44123

(216) 731-0234

Visit our home page at: http://www.willese-press.com

A Peacock or A Crow:

Stories, Interviews and Commentaries of

Romanian Adoptees

Printed in the United States of America

B C D E F G

ISBN 1-893435-02-4

This publication is designed to provide accurate and authoritative information with regard to the subject matter involved. It is sold with the understanding that the publisher is not engaged in rendering legal, accounting or other professional advice. If legal advice or other expert assistance is required, the services of a qualified professional person should be sought.

-From: **A Declaration of Principles**, jointly adopted by a Committee of the American Bar Association and a Committee of Publishers and Associations.

Editorial Services and Cover Design: CCS Associates, Hudson,OH
Cover art copyright www.arttoday.com
Cover photo by Tina Leto

Dedications

To my grandmother, Verona Bodea Groza Deac, and my Aunt, Florence Smith (Florica Deak), who taught me the most about being Romanian.

victor groza

Pentru mami, tati, Stelian, Dan si maica: multumesc pentru sprijinul si dragostea voastra. ….also dedicated to the one I love, Donald T. Noda.

daniela f. ileana

To my wife, Elsie Vazquez Irwin. Stiu puritatea!

ivor irwin

Table of Contents

The Crow   vii

Acknowledgments   ix

Introduction   xiii

Chapter 1:   Romania: History, Mentality and Culture   1

Chapter 2:   A Family Tells Their Story   21

Chapter 3:   Dickens, Boys Town or Purgatory: Are Institutions a Place to Call Home?   25

Chapter 4:   Ivan and Ciprian: A Child Lost and Found   43

Chapter 5:   The International Adoption Circus   51

Chapter 6:   Adoption Stories During and After the Chaos   61

Chapter 7:   The Children Adopted from Romania: Myth and Reality   97

Chapter 8:   A Spiritual Calling to Adopt   111

Chapter 9:   Saints, Charlatans, Witch Doctors and Good Nails   125

Chapter 10:   Adopting a Child from Overseas   151

Chapter 11:   Lessons Learned   163

Epilogue: The Road to Hell Is…   171

Afterwards: When Three Paths Crossed   175

Appendices   189

The Peacock   195

The Crow

Once upon a time…a raven clan wasn't sure that a crow quite fit into the family. The crow, not sure if he was wanted, decided to venture away from home and friends. Suddenly, in a farmyard, he met a pair of peacocks. What wonderful birds they were! The crow had never seen such beautiful feathers, and he timidly asked the regal-looking birds what they were. "We're peacocks," one of them replied, spreading its tail. And as the peacock strutted about, showing the crow his magnificent feathers, he screamed, as peacocks do. From that day on, he could not help thinking about the peacocks and his own plain feathers. "What fine feathers! They must be so happy, being so beautiful. Surely, everyone loves and admires them" And he gazed down sadly at his own ugly plumes. He even stopped looking at himself in the pond water, for every time he did so, it made him even more depressed. He got into the habit of spying on the peacocks, and the more he watched them strut royally around, the more envious he was of their beauty. One day, he noticed that one of the peacocks had dropped a feather. When the sun went down, the crow picked it up and hid it away. For days on end, he watched the peacocks and found another feather. When he had four, he could wait no longer: he stuck the peacock feathers onto his own tail, using pine resin, and started to parade up and down for his family and friends to admire. "Just look at my gorgeous tail!" he said proudly. "I'm not ugly! Out of my way, you moth-eaten ravens!" The other birds' amazement soon changed to indignation, and then they started to laugh. "You're nothing but a crow yourself, even with those flashy feathers!" they jeered. So off he went to live with the peacocks. When the peacocks set eyes on the stranger, they thought the crow was just another peacock who, for some reason, had lost most of his feathers, and they felt sorry for him. But the crow wanted to attract greater admiration and a foolish idea came into his head. He tried to scream the way the peacocks do when they fan their tails. But the harsh "Craw! Craw! Craw!" quickly betrayed the crow. The furious peacocks pecked the stolen feathers off and chased the crow away. Poor crow! For when, sad and downcast, he went back to his family and friends, he was also given rough treatment. Nobody would speak to him and all the birds turned their backs on him for trying to be what he was not, as well as not being what they expected.

Adapted from: <http://www.geog.umd.edu/EdRes/ReadingRoom/Fiction/FairyTales/vain-crow>

Acknowledgments—Victor Groza

The research and information for this book would not have happened without the help of many agencies, students, colleagues, and friends. The American agencies include The Rocky Mountain Adoption Exchange in Colorado, Four Oaks in Iowa, The National Resource Center for Special Needs Adoptions in Michigan, the University of Iowa, and the Mandel School of Applied Social Sciences (MSASS) at Case Western Reserve University (CWRU) in Ohio. The Romanian agencies include Holt International-Romania, Speranza, University of Iasi, and World Vision-Romania. American colleagues and friends that I wish to express appreciation to include (in no particular order): Dixie Van De Fleur Davis, Mary Sullivan, Anne Gruenewald, Jim Ernst, Karin Turner McKeone, Kelly Corcran, Don Kiesewetter, Joan Heifner, Leon Ginsberg, Katie Dunlap, Maureen Marcenko, Sandy McLaughlin, Sister Katherine Kooney, Katherine Springer, Kathy Remias, Sharon Cermak, and Sana Loue. Special thanks to Alice Johnson—her passion and commitment to Romania is quite remarkable. Romanian colleagues I want to acknowledge: Mihaela Ianasi, Ovidiu Gavrilovici, Martha Iliescu, Violeta Stan, Viorel Prelici, Tibiu Mircea, Maria Roth, Denezia Gal, Dean Dima, Mr. Miftode, Lila Onu, Carmen Luca, and Mia Farkas Spanu. Much appreciation to my Romanian host family—George, Maria, and Ciprian Alexandrescu. I would also like to acknowledge those who worked with me as students between 1991 and 1997: Mark Haines Simeon, Karen Berlin, Steve Pohlmeyer, Joan Shroeder, Steve Marinan, Kathleen Ruyle, Owen Groze, Mary Adams, Harold Ritscher, Cathy Laube, Beth Leakey, Marcy Phillips, Helen Jean Pratt, Scott Gee, Claudia Rose, Joy Bourhill, Sandy Hamilton, Jane Robertson, Patricia Barto, Beverly Vermeer Carol Dankert, Beth Steinberg, Irene Quinlen, Magdalena Wolinski, Beth Steinberg, Carol Cieplinski, Kelly Williams, Barbara Wright, Joanna Johnson, Scott Wasserman, Linda Bailey, Jenny Kattlove, Sarah Kautz, Rachel Foster, Katherine Marks-Caruso, Steve Plumb, Bonnie Eidens, and Darilyn Cardona (sorry if anyone was left out). I had contact with adoptive parents who helped by either reviewing a preliminary draft of the questionnaire used in a survey of adoptive parents of Romanian children, providing us a mailing list, distributing questionnaires to adoptive parents, or providing us with an interview and/or photographs. I want to acknowledge the assistance of Mary Thomas, Alison Pentlock-Folk, Carol Jansen, Carole Stevens, Gloria Smith, Karen LaGripo, Kathy Swanson, Mark Treon, Barbara Knowles, Chris Kleimszak, Kathryn Creedy, Marie Mercer, Pat Denlow, Thais Tepper, Susan Miller, the Meckes Family, the Ficken Family, the White Family, the Korponay family, the Goldstone Family, the Korshak family, the Granade Family, the Smith Family, and the Johnson family. This book represents the combined contribution of these people and organizations who helped us understand the complicated issues in Romania, in Romania's child welfare system, international adoption, and life after international adoption.

ACKNOWLEDGEMENTS

Second, I want to thank the many people who typed interviews, read chapters, and searched archaic sources–all of whom contributed to the development of this book. This includes Deborah Horne, Theresa Wilson, Curtis Proctor, Karen Kaye, Ann Toomey, and Karin McKeone.

Third, I want to thank the Dean of MSASS, Dr. Darlyne Bailey, who provided funding for two years to follow-up parents who adopted children from Romania. Without this funding, the impetus for the book would not have happened. I appreciate all the support we have received from her.

Finally, I want to thank all the families who provided us information and insight. Without their help, willingness to provide information, and dedication, there would not have been a story.

Acknowledgments—Daniela Ileana

I want to thank my parents for taking such a big leap of faith by immigrating to the United States. They left everything they had, including their immediate and extended familes. They left it all so their children could have better lives: freedom, opportunities, and a life without fear of oppression. For their sacrifice, I will always be grateful. A huge thanks to my brother, Stelian, who risked his life by escaping across the Romanian border to try to help our family leave Romania. He strongly believed that medical treatment for my illness, epilepsy, would be better in America. He was right. Thanks, Stely. Thanks to my twin brother, Dan, for encouraging me to go to college, for always believing in me, and for watching out for me for so long. I am grateful to my colleague and friend, Jane Sibley, for her love and support during this project, during graduate school, and through my personal life transitions. I also want to extend a special thanks to the CWRU-MSASS students that traveled and worked with me in 1994 and 1995; I want to include acknowledging Justin Henry and the Romanian project leader from Timisoara, Lila Onu. Last but not least I want to thank my little nephew, Jonah Benjamin Ileana, for being such a great source of joy and inspiration for my soul.

Professionally, I want to extend a special thanks to Hill House for giving me the opportunity to take the time off I needed to go back to Romania and work on projects. I would not have been able to go back to school and complete my masters degree if Hill House had not been so flexible in accommodating my work schedule. Special thanks to Lisa Middleton-Courtot, who taught me how to be a professional. You will always be an inspiration and great role model to me. Thanks to Dave Titus for his support and to Judy Peters. Judy, as I am writing this, I am sending you my best wishes.

Acknowledgments—Ivor Irwin

First and foremost, I want to acknowledge my long departed grandmother, Rachel Israelovich, for planting the seeds of curiosity in my head concerning Romania and Romanians. We were uncouth. We talked as we ate at a breakfast table that was dense with repartée and curiosity. I was brought up to believe that truth was not expedient. "Du must mach zich nit visendik!" That means, more or less, "You must only pretend to be ignorant." Expedience, materialism, and ignorance always win in the short run; still, nobody knows better than the Romanian people themselves that although hanging in there and shouting out the truth may lead to the destruction of the physical body, it cannot hinder the soul or spirit.

There are many people who helped me get the writing right. James Walton-Myers of Evanston, Illinois; Pastor David Minor of the Gospel Tabernacle Church of Coudersort, Pennsylvania; Shennan Muriel, Director of the Department of Children and Family Services in Springfield, Illinois; Nancy Cocoriu of the M. C. International Adoption Agency of Bloomfield, Michigan; Doctor Mark Braun of "Doctors without Borders" of Chicago, Illinois; Patricia 'Poodle' Popescu of Manchester, England; Professor Peter Schneeman of Pennsylvania State University; Nina Cassian, Richard Elman, Sabastian Taralunga, Arpid Müller, Tina Leto, Kevin Craig; and, my heroine, the righteous fighter of the good fight, Nancy Wellhousen, rarely home in Tulsa, Oklahoma, mostly found in Suceava, Romania, building 'Bridges for Children' in Romania.

The two people who really helped me keep a sense of truth and perspective are Danny Gaga of Iasi and my wife, Elsie Vazquez Irwin. Danny, you taught me so much. Unfortunately, as you insisted, the "powers" are everywhere; they speak in righteous terms, own sharp knives and have compromised everybody, especially themselves. Over endless shots of tzuica, you taught me to toast, "Ultima Solutie, inca o revolutie." Indeed, the final solution is not a revolution. Life goes on, Danny. I miss you and the hospitality of your family. And, no! The colleagues I wrote this book with are not members of Securitaté.

Last, but not least, comes my long-suffering wife, Elsie. You carried our son, worked and kept things sane while I wrestled the anaconda of writing three different books and teaching. More than that, you're a damned good editor.

Introduction

Long before children suffer a physical death, there is the spiritual and emotional death that occurs when they are not loved, nourished, cherished, or cared for by a family. Children suffer silently, since they have no voice in the decisions made about their lives. They languish when they have no place to call home. They are vulnerable. When there is no one to protect them, they are exploited and hurt. Children, and their plight, capture our hearts. It is up to us to speak for them, to guard them, and, when they can't stay with their birth families, to find them homes.

A Peacock or a Crow: Stories, Interviews and Commentaries on Romanian Adoptions is about the children from Romania. The stories told and the lessons learned have much broader implications than just understanding Romanian adoption. If you are an adoptive parent of a child from overseas, this book will confirm your feelings and experiences. However, it may also challenge you to look at your child and circumstances differently. If you are thinking of adopting, this book may help you understand the many, complicated issues in international adoption. If you are a professional working with families who have adopted, this book may help you be a better practitioner in unraveling issues that families face. Finally, if you have any interest in history and Eastern Europe, this book can help you understand and look at Romania from a unique perspective.

At the core, this is a book about hope, about ordinary experiences, and about uncommon events. Life as an adoptive family and for an adoptee is unique. In fact, the beginning of life for many of the children adopted internationally was particularly unusual. They start life in a country far from where they will be raised. Understanding the country where children are born—the history, folklore and tradition—serves a few purposes. It lets parents know how their child may have become available for adoption. It could help adoptive families understand how they are perceived abroad. It may serve a more important purpose later. Children, as they get older, may want to understand more about their lives before adoption and about themselves as cultural or ethnic persons. Families can help their children in this quest and answer their questions if they have information to share with them.

Not only are early experiences for adoptees unique, they may also be traumatic. Most of these children have spent time in institutions. To understand this, we describe Romanian institutions and their effects on attachment and development. We also discuss how some of these effects may be reversible while others leave long lasting impressions on children, affecting their behavior and health for many years.

Parents who have "been through it" have valuable insight and can help in the preparation of new adoptive families. Agencies can use the information to educate potential adoptive parents, as well as help parents process what they can and cannot accept in adoptive placements. There is a warning here, however. You cannot take information about the group and apply it to a specific individual. For example, while we know that the longer children stay in institutions, the greater their delays in their development, we cannot say that since a specific child spent a year in an institution that he or she will be a year behind. Each child is different. Also, because we collected information about children at a specific point in time, we cannot say conclusively which is cause and which is effect. Many Romanians believe that only developmentally-delayed children are put in orphanages and institutions. Our knowledge from working and visiting Romania, along with 90 years of previous research, tells us otherwise. Finally, the information presented here relies on parent perception as well as our own analyses and interpretations. Parents' perceptions are critical for understanding the benefits and stresses of adoption. However, parent reports often differ from reports of professionals from the multiple disciplines that evaluate children. The fact is that there are many ways to understand children and look at the information—all can be accurate, even if they are very different.

All parents profit from knowing the benefits and the risks in international adoption. There should be no filtering of information for families—families have to be seen as capable of handling any information given to them. Some families, having been given accurate information about international adoption, adoption issues, and the adoption process, will choose not to pursue adoption. They recognize that they may not be successful or that there is a problem between their expectations and the realities of adoption. Still, most families are able to make the changes necessary to be successful in adoption. Success in adoption depends less on the issues that children bring to families and more on the characteristics of strong and successful adoptive families. While results to date are very positive about international adoption and about the children adopted from Romania, there are also areas of concern. Parents need complete and accurate information so they can make the best decisions about this option for building a family.

We wrote this book to accurately reflect the realities of adoption from Romania. We are not media hounds looking for a sensational story—the media has not given accurate information. What we found were many remarkable stories about Romania and the adoption of children from Romania. We hope that the person reading this book will have a better understanding of the many complicated issues in international adoption in general, and about Romanian adoptions in particular.

Chapter 1

Romania: History, Mentality and Culture

Here is the dialogue that led to the onset of this book—it was one of many conversations the authors had in an attempt to try to understand what happened in Romania. The authors begin with a heated discussion as they try to unravel the reasons why so many children are in institutions. They delve back in history to events that brought them together and focused the world's attention on Romania.

Ivor: We have a nation of people in denial. But, if you knew it, and you were just a kid, everybody in town must have known what was going on with those children. Why is it that every Romanian I talk to says, "We didn't know!"

Daniela: They didn't know about the institutions. You try to survive. That's all you were doing. And rely on the mass media and politicians to give you the truth.

Ivor: All right, look, you know, I'm a Jew and I'm sensitive about this stuff. But I don't believe any older Germans who've said to me: "We didn't know what was happening to the Jews." Well, it wasn't on Nazi radio. But didn't they talk about it to each other? I don't believe it. It's a big lie.

Daniela: You're personalizing it. To this day, you go to Romania and you ask about institutions for "irrecoverable children." They're going to look at you like, "What are you talking about?" It's not on the radio. It's not on the television. They don't know.

Ivor: It's almost incomprehensible.

Victor: On some level, but on a preconscious level. In the community and in discussions the plight of the children would never be discussed.

Daniela: They thought that they [the state] were going to take care of them and train them. They didn't tell the parents that some children went to the institutions for the irrecoverable.

Ivor: It's not a matter of believing. It's understanding the mentality. I think they knew. You know, massive societal denial—I think they did know...I can't prove it and you can't disprove it. It's like mass brainwashing.

Victor: It's real, but it's not real. It may exist, but because we cannot talk about it, it does not exist...If you live that way long enough, then.... It begins to drop back to the recesses of your mind. So if you're confronted with it, your choice is to be shocked or to be angry and deny it.

Daniela: The whole Romanian nation is in denial about it.

The Country of Romania: Geography And History for The Novice

Romania can be thought of as the intellectual and spiritual intersection between the East and the West. It is surrounded by water, with two-thirds of its borders formed by rivers and the sea. Resting on the northern part of the Balkan peninsula, to Romania's east lies the country of Moldova—a source of tension with the former Soviet Union since it was once part of Romania Mare (Great Romania); to the north is located the Ukraine; to the south and southeast are Bulgaria and the Black Sea; the west and southwest are bordered by Hungary and Serbia.

Romania is divided into five regions—Banat, Dobrogea, Moldavia, Transylvania, and Wallachia—all ruled out of Bucharest, the capital. Incorporated into Romania in 1918, Banat (Western Romania), because its geography is part of the great Hungarian plain, is often mislabeled by non-Romanians as being a part of a greater Transylvania. It is not. The Banat, especially the area around Arad, is hard-core warrior territory. They fought savagely against the Turks, Slavs, and other groups through the centuries—at Paulis in 1848 against the Austro-Hungarians, and, in 1944 against the *Einsätzgrüppen* of the German S.S. The Revolution (or coup) of December,

1989 began there in the baroque-influenced town of Timisoara. There are many ethnic Hungarians, Germans and Serbs here; more so than in other parts of Romania, these ethnic groups tolerate each other.

The beautiful, fertile delta of Dobrogea of Eastern Romania is the home of the Danube Canal, which connects shipping throughout Europe to the Black Sea. It's largest city is Constanta, most famous for being the exile home of ancient Rome's great poet, Ovid, after he was caught despoiling the Emperor's daughter, Livia, in AD 9. If you visit Constanta, you'll find wonderful Greek and Roman ruins, and a handsome mosque a few doors away from the main Orthodox cathedral. A sizeable population of Romanians with Turkish ancestry reside here. There is a marvelous statue of Ovid in the Piata Ovidiu with an inscription of *Tristia* (Sorrows). In and out of Turkish hands over the centuries, it was ceded to Romania by the Treaty of Berlin in 1878. Dobrogea's crowning architectural glory, the Romanian royal palace at Balcic, was, however, taken away in the same treaty. Now a part of Bulgaria, Balcic is a bone of eternal contention between the two countries.

Speaking of contentions, there's the province of Moldavia in Northeastern Romania. The Russians, Ukrainians, and Austro-Hungarians have been fighting over its ownership since the middle of the 14th Century. "Ownership" has gone back and forth, although the last word was spoken by Josef Stalin when he ripped the province in two, forming the Soviet republic of Moldova from parts of Romania which were formerly known as Bessarabia. In fact, parts of Moldova were also given to the Ukraine. Too many Moldavians spoke their own "Moldavian" language (sounds like Romanian), so Stalin brought in a huge population of ethnic Russians to Russify the land, adding about 40% of ethnic Russians to the population. The Romanians did nothing— Gheorgiou-Dej and Ceausescu needed to be nice to Russia for the sake of Marxist brotherhood. The bear's claws aren't so sharp these days; however, remnants of Securitaté (the secret police) are keeping the pot boiling on the Russian side of the ten meter high fence Stalin built. Nationalists would like Moldova to rejoin Romania. In the early 1990s, when there was movement in this direction, the Russians, under the leadership of Alexander Lebed, moved troops into the area to squelch any such inclination. A Slavophile with a tendency to favor Serb and Ukrainian interests, Romanians hate Lebed and fear him, particularly during the time he served in the cabinet of President Yeltsin.

Moldavia is one of the 'purer' pastoral parts of Romania. Until the mid-1990s, Moldavia had few new buildings and little in terms of modern technology. It has only one major city, Iasi, and looks more or less as it did a century ago. In the countryside, the houses, simple and tall, often lack indoor plumbing. The landscape, however, can be breathtakingly beautiful: lush green fields, rich floriculture, and stunning mountain vistas. Monasteries and churches seem to be everywhere. At Agapia, you can see the icons painted by the famous Romanian painter Nicolae Grigorescu.

Ivor:	I well remember my visit to the cathedral at Agapia. Obviously a foreigner, I was amazed at seeing so many horse-and-buggy contraptions.
Victor:	The monasteries are world renowned—Voronet, Moldovita, Putna, Humor. The folklore is that every time Stefan Cel Mare (Steven the Great) won a battle with the Turks, he had a monastery built in thankfulness to God.
Ivor:	Evidence I've gathered from personal observation, tourists, and Romanian city slickers suggests Moldavians are superstitious.
Victor:	I agree about superstitious, although I think spiritual is a better word. It is a mystical part of Romania but is also known for its hospitality. Particularly when you leave the city, people get friendlier.
Daniela:	Peasants remain peasants in the true sense of the word in Moldavia; they prefer a simpler way of life.
Victor:	And peasants are the backbone of the country. Their work ethic, pragmatism and relative separation from the political ideologies which changed in Romania have resulted in the culture, values and beliefs remaining intact—at least in the countryside. Romania is only as strong as its peasants.

Iasi is the cultural capital of Romania; it is *the* place to visit in Romania. Iasi is a beautiful city filled with ancient royal tombs that give a true sense of the complex depth of Romania's history. The church of the *Trei Ierhari* (Three Hierarchs), built in 1639, has an outside design—the most intricate elaborate stone carving—that will truly take your breath away. Folklore says that originally the building had gold inlaid into or on its elaborate carvings. During one of the battles with the Turks, the gold was looted by being burned away from the building. What is left are elaborate stone carvings.

Transylvania, the Central Region to the north of Bucharest, forms its western border with Hungary and is probably the most interesting province in Romania. It is certainly the most misunderstood by outsiders. For a start, no matter what Universal Pictures, Bela Lugosi and Bram Stoker have to say, it's not the home of Vlad Tepes (aka Dracula). The "impaler" was actually from Wallachia and it's a minor irritant to Romanians if you suggest otherwise (kind of like suggesting to Chicagoans that Al Capone was San Franciscan just because he paid a long visit to Alcatraz). What's ironic is that, in 1579, Transylvania was the first country in Europe to declare, by law, freedom of religion. From Transylvania we have the origins of the Unitarian Church and—while religious freedom was declared and is still conceptually respected—ethnic intolerance runs amok in some areas. Yet, if you talk to Ardealians (*Ardeal is another term for Translyvania*), they will tell you how well everyone gets along. They'll say that tension is a creation of politicians. But, there is only a thin veneer of liberalism once you talk about particular groups—the most obvious targets of scorn are the gypsies, followed only by the "nationalistic" Magyars who want schools, newspapers and signs in their "vulgar" language. As you hear often, "You know their language is barbarian."

History has seen ownership of this region shift back and forth. Anthropologists and historians have argued for centuries over who came first, the Dacians (who joined with Italians to become Romanians) or the Magyars (Hungarians). Germans with roots in Saxony have been there 800 years. The bottom line is that the Hungarians ruled from 1691 to 1918. From 1918 to 1940 it was given to Romania by Britain and France. In 1940, Hitler gave it back to Hungary; and, finally, in 1945, Stalin returned it to Romania. Even taking into consideration the natural Romanian foible of massive exaggeration and hyperbole, there is ample evidence of massive numbers of atrocities on both sides (with the large numbers of Germans, Jews and Gypsies always caught in the riptide, forced to pick sides, and usually the first to be raped and butchered). There have been enough defiled, murdered corpses to form a layer at least three high across every centimeter of these two small countries.[1]

More recently, Nicolae Ceausescu, surely the most colorless dictator ever to claim a cult of personality, began a policy euphemistically entitled 'rural systemization.' Villages were destroyed, families forced to move from ancestral lands, and large, concrete apartments/tenements were built to collect the rural peasants in one location. Hungarian schools which only taught in Hungarian were banned. Hungarian names of cities were 'Dacianized'; Hungarian, Roma (i.e., gypsy) and some Romanian villages were burned as part of systemization, and there were rumors that any couple with a trace of Magyar blood were taxed as a punishment for producing more than two children.[2] This, naturally, helped disproportionately populate the orphanages of Sighisoara, Sibiu, Cluj, and Brasov, compared to the other regions.

Human atrocities aside, Transylvania is beautiful. It is a climber and hiker's paradise and the peasantry is very friendly to visitors. If you're into raw nature, the Fagaras mountains are awesome. This is not Colorado or Switzerland, however—bring whatever supplies you need *with* you (and be prepared to pay the necessary tithes at customs for expensive equipment). There's a lot to see and do around Brasov, including one of the best ski resorts in Europe. In fact, everywhere you go you'll find dense forests, medieval castles, hills and more hills. Rent a car and drive through this wonderful country, especially between Brasov and Sibiu.

Wallachia, Central and Southern Romania, is the richest and most influential region. The capital, Bucharest, is there. The Danube, vast as a sea in some places, forms the country's southern rim. To get a true sense of historical and geographical perspective, visit the Iron Gates (*Portile de Fier*) next to the ancient Roman town of Drobeta-Turnu Severin. Both a bridge to Serbia and a hydroelectric plant, 448 meters long and 30 meters high, it produces 20 billion kilowatts of electricity a year. Through a complicated system of locks and dikes it allows free passage to huge amounts of shipping and holds back the enormous amount of water pushed into the Danube (the Dunarea to Romanians) from the Black Sea Delta. Such a feat of engineering may sound boring but, standing there, surrounded by a magnificent vista of mountains, you get a true sense of how supremely isolated this country was (and some say still is) from the rest of Europe and how it was once completely subject to the vicissitudes of nature. The Danube is so vast here that it will truly take your breath away. While you're in Turnu Severin, go see the Roman ruins and visit the Iron Gates Museum.

As you head northeast toward Bucharest, *the* must see Wallachian place is the market town of Tirgu-Jiu. It's not a particularly attractive town but there's the mausoleum and birthplace of the proto-feminist martyr/warrior heroine of the First World War celebrated by Romanian poets, Ecaterina Teodoroiu. Even more important, in the park on the River Jiu, are the phenomenal works of the father of modern sculpture, Constantin Brancusi. A memorial to Teodoroiu and the dead of World War One, it is called the Column of Infinity and features pig-iron sculptures entitled the Table of Silence, the Gateway of the Kiss, and the Avenue of the Kiss, all of which connect with the one hundred and five foot high, copper-coated pig-iron Endless Column. Seeing these sculptures reproduced in books can in no way substitute for the emotional experience of seeing them in their natural surroundings.

Brancusi, born about 20 miles away in the village of Hobnita, is a Romanian hero. Even during the most oppressive period of Ceausescu's rule, the locals, primed with tzuica (plum brandy), temporarily forgot about Securitaté and told hilarious tales of 1948. The politburo in Bucharest, it seems, wanted Brancusi's decadent degeneracy removed from the park and an army of can-do apparatchiks, armed with tractors, tried to do so. A tractor attached a steel hawser to the mighty column and attempted to rip it away. The structure was so well built, however, that the tractor's suspension was torn off. This lead to two even bigger tractors, specially brought in from Bucharest, being commissioned to do the job. They too lost their suspensions. Humiliated at the idea of requesting any more Russian tractors from party central, the Communists gave up.

Fifty kilometers from Tirgu Jiu, east of the village of Pologravi, is the Hurezu Monastery featuring the miraculous architecture of Count Constantin Brincoveanu. Here there are fantastic frescoes, massive carved pearwood doors, and various wonderful icons. At certain times of the day, in lieu of church bells, the monks beat out a rhythm with mallets on a beechwood instrument called a *toaca*. The contrapuntal dexterity of these monks is up there with the percussive kind of jamming you'll hear in the Afro-Cuban jazz of Mongo Santamaria and Tito Puente. In some of the monasteries, it is the nuns and not the monks who beat the toaca.

Finally, there's Bucharest.

Ivor: My grandmother told me it was the Paris of the East, but…she never visited Paris. Sure, it has two huge boulevards, Calea Victoriei and Bulevardul Magheru, and many locals look jaunty in berets, but I fear that spirit went off into exile along with Ionesco and Brancusi. There were a handful of Frenchmen staying at the Intercontinental the last time I was there; hard looking fellows doing their best to look Belmondoesque. Chain smoking Gitanes, they were recruiting young ladies to work in the porno industry in Budapest.

Victor: There is another part to this city. A sleeping grandeur that is starting to wake from a long, tortured sleep. Bucharest is urban renewal at its finest with money being poured into restorations and developments. But, juxtaposed against ancient synagogues, churches, art and neoclassical homes and office buildings are all the neons, smells and sites of western capitalism—McDonalds, KFC, Pizza Hut.

Ivor: It's a filthy, polluted, gray city.

Daniela: It is a leviathan, waiting to eat you and destroy your soul.

Victor: It is beautiful and disgusting. It was wonderful and has potential. It needs a lot of work!

Most of the good nineteenth architecture was forcibly removed by Ceausescu in an orgy of Stalinist "modernization." Well worth searching for and checking out are: *Ateneul Roman*, a beautiful concert hall modeled on the Parthenon, located on Calea Victoriei by the Stirbei Voda; on the same street is the National Art Museum, which includes work by Brancusi and the unsung impressionist paintings of Grigorescu, Tonitza, Pallady, and Luchian. Close by, on Postei Street, is the *Biserica Stravopoleos*, a sort of 18th century folk culture church. The Village Museum on Calea Kiseleff has some unique peasant architecture on display. The *Tempul Coral* synagogue, a gorgeous temple that was once the center of the Jewish ghetto of Vacaresti, should be explored. The most visually attractive place in the city is Herestrau Park. Lined with magnificent oak trees that somehow seem to be the only natural thing in the city to remain unaffected by the pollution, it's well worth a visit.

Last, but not least, for those who like gritty street life, there's the Strada Lipscani. It's a lively street market between Lipscani and the banks of the Dimbovita River. The best cheap food in the city is here; there are locals, country folk, Gypsies, Turks and Arabs hustling their wares old-fashioned artisans who work in wood, leather and clay, all kinds of cool things to take back home. Still, beware of the army of pickpockets and beggars, especially the endless onslaught of Gypsy children who can't keep their hands to themselves. Keep your wallet some place safe and don't put your cash in your trouser pockets.

A sprawling mass of curving streets and identical concrete apartment blocks that seem to go on into infinity, the city is easy to get lost in. You cannot trust the maps of Bucharest, which make it seem gridded and logical.

Downtown Bucharest (Centru) is a little easier on the eyes but little, save perhaps for the perverse architecture of the Palace of the People, is clean. The best way of getting a sense of the layout of the city is to check it out from the upper part of the Intercontinental Hotel; better yet, make friends with the locals and be generous to them. Being dependent upon your cab driver often proves to be much more stressful and expensive—they are known for their corruption and greed. Always negotiate the amount of the fare before you enter a cab. Better yet, walk or take the metro whenever you can.

Up until the mid-1990s, everything here was neglected. It is not the elegant decrepitude of a New York or Napoli. Everything you touch is covered with a layer of soot. Public drunkenness seems to be an accepted fact of life, as in Moscow. Pollution and hard times have affected everybody. This should go without saying, but, be careful at night when you're walking the streets, especially if you're beyond the Centru (central part of town). Consider Bucharest as if it were a giant set of projects. There are many sad, desperate people out on its streets.

Why is this history and geography overview important? It provides part of the answer to understanding how different parts of Romania developed, solved problems, and dealt with their social problems. The result is different patterns of institutionalization in various regions and unique efforts to respond to abandoned children and at-risk children in each of the five regions. The review also underscores that while there are many similarities between people in a country, there are also many differences as a result of history and geography. To understand Romania, or any country, it is important to understand what is alike and what is distinct about each part.

Romania: A Mentality Forged through History

You hear it every time you speak to someone who has spent any time in Romania—the "Romanian Mentality." What is the Romanian mentality? It is deep-seated xenophobia, anti-Semitism, and pervasive corruption, which lives side by side with a culture that loves strong leaders. It is sarcasm, wit, feeling deeply about every issue, and being emotional about *all* of life. It includes a touch of hedonism. Additionally, Romania is a pervasively macho, super-chauvinistic society; the only means of equal opportunity allowed to women has been through working for Securitaté. It is also the "victim" mentality that so permeates Romanian society—the fear cultivated by politicians of being a Latin people in a "Sea of Slavs." It is the anathema of the culture of enthusiasm, eternal hope, rugged individualism, and ambition that permeates the American psyche.

Romania's history goes back at least 10,000 years. Written history shows the country being invaded by Persia in 514 B.C. and conquered by the Macedonians under Alexander the Great in 335 B.C. The Roman Emperor Trajan arrived in A.D. 106. Romans were followed by Germanic tribes, Huns, Ostrogoths, Goths, Gepidae, Visigoths, Vandals, Lombards, and, finally, Slavic Avars. After three or four centuries of relative peace, small Romanian states began to form in Dobrogea, Wallachia, Moldavia, and Transylvania, but these were then invaded by Magyars, Cumans and Pechenegs. In Medieval times, Romanian kings and barons began to control vast amounts of land, but there were always wars with the Teutonic Kingdoms, Poland, Hungary, the Tatars, and, finally, the Ottoman Turks, endlessly, from 1369 when they invaded Wallachia. You get the picture? Perpetual, interminable war. The only reason Vlad Tepes is remembered out of all the Romanian warrior barons is because of the ruthless way he fought the Turks and those who dared rebel against him, and *won!*

Seen from a Romanian point of view, their people have been the "Tar Baby" of Europe. They have suffered mightily to save the rest of the caucasian, civilized world from further encroachment by the infidel Moslem Turk. The West owes Romania, according to a fixed Romanian mindset. Romanians, like elephants, Hungarians, Croatians, Serbians, Jews and Africans, *never forget.* Telling them that their country's geographical placement is one of the accidents of history does not work with Romanians.

After the Turks came the more benevolent Austro-Hungarian Habsburgs, and, finally, independence between two world wars. Independence? Freedom? Nah! It's complicated—readers are referred to the books at the end of the chapter for details. Suffice to say that the beloved of the Orthodox church, King Carol, tried to rule as a Tsarist autocrat, flaunting his mistress, Magda Lupescu (the Calea Vacaresti's ghetto poster girl for anti-Semitism). He forced all the great intellectual minds of the country into exile and flirted disastrously with the green-shirted Fascist thugs led by the beloved-of-the-rural-masses, Ion Antonescu. By the time Antonescu staged a coup and sent Carol and his mistress off to exile in Portugal, Romania had been pulled into World War II on the Nazi side. Sure, things were really bad in two world wars—most of the Jewish population were cooked up for Hitler's supper or gone in exile. Millions of Romanians were dead, too—but once the rebellion of August 23, 1944, took place and peace was made with the Soviet Union communist state, the *real* decivilization of Romania truly began.

Victor:	A cynic might say something like "but you're not Romanian."
Ivor:	That's obviously true. Nevertheless, in my experience, having spent twenty-two years domiciled in these United States, despite a worsening racial divide, the collective acceptance of a division between rich and poor, and a shrinking middle class, we still have a culture of unbounded metabolic vitality. Fueled by a relentless orgy of buying, selling, and mass culture; we trade jobs, homes, partners, and goods as speedily as those automatic weapons sold to our little gang-banger monsters spit out bullets. Indeed, our high-speed capitalism, despite a post-communist malaise, seems to be catching on like wildfire in Russia, Hungary and the Czech Republic. Organized crime may have risen to epic proportions over there and the losers often cry for the return of

Stalinist simplicity, but the genie is out of the bottle and our gifts of stock options, MTV, CNN, heroin, pornography, and fast food are here to stay.

Victor: Despite the negatives, Romanians are incredibly friendly, warm and generous. The first year I went, in 1991, a man from the crowd at the Romanian-American conference—the first ever held in Romania—befriended me. He introduced me to his family, helped me navigate the city, took me on a walking tour, helped me change money, gave me advice—he wanted to make my visit pleasant and memorable. At first I was suspicious, thinking: "What did he want?" That is the American mentality—suspicion and fear. His generosity the first year I was there made me fall in love with the country. To this day, he and his family have become my Romanian family (George, Maria and Ciprian Alexandrescu).

Ivor: In lieu of looking like a hypocrite, let me now contradict myself and add that I've also found Romanians to be incredibly friendly and warm. Make an effort to speak their language, listen to their complaints, accept their hospitality, get past the surface stuff, and you'll find them wonderful. It's a vociferously Latin culture. They're Italians who got lost, physically and metaphorically.

So, taking all that into consideration, what happened in Romania? Well, you can't avoid a history lesson. Romanians, despite their Italian ancestry, were never exposed to the Roman Catholicism that touched their western blood brothers. They are members of the Orthodox church. Orthodox philosophy and theology stress communality. Orthodox philosophy also stresses building an inner life rather then a reliance on external acts. It's no accident that there was never any kind of reformation in Orthodox countries. Individualism has always been frowned upon. Americans take the Protestant fixation with individual obligation—making up our own minds as to that which is right or wrong—and create a more personalized obligation to take whatever action might be deemed necessary to support it. Americans live for the individual, Romanians live the internal and the communal—family, neighbors, friends, and church.

Ivor: I well remember sitting in a tavern in Iasi watching Gheorge Hagi, Romania's reigning football genius, executing a gloriously individual run during an international game. Unfortunately, his shot was saved brilliantly by the Russian goalkeeper. This marvelous bit of individualism, unusual for an over-coached, ultra-defensive team, drew a totally negative reaction from the crowd of fans. He was booed and cursed in the most vituperative way. Afterward, my friend

Nicu said it would have been just as negative even if he had actually scored a goal. It was an irrevocable mistake, he said, an embarrassment to his country and countrymen.

Romanians have always looked enviously toward the West; theoretically, at least, always longing for freedom of speech and material goods. Now that freedom is at hand, however, a time when innovators must step forward and work their will, the Romanian people as a whole are still sitting on their hands. Atypically, Romanians have always, and still do, put the blame for their problems on everybody *but* themselves. You can't have your cake and eat it, too—but Romanians try.

Communism and the Romanian Mentality

It's important to realize that the Stalinistic-like dictators who ruled Romania gave the people forty-five years of peace. No one had been unaffected by the carnage caused by the two world wars. The two dictators, Gheorghe Gheorghiou-Dej, who ruled from 1948 to 1965, and Nicolae Ceausescu, who ruled from 1965 to the 'revolution' in 1989, were ruthless, mean-spirited men, but they kept the peace and put food on the table for most of those years.

Gheorgiou-Dej was more or less a Soviet apparatchik puppet. When Ceausescu took power, however, he consolidated his own position at the expense of the central committee, instituting a more nationalistic 'cult of personality', building up his secret police force (*Securitaté*)—to the point where about one million of the nation's population was in its employ. In 1974, after nine years in power, he appointed himself President and began to set in motion a series of diabolical plans. Along with his wife, Elena, a semi-literate creature of unquenchable greed and egotism, Ceausescu set about converting Romania into the Oceania of Orwell's *1984*—not a novel or a movie, but real life. It's not our job here to recount their horrific crimes against the Romanian people. One can easily find erudite epigraphs alluding to the banality of evil, for there were never a pair of duller, meaner peasants than these two. For them, in the words of sociologist Eric Fromm: "Power is not a means; it is an end. And power means the capacity to inflict unlimited pain and suffering to another human being"[3]. The horrors we'll recount here are only meant to help the reader gain an understanding of the modern Romanian mind as shaped by communism and dictatorship as well as explaining the causes of Romania's orphanage crisis.

Aside from becoming rich, the Ceausescus had three particular obsessions. One was to monitor the activities of every single Romanian citizen. Absurd as this may sound, they pretty well pulled it off. Its *Securitaté,* Romania's secret police, found a way to compromise every single citizen who had *any* kind of job. To get a good job meant party approval in the first place. Thus, everybody was expected to report on their fellow workers and members of their family a minimum of once a month, either to the "Block" or "Street" Committees of their neighborhood, or directly to secret police headquarters. All teachers, for example, were expected to not only lecture the party line, but to also report on their colleagues and students.

This insidious *status quo* helped set in place a sort of cradle-to-grave snitching.

Daniela: You couldn't trust anybody. My parents always told me that every other person is a securitaté person. Even your brother would report on you. You had a world inside your mind and that is where you kept it.

If that's not enough to addle the Western mind, there was the DGTO (Directia General de Technica Operativa), or General Directorate of Technical Operations, and Directorate IV (Military Counterintelligence). By 1954, the KGB-trained Directorate IV was monitoring the homes of all military officers through the use of microphones. Once Ceausescu took over, DGTO set about monitoring the homes of every member of the party, including every ranking member of the Politburo. According to Ion Pacepa, formerly the head of Romanian Intelligence until his defection to the United States in 1974:

> When he came to power in 1965, the Romanian security forces had one central and eleven regional KGB-designed electronic monitoring centers and five central mail censorship units around the country...The DGTO had, as of March 1978, ten central and 248 peripheral automated electronic monitoring centers, plus over a thousand 'portable' units covering small towns, vacation resorts, and the picturesque, historical monasteries favored by Western tourists, as well as 48 mail censorship units.[4]

On March 28, 1978, Ceausescu ordered that every one of over 3,000,000 telephones in use in Romania be replaced with a new one. These phones, created by the President's "security scientists," in addition to their normal function, were very sensitive microphones capable of recording every conversation in the room they had been installed in, whether the phone was in use or not. For those who didn't own phones, especially in rural Romania, there were ashtrays, vases, radios, and televisions. On any given night between 1985 and 1989, DGTO was capable of monitoring the goings-on of the public simultaneously from ten million microphones.[5]

To further control the population, Ceausescu instituted "systematization" as a policy for creating new culture. It included massive relocation of both historic rural villages and city centers, replacing them with apartment buildings and high-rise commercial complexes. This policy dismantled neighborhoods and extended family networks by forcing relocation into large block complexes where a family was assigned to live, often with other people who they did not know. Obviously, it was much easier to control a population when people didn't know or trust each other. It is also easier to control people when they are in one place rather then spread out through the countryside.

The other two obsessions went hand in glove. Elena and Nicolae had big dreams; they were obsessed with creating a neo-Roman Empire. Surrounded by ethnic enemies and dependent on the benevolence of the Soviet Union, the Ceausescus dreamed of a mighty conquering Socialist military machine superior to the Red Army, able to repatriate Soviet Moldova, the Banat region of the former Yugoslavia, and the parts of Bulgaria that had been "stolen" from it. They also dreamed of being an economic and industrial power. To do that, certain things were absolutely necessary. First and foremost, they needed a totally obedient population. As we've already discussed, Securitaté had already begun to set that plan in motion. Paranoid, the Ceausescus also wished to remove the indigenous "non-Romanian" population. All outsiders—Gypsies, Hungarians, ethnic Germans, and the few Jews who'd survived the war—were to be removed, forcibly or otherwise. "Otherwise," in the case of the Germans and the Jews, meant that that they were available to West Germany and Israel. At $5,000 to $10,000 per head, Ceausescu sold citizens abroad for almost two decades, helping to create a huge Swiss war chest. If the Israelis and the Germans stopped paying, the little dictator had more insidious plans that smacked of Hitler's Final Solution.[6]

Still, to own a massive military and economic machine, one must have bodies. According to Pacepa, the party's paperwork found that there were only ten million citizens of "pure blood." There needed to be a massive increase in the Romanian population. In 1984, the party ordered each family in Romania to produce at least five children. There were incentives and punishments to the mandate. Families were taxed if they did not fulfill their obligation to the state, as much as 30% of their income[7]. Large families were rewarded. As Popescu noted: "mothers of more than five were declared '*hero mothers,*' paid a state allowance, and given priority in housing" (p. 110)[8]. The plan was that, within a decade, the population would be 40,000,000 strong, from the current 23,000,000. To whit, according to the same decree, any woman who had an abortion and any doctor who carried such an act out was subject to imprisonment or condemned to death. "Pregnant women were frequently checked at their workplace to ensure they were not having abortions. Women who had them anyway lost their jobs"(p. 96).[9] Thus, by the turn of the century, the Ceausescus would be ready for war as well as be an industrial power in Europe.

In practical terms, this decree was a recipe for pure disaster. Romania was bankrupt; any remuneration Romania received for its low-priced agricultural crop and manufacturing (a tithe to keep the Soviet Union appeased), as a result of its blackmailing of West Germany and Israel, or the benefits of "most favored nation status" with the United States, ended up being spent on the monolithic presidential palace in downtown Bucharest or deposited in private Swiss bank accounts. Albania aside, it was the poorest country in the communist bloc.

Meanwhile, in the countryside, having not learned anything from the mistakes of the monster Stalin, hundreds of thousands of peasants were forced to move to the cities to work in factories. Consequently, less and less food was available because fewer peasants worked the land and collective farms reduced productivity in agriculture. Romania's whole system became fed by a darwinistic (illegal) black market economy, and, meanwhile, the population kept growing and growing.

The pitiful economy, coupled with the draconian laws *Securitaté* enforced against abortions and abortionists, led to unforeseen circumstances. Thousands of children were simply abandoned in maternity hospitals and then placed by the authorities in orphanages. Families couldn't feed all the children they had, and so they left them in the hospitals. Children with minor difficulties couldn't be cared for at home because there was little family support. In the past, the extended family and neighbors were able to help when there were too many children or a child had a special need and extra care was required. Unfortunately, as "systematization" was enforced, those old social networks were dismantled. Finally, years of propaganda resulted in people believing that the state would be responsible and take care of their children if they could not. The Ceausescu government developed a solution for families who were unable or unwilling to keep their children at home—the solution to the problem was institutionalization.[10]

Institutionalization took place for other reasons also. Children could be placed in institutions because of a physical and mental disability of the child or his or her parent, family dysfunction, poverty, repeated hospitalization for medical problems, and juvenile delinquency.[11] Unfortunately, once a child was institutionalized, it was almost impossible to change the decision. Children were not re-evaluated and the people in charge of child placements didn't usually recommend that children return home. The prevailing myth and mentality that developed was that institutional care was better than family care, particularly for children from poor families. In addition, for children who had serious health needs, often the only way to get the medicines that they needed was through institutionalizing them.[12]

The institutional system expanded rapidly once it was developed. It had several serious, negative consequences. The first consequence was that it disrupted parent-child bonding. Mothers were allowed to visit for only one hour per week and even then could only sit by the bed; they were not allowed to hold the baby or child. Because of general poverty and long distances, traveling was expensive and difficult. It wasn't long before many children were left without being visited—families couldn't afford the travel cost or the time away from the job to travel.

Another reason the institutions grew concerned the long convalescence periods from illnesses. Many children were born with low birth weights, due to diet restrictions, and needed long-term recuperation periods that could not be provided for in the home. Low birth weight babies were 100 times more likely to be institutionalized.[13]

This did not faze the Ceausescus, however. Each abandoned child was a child of the party. It is no exaggeration to state that the Ceausescus saw each orphan as a future Securitaté assassin/operative. In fact, there is enough anecdotal evidence, along with leftover Securitaté files, to suggest that the most obedient secret police operatives were, for three generations, products of state orphanages.

When the end finally came in 1989, it was accompanied by an emphysemic whimper. In a scam of scams, perpetuated by Securitaté on CNN, in particular, and the gullible world press in general, what was disguised as a revolution turned out to be a coup. The jaded, exhausted Romanian people were not fooled, though. (Anyone interested in deciphering something approximating the truth about what actually happened would be well served by viewing *Requiem for Dominique*, a fine French-Romanian film.) The issue of orphanages, institutions, and orphans is a national embarrassment to Romania. Naturally, when dealing with the Romanian people, you will find an almost truculent kind of defensiveness concerning this issue. A people kept under a state of civil siege for close to fifty years do not take to constructive criticism well.

After the "revolution," the laws concerning orphans changed often, almost every day. Many nationalists, especially the most obdurate rightists in the Peasant Party, use xenophobic language alluding to the former Iliescu government's mortgaging off of Romania's future.

The markets of Bucharest, Iasi and Timosøara are now full of food. There's not much money available to buy it with, but, in the mode of 'meet the new boss, same as the old boss,' old Securitaté apparatchiks now own Pepsi, Pizza Hut and McDonald's franchises. Somebody's got money, obviously. Forgetting would, of course, be a lot easier if the same people weren't still succeeding and the foreign tourists and media weren't still harping on the orphan issue. Until these institutions are depopulated, the Romanian people will not heal. The orphans are, ultimately, both a mental and physical metaphor for an unending malaise.

The Romanian Spirit

Ivor: We are done with this chapter.

Victor: I don't think so. It needs balance. It doesn't look at or highlight the positive contributions.

Daniela: I agree. Since 1990, endless articles and books have been written on the politics of Romania, the Nazi-like personality of the Romanian nationals, and the "Romanian way of handling things." Some people write about how rude the Romanians are, how inferior and backwards they are—not to mention how dishonest they are. While I respect all of those people's views, which are extremely negative and based on maybe a few months' experience, I also resent it. If anything, Americans always say, "don't generalize." Well? Nobody talks about the positives of the

Romanians, about their generosity and loving spirit. As a Romanian-American, I know not to generalize about all Romanians. Different regions will present you with different personalities.

Victor: Then, that is also what we need to bring out. It gives better balance.

Ivor: We are not writing a tourist manual here.

Victor: Right, but we are trying to present a balanced view and a context for understanding what happened. It needs something more.

Daniela: Well, I could go on and on telling you stories about the other "side" of Romania, but it's not my role here to do that or defend Romania. But, we must give the other side.

Victor: Truth is like a diamond which has been shattered. Our job is to find the slivers and let someone figure out how they all fit together when they contradict or do not fit exactly with each other.

Romanians have a good sense of humor. The humor has a sharp edge; it often is sarcastic and witty. Rarely will they say something nasty directly. Personal attacks are subterfuge and innuendo is a way of life. Indirect criticism, particularly concerning politics, is valued and developed into a highly prized skill. Cynicism is a dominant personality trait.

Rumor is the lifeblood of the community. All of life's events are subject to multiple interpretations. Romanians feel strongly about everything. They are quick to love but quick to anger. They are pliable and stubborn.

Romanians love celebrations. And Romanians know how to celebrate! There is nothing like a Romanian party, regardless of the reason for the celebration. Songs, food and traditions are part of the rich culture life of Romanians. Many owe their origins to old pagan festivals. Much of Romanian culture is a blend of ancient paganism and Christianity.

One of the fabulous characteristics of the Romanian people is their hospitality. If you go in a Romanian's house, he/she will serve you the best meal ever, even if that means putting the last of the food on the table for you. They will do whatever it takes to make you feel like royalty. Sometimes what you get served may look awful to you; maybe the roasted chicken looks like a roasted pigeon, but to the Romanians you are served the best they have to offer. If you stay for awhile, even if its for a short period of time, there is a good chance you will leave the house with a gift that probably is made by your hostess. The family will ask you many questions, will compliment you, admire you, respect you, thus making you feel like you are the most important person, even if it's only for one hour, a day or a week.

Another positive characteristic of the Romanian people is the way they love their families and each other. This may sound strange after reading how the Romanians treat their abandoned children! But, Romanian parents love their children. They will work extra shifts and do whatever it takes to get their children the best education and healthcare, even if it means bribing. They will do as much as they can. The children, in return, take care of their parents as they get older. Nursing homes are not an option unless there is a severe mental or physical handicap. Most people in nursing homes are there because they have no one to take care of them. Grandparents, taking their turn, take care of the grandchildren, this making for a full circle of caring and meeting mutual needs within the family. It is not uncommon for a Romanian family to be composed of three generations still living under one roof.

Once the children are grown up and marry or move on, it is not unusual for the parents to continue to provide monetary support. One reason for this is because Romanians don't believe in debt.

Romanians are a very passionate people; they fall in love and are very dramatic about it. Romanians love to give and share. Friends give things to each other and share everything. For children with families, living in Romania means a beautiful childhood. Children play outside of the house with other children in the neighborhood. They are not afraid of being kidnapped or being the victims of a drive-by shooting. They are not sitting in the house watching television all day, their skin growing paler and paler. Kids are happy. Romanians hug and kiss a lot; they are very expressive both physically and emotionally.

Finally, Romanians have strong traditions, stories, beliefs and a commitment to keeping and maintaining rituals in the family and in the community. As Anton[14] states: "Dominated by foreign power and subjected to corrupt leadership, first foreign and then native, Romanians survived as a people primarily through the shared experiences of telling stories" (p. 30). The Romanian culture is very rich; they celebrate all events and holidays reflecting the richness of this beautiful country. In addition to the celebrations of life, Romanians have a flair for the melodramatic and traumatic. The folk stories and songs, like those of many cultural groups, are imbued with themes of love and loss, yearning, sadness and tragedy. Many are tied to the important moments in a person's life—birth, marriage, death, military service—or other events or festivals, such as those involving seasons, religious holidays and occupations.

Conclusion: a Nice Place to Visit, But...

The atrocities of communism and the Ceausescu dictatorship were replaced by a newer, slightly more benevolent mode of oppression, killings, and pseudo-changes in the politicos who seized power after the "revolution." Protesters were beaten twice by "miners" in Bucharest between 1990 and 1993. The secret police, after a re-organization, are still a force with which to reckon. Dissidents immigrate or, sometimes, are found dead—sometimes of explainable causes, sometimes under curious circumstances. The social democrats, communist wolves in democratic-sheep clothing, profited from the chaos created by the political and economic changes. The reforms that took place were not the sweeping changes necessary for economic revolution to a market economy. Most of the people in the new government are the old guard of the former government with new labels. The changes made were largely cosmetic and did not represent a change from the superstructure that existed under communism. One of the real changes was the opening of the borders to people, goods and information. In the years after communism, this is the only true catalyst of changes that are occurring in the late 1990s.

As of this writing, there are more children in institutions than there were before the "revolution." The election of 1996, however, may prove to be a means of genuine change. The new President, Emil Constantinescu, an academic out of the University of Bucharest, is attempting to overhaul an unwieldy constitution and replace the last vestiges of communism with qualified technocrats and professionals, many of whom have returned after decades in exile. Still, there is deep-seated corruption. Many of the former communists are still in positions of power in both the public and private sectors. There are remnants of the secret police still operating. There are unanswered questions about the revolution and Ceausescu's fortune. Fascism and nationalism are on the rise and sanctioned. But, things do seem to be improving, albeit at a turtle's pace.

Recommended Readings about Romania

A history of Romania. (1997). Iasi, Romania: The Center for Romanian Studies.

Anton, T. (1996). Eros, magic, and the murder of Professor Culianu. Evanston, IL: Northwestern University Press.

Behr, E. (1991). Kiss the hand you cannot bite: the rise and fall of the Ceausescus. New York: Villard Books.

Bock, J. (1997). Ethnic vision: A Romanian American inheritance. Niwot, CO: University of Colorado Press.

Codrescu, A. (1991). The hole in the flag. New York: Avon Books.

Kaplan, R. (1994). Balkan ghosts: a journey through history. New York: Vintage Books.

Pacepa, I. (1987). Red horizons. Washington, D. C.: Regnery Gateway.

Popescu, P. (1997). The return: A family revisits their eastern European roots. New York: Grove Press.

Recommended Websites about Romania

Romanian Friends and Partners

<http://www.friends-partners.org/fpromania/index.html>(opt,mozilla,mac,english,)

Romanian Poetry

<http://www.users.interport.net/~radvel/poezii/>

The Center for Romanian Studies

<http://www.romanianstudies.ro/>

Virtual Romania

<http://www.info.polymtl.ca/Romania/>

Notes from Chapter 1

[1] Nagy, F. N. (1970). The green shirts and the others. Palo Alto, CA: Hoover Institution Press of Stanford University. Parzan, V. (1973). Dacia. Boulder, CO: Eastern European Quarterly Press.

[2] As many Romanians are quick to point out, similar events of changing names and taxing Romanians occurred when the region was part of the Austrian-Hungarian Empire/Kingdom. These incidents are not easily forgotten here and are often used to justify current inhumanities.

[3] From Eric Fromm's introduction to George Orwell's 1984.

[4] Pacepa, I. (1987). Red horizons. Washington, D. C.: Regnery Gateway.

[5] Pacepa, I. (1987). Red horizons. Washington, D. C.: Regnery Gateway. Pacepa's claims have never been verified. Recent media reports suggest that the figure was closer to 1,000,000. However, regardless of the figure, fear and suspicion of being monitored were rampant, exerting great control over the majority of the population.

[6] Pacepa, I. (1987). Red horizons. Washington, D. C.: Regnery Gateway.

[7] See Johnson, A., & Groze, V. (1993). The orphaned and institutionalized children of Romania. Journal of Emotional and Behavioral Problems, 2(4):49-52. However, while 30% is the figure often quoted, the exact figure, as specified in policy, was less than 10%. There seems to be regional differences in how this policy was enacted and enforced.

[8] Popescu, P. (1997). The return: a family revisits their Eastern European roots. New York: Grove Press. However, the policy actually stipulated that mothers having 10 or more children were "hero mothers." Similar to taxation, there seems to be regional differences in how this policy was articulated and enacted.

[9] Codrescu, A. (1991). The hole in the flag. New York: Avon Books.

[10] Johnson, A. K., Edwards, R.L., & Puwak, H. C. (1993). Foster care and adoption policy in Romania: Suggestions for international intervention. Child Welfare, 72(5), 489-506.

[11] Kaler, S. R., & Freeman, B. J. (1994). An analysis of environmental deprivation: Cognitive and social development in Romanian orphans. Journal of Child Psychology and Psychiatry and Allied Disciplines. 35(4), 769-81.

Stephenson, P. A., Anghelescu, C., Bobe, N., Ciomartan, T., Gaistenau, M., Fumarel, S., Goldis, C., Georgescu, A., Ionescu, M., Iorgulescu, D., Lupu, R., McCreery, R., McKay, S., Manescu, V., Mihai, B., Moldovanu, F., Moldovan, Z., Morosam, I., Nanu, R.,

Nicolau, A., Palikari, G., Pascu, C., Popa, S., Popescu, P., Raican, A., Stanescu, A., Stativa, E., & Stoica, M. (1994). The causes of childrens' institutionalization in Romania. Child Care Health and Development, 20(2), 77-88.

Johnson, A., & Groze, V. (1993). The orphaned and institutionalized children of Romania. Journal of Emotional and Behavioral Problems, 2(4):49-52.

[12] Stephenson and colleagues. (1994). The causes of childrens' institutionalization in Romania. Child Care Health and Development, 20(2), 77-88.

[13] Bascom, B. B., & McKelvey, C. A. (1997). The complete guide to foreign adoption: What to expect and how to prepare for your new child. New York: Pocket Books

[14] Anton, T. (1996). Eros, magic, and the murder of Professor Culianu. Evanston, IL: Northwester University Press.

Chapter 2

A Family Tells Their Story

There are all kinds of stories from people who've adopted from Romania. People who live all over the U.S.—this is the first of several that you will read. All are interesting. But, the insatiable media monster has exploited so many families that many people were very reluctant to speak out for fear of distortion. Still, we found families who were eager and willing to share their stories. A certain number of editing changes had to be made for the sake of clarity, conciseness and continuity in the various stories. As you'll see, we've run the gamut, from the simply heartwarming to the heartbreaking, and included various formats, including the straight first-person narrative, monologues, daily journals, and a more journalistic Question and Answer. We've interviewed the rich, the middle-class, the unemployed; Christians, Born-Again Christians; a "street-fighter", moralists, egocentrics, atheists and plain-old nice folk—all who have been through an experience that has changed them forever. It's to be noted that many of the stories, especially those based around the madness that took place in 1990 and 1991, offer scenarios that are no longer applicable. They're all engaging and insightful, at any rate. In addition, while adoption is regulated now and there are official guidelines, about 10% of adoptions each year are still going on through illegal or unsanctioned approaches—so some of these stories may still be relevant for families who adopt in this way. While families consented to these interviews, to afford them some protection and privacy we used only their first names and made ambiguous their geographic locations.

Janet, Dave, Reid and Ethan: An Aradian Odyssey

There is an old, well-known anonymous poem that reflects our attitude about adoption. It goes like this:

Not flesh of my flesh,

nor bone of my bone,

but still miraculously my own.

Never forget for a single minute,

you didn't grow under my heart, but in it.

My husband, Dave, and I built a family through adoption, and our youngest son, Ethan, is part of that small group of Romanian children adopted in 1990 and 1991. Ours was an odyssey that began when we saw the story about the first Romanian adoption on the TV program *20/20*. We had already adopted our oldest son, Reid, through Lutheran Social Services and were pursuing another domestic adoption. Because of the many delays and uncertainties involved in U.S. adoptions, however, the time seemed right for us to be adventurous. Through some lucky contacts, we were taken on by an adoption agency in another state in order to begin the myriad of paperwork and the emotional seesaws accompanying international adoption.

Our journey began November 9, 1990, with an eleven-hour plane ride from Chicago, followed by another eleven-hour train journey over the mountains from Bucharest to Arad. Reid, who was seven at the time, accompanied us. In retrospect, we are so happy Reid had the opportunity to share this important experience in our lives; but, at the time, I spent many sleepless nights worrying about whether we were making the right decision in taking him with us. Reid has asthma, and I was very worried about his having an asthma attack in a very polluted country. I packed my purse with an arsenal of medications and prepared for the worst. Reid came through the trip beautifully—with no asthma and with wonderful memories of the watershed event in our family's history.

Upon arrival in Arad, we were immediately filled in about adoption in Romania and learned that the process would probably take longer than we had hoped. "Overburdened" was how one adoptive parent we met described it. We soon met our lawyer, Cornel, who was very conscientious but overworked. Although he was trying to take care of eight adoptive families at once, he was the person who opened the door to the entire Romanian adoption process for us.

When we left home, we knew that we had already been assigned a child; however, we never saw that child, nor had any proof that he even existed. The name was simply our ticket into the orphanage, which we visited November 13. Prior to our arrival in Arad, Dave and I had done our homework. We talked to other adoptive parents and took their advice and direction in choosing a child. We decided that we would give preference to a male baby with good motor skills. That decision sounds hard-hearted, but we knew that, with so many children to choose from, we had to put reason above emotion and be decisive about the child we wanted.

We chose our child during that first day at the orphanage. Paul (now renamed Ethan), a six-month-old boy with curly brown hair and dark brown eyes, appeared healthy. Some of the children we saw were so weak that they couldn't even hold their heads up because of poorly developed neck muscles. Most of the children had colds or sniffles, and even Ethan, who had a strong neck and arms, had a little cold. In addition, the babies were wrapped in huge diapers that made leg movement nearly impossible. Ethan was strong, but he didn't stand well because of his diaper.

After our decision had been made, we met our attorney at the orphanage and gave him the information he needed regarding Ethan. Despite earlier warnings that the adoption could take longer than we anticipated, we were contacted by Cornel that same evening to say that Ethan's birth parents would meet us the next morning. We could hardly believe how smoothly things were progressing.

Ethan was not a true orphan, just as most of the children in the orphanage were not. He was, rather, a victim of Ceausescu's economic and population policies. His unmarried mother was simply too poor to take care of her son. Unfortunately, Ethan was never in a traditional home; he was put in the orphanage shortly after his birth.

The meeting with Ethan's birth mother took place on November 14. On the very next morning, we got permission to adopt from the orphanage. Getting the orphanage's permission was an informal courtesy on our part; the formal process involved both birth parents agreeing to a home study and allowing us to adopt the child. Dave and I had to sign an affidavit stating our intention to adopt before a lay magistrate. In addition, I signed over my full power of attorney to Dave, who would act in my absence, since Reid and I would soon be returning to the United States.

On November 22, Thanksgiving Day, Reid and I left Ethan in the orphanage, said goodbye to Dave at the train station, and began our long trip home. Both Reid and I were in tears; it was very emotional for us to leave Dave halfway across the world. I also became very emotional about saying goodbye to our hosts in Arad. The people we stayed with, Gheorge and Anna, were wonderful people. They lived very simply in a clean but primitive house. They didn't have running hot water; instead they had a hot water heater that needed to be fired up by cobs and wood, which they only started up twice a week so that everyone could take an occasional shower. I was also surprised that their beds, which were all day bed sized, were in every room, including the kitchen. The day-bed in our room had to fit both Dave, who is six-foot-seven, and myself; there was also a small crib that Reid used. Reid will never forget being seven years old and sleeping in a crib!

Before Reid and I left Arad, we spent a lot of time at the orphanage visiting Ethan and playing with the other kids. Dave continued to spend time there. Alone on November 24, he fed Ethan for the first time. Ethan's bottle was filled with a thick gruel eaten out of a nipple with a very large hole. On November 26, Dave wrote in his dairy, "I was pleased with Ethan today. He immediately recognized me and was anxious to come. This is the first sign that I have seen in him that he has any recognition of my face."

While waiting for the final court date, Dave also had time to visit Ethan's birth parents. With the help of an interpreter, they talked for six and a half hours. Then, on November 28, Dave had the final court appearance and was finally able to take Ethan out of the orphanage. It was a rainy, miserable day, but, despite the downpour, Dave brought Ethan to our host family's home and felt a sense of accomplishment and relief. Ethan went to sleep at 8:30 p.m., but he woke at 11:30 and vomited all over. "He finally quieted down without us being able to do much for him," Dave said.

Two days later, Dave and Ethan caught the express train from Arad to Bucharest, and the rest of the adoption process began. Dave described the paperwork and rushed appointments as "frustrating." In addition, Ethan was sick with a fever; he had a cold, teething pain, and an upset stomach from the sudden change in diet. He was very fussy, probably from all the change as well as being sick. Dave's host family in Bucharest gave him plenty of help and support with a colicky Ethan. "I was fortunate to be staying with a family who were perceptive enough to understand the situation, even though they spoke no English whatsoever," Dave said.

Dave left Bucharest laden with camera equipment, luggage, a painting we had purchased, and Ethan. The trip drained him both physically and emotionally. He will never forget the kindness of a woman from South Dakota, who cared for Ethan on the final leg of the journey home. Dave thought of her as literally a lifesaver. Understandably flustered, he neglected to get her name. Last fall, he wrote a note of thanks to the local newspaper in the town she came from, and, just recently, her husband called to identify his wife as Dave's helper. Our hearts are still full when we think of all the kindness of people, both in Romania and at home.

Reid and I met Dave's plane at 10:30 p.m. in the airport. Dave was the last person off the plane, but everyone on the flight stayed to watch our reunion.

I'll never forget Ethan's perception of the world on his first day in the United States. His eyes were wide as he looked and looked. He was obviously seriously over-stimulated by all the sights and sounds of a new country. Ethan was also taken to school shortly after his arrival so that Reid could introduce his new brother to his classmates.

In the years that Ethan has been part of our family, he has grown into a bright, enthusiastic, social boy. He has always been extremely active and has more energy than both his parents put together, although he has settled down a lot more as he has gotten older. He attends pre-school, likes baseball and can hit a ball very far for someone his age; he also enjoys building with Legos and being with his friends. We've always said that God had a plan for our lives, and so we become spiritual when we think of how our family came about. We can hardly imagine what Ethan's life would have been like had he remained in the Romanian orphanage system. We thank God every day that he is a part of our lives instead.

Chapter 3

Dickens, Boys Town or Purgatory: Are Institutions a Place to Call Home?

Institutions for Children in Romania

As mentioned in Chapter 1, the Ceauscescu government developed a solution for families who were unable or unwilling to keep their children at home. The solution to the problem was institutionalization. The exact figures are as yet unavailable and may never be known, but, by the end of the Ceauscescu dictatorship in December of 1989, it is estimated that there were 600-700 institutions in Romania that provided residence for an estimated 100,000 children.[1]

Just as problematic as the number of children residing in institutions under Ceauscescu is the number of children placed in institutions *after* the dictatorship. According to UNICEF, following decreases in the number of children in institutions in 1991 and 1992, by 1994 the numbers had increased and become greater than the number of children in 1990. UNICEF reports that in 1990, about 86,000 children were in institutions. In 1992, only about 73,000 children were in institutions, largely due to international adoption. By 1994, however, the numbers had increased to over 98,000 children.[2] In these institutions, about 24% of the children are under the age of 8, 20% are 9 to 11, 31% are 12 to 15, 19% are 15 to 18, and about 6% are over the age of 18.[3]

Children continue to be abandoned, mostly in the maternity hospitals. Mothers will deliver at the hospital and, simply, walk away. The hospital staff can tell who is most likely to abandon their child. There is a typical profile. It is a women who shows up at the maternity hospital, ready to deliver, without her official papers. She will be from out of town. She will be a single mother or a mother who already has several children. Once she delivers her baby, she may give the child a name but often does not. Without a name and the official paperwork, the child is instantaneously placed in legal limbo. You can't track the mother because there are few social workers to do outreach and you don't know if you have the correct information. The child cannot be adopted because, under Romanian law, the child is not legal—he or she is nobody's child.

> *(From Victor's diary and notes):* Ancuta was 19 years old, from a village near Brashov, in Transylvania. Her water had broke by the time she arrived at the maternity hospital. She had traveled in the morning by train, arriving at Gara de Nord (the north train station and main station in Bucharest) around noon. She told the doctor that she was in a rush after the contractions started and forgot her papers. However, she promised that her family would be bringing them when they came for a visit after the baby was born. Ancuta was unmarried and the father of the child refused to marry her or claim the child. In fact, they had broken up over the pregnancy. She had a previous pregnancy a year ago that she terminated with an abortion—it was so painful she decided not to have a second abortion. She worked on her parents' farm. The interview was interrupted when her contractions increased and she was taken for delivery. A day after she delivered, the mother

was gone and the little girl, whom she named Ana, was left in the maternity ward—with a name but with no registration and no way to track the mother. She would stay at the hospital for about a month and then be assigned to one of the state orphanages.

The hospitals will keep children up to three months, but then they must be moved. It is chilling to walk into the nursery at a maternity hospital. Instead of hearing children crying and seeing them move around, they are quiet—too quiet. It's not natural. The children, if their eyes are open, stare blankly into space. While the wards are generally clean and the necessary medical supplies are available, they are eerie—silent and abnormal without child activity.

There have been many official and some unofficial reports about the structure of the child institutions in Romania. The following has been pieced together from official documents, unofficial reports, and personal experiences.[4]

Under the old regime, up until the age of three, children were placed in institutions called orphanages or *leagane*. These residential facilities were under the direction of the Ministry of Health. It appears that, at around the age of 3, the children in these orphanages were divided into two or three groups. The first group were 'normal children.' Children were classified as normal if they could pass an assessment conducted by a physician or, in some institutions, a team of professionals. There was little training in child development for the persons conducting the assessments and a lack of uniformity in assessment techniques; children were generally considered normal if they could talk, were toilet trained, and suffered no apparent physical difficulty. These children were sent to training schools where they were fed, clothed, sheltered, and received an education. Interestingly, few gypsy children were judged normal. The "normal" children were under the guidance of the Ministry for Education until the age of 18.

The second group was made up of those children who had minor handicaps. There was one school for the deaf, one school for the blind, and other schools classified as "special schools" or "special hospitals." "Special school" may have been the words used to describe the place, but there was nothing "special" about the program. They were not as well supplied as the normal schools, but these children were still at least seen as salvageable and educable. These children were also under the Ministry of Education.

The children who belonged to the last group were diagnosed with physical, medical, or psychological problems that were considered too severe for either of the placements mentioned above; therefore, they were sent to an institution for the 'Irrecoverable.' These were children who were considered unsalvageable. The children in this group included those with major mental and physical defects, as well as children with medically correctable handicaps such as crossed-eyes or club feet.[5] The main purpose for sending these children to institutions of this sort was to hide them away, helping only to maintain the belief that Romania did not have any social problems or handicapped children. These children were under the direction of the Ministry for the Handicapped.

> I remember that first year so vividly as we drove from Bucharest to the Institution for the Irrecoverables in Videle. After two hours of driving, through black, oil-drenched fields where cows walked around the oil slicks, we arrived at the village. We stood at a large compound of white buildings that, from the outside, looked like they needed a lot of work. The paint was chipped with big splotches of unpainted cement. Electric wires were dangling and blowing back and forth. Many of the windows were missing. Between bricks, mortar was gone. It was hard to believe that anyone could live here! The front gate was probably about 8 feet tall; next to the gate was a guard station and a large fence circled the entire complex.

> We were escorted from the front gate to the back of the complex by the guard and an official from the Ministry for the Handicapped. At the very back of the complex, surrounded by raven-colored fields on three sides sat another of those white, three-storied buildings with a large white stockade fence that fortified the alcazar. You could see the faces of children peering through heart-shaped grates, black and rusting, which covered the windows and the doors—vacant eyes, older then they should have been, looking at us through black, rusted hearts. More dismal then the building was the screams and cries that echoed out and through the gates while we waited to enter. Here were the Irrecoverables—hidden from most of the populace and obscured in the back of a large compound, children screamed from the pain and purgatory of institutional life.

The three-tiered-system of institutions had very different physical conditions as well as child care standards. The most horrendous conditions were found in the institutions for the Irrecoverables and the images seen in the media such as those presented in the *20/20* special "*Shame of a Nation*" were from these settings. Romania was not unique in this system of institutions. It appears that there are similar institutions and tiered systems in Russia[6] and the Baltic States,[7] with a range of quality in their atmosphere, staff, and programs.

Normal Child Development—Keeping Perspective

By understanding what is typical, healthy development, we can better understand how life can be complicated for children growing up in an institution where there is an interruption in the normal path of development. Normally, children develop and grow according to a set schedule. Growth and development begin prenatally and we know that maternal health, nutrition, exposure to stress or toxic chemicals, and the quality of life in general have a profound effect on the developing fetus. After birth, while children vary in their rates of development, they all proceed through the same sequences.

A PEACOCK OR A CROW

Normal development is governed by intrinsic maturational factors and environmental conditions. Initially, there are rapid changes and gains made in physical development—children gain weight and grow—as well as the mastering of physical tasks such as the gross and fine motor skills that allow children to eat, cry, smile, turn over, crawl, stand, walk, jump, etc. To maximize normal growth and development, children need proper nutrition, sunshine, hygienic conditions, warmth, stimulation, attention, and love. At the same time as this is occurring, attachments begin developing, usually between mother and child. At first, the infant becomes attracted to all objects; it is only after several weeks that they begin to prefer humans to inanimate objects. Children will, from birth, give cues to their needs, that, if they are well cared for, will be met by a parent or whoever cares for them. For example, when they are hungry or uncomfortable, they will cry. When they express a need and the need is met in a consistent and timely manner, this results in a foundation of trust for the child toward the attachment figure who is fulfilling their needs. From the first weeks of life, there is a clustering of attachment behaviors that influence both how the child responds to the parent or caregiver as well as how the parent responds to the child. While, initially, children do not differentiate between caregivers, at three-months-old an infant begins to smile more at his primary caregiver than at strangers. By the end of the first six months of life, they learn to discriminate between familiar and unfamiliar attachment figures. From the first year of life, approximately up until the age of three, children will begin to protest when attachment figures leave them and they will engage in various behaviors to remain close to the attachment figure. If an infant develops a trusting relationship with the primary caregiver, the infant will desperately seek to always stay with that one attachment figure. This attachment will enhance the parents' effectiveness in the later socialization of the child.[8]

In addition to attachment behaviors, as a child's cognitive abilities develop, he or she develops ideas about relationships and the manner in which the world works, based on these experiences. These changes in their cognitive and intellectual development affect their personality, moral reasoning, and critical thinking skills.

During the first year of life, children begin to acquire language skills. The first skills are sounds such as cooing, crying, laughing, etc. Often they are introduced or reinforced by the primary caregiver. At a later point, children begin to organize the sounds that will eventually become language.

Finally, all these developmental tasks and activities—physical growth, attachment, cognitive development, the learning of language—influence the child as a socially skilled being. Obviously, social skills are important for the development and maintenance of the social relationships that are to soon follow. This includes relating to siblings, peers, extended family members, neighbors and community members at large. Social skills are important by the time children are ready to navigate and negotiate their way to preschool, kindergarten, and other activities outside the home.

This overview of a reasonably normal childhood is important as we look at what happens to children who are institutionalized at an early age. More often than not, they are not exposed to the stimuli of relationships or placed in an environment where the usual needs can be met and the average tasks of childhood are not accomplished.

Recent research strongly suggests that many of the tasks and developmental achievements, those which are not organically or physically based, influence the neurological and biochemical development of the brain. Unfortunately, such ideas are largely based on theoretical models and related research on animals. The degree to which they accurately reflect the capacity of children's brains to be able to reverse childhood trauma is not well known.

In 1996, a new round of sensationalism was added to the media coverage of the problems associated with children who have been institutionalized before adoption. Family tales of suffering and soft science met on TV programs. Adopted Romanian children were treated as guinea pigs as the news media touted brain scans for children who had been institutionalized early in life. Despite all those visual images of all-black brain scans and patches of blue and red activity areas in their brain, most children look good. This type of information, black brain scans, was taken from a very small group of children and is meant to be gathered for research. Indeed, the information from this type of research is still very much in the early stages. The danger, concerning the media in this case, is that it gives the public a skewed, simplistic view of an issue that is as complicated as the brain itself. Knowing that a part of your child's brain isn't functioning doesn't give you any information about what you can do differently. It creates anxiety and fear, but doesn't tell a family or a practitioner what can be done to improve upon the actual problem. Children's brains have amazing recuperative powers. The fact is, that despite the media's relentless attempts to sow panic among a susceptible public, it's still too early to come to any absolute conclusions.

What is certain is that the quality of a family and social environment is crucial. If we accept that a family is an ideal environment for a child, then we need to understand what happens to children who spend their formative years in some kind of group or institutional setting.

The Effects of Institutionalization

The negative effects of early institutionalization have made headlines in England and America for the past 90 years. Institutionalization early in life interrupts the parent/child cycle of bonding, which results in attachment difficulties as well as slowing emotional, social, and physical development.[9] Early deprivation can affect a person's ability to make smooth transitions from one development stage to another throughout life.

A PEACOCK OR A CROW

Henry Dwight Chapin[10] was one of the first researchers to examine child development in institutionalized settings. The director of pediatrics at Columbia University Medical School, Chapin began his work after realizing that, by the turn of the century, the infant mortality rate in institutions had reached an astonishing 100%. Chapin discovered that there was a critical period for development in institutionalized infants—that the first year of life is absolutely crucial for normal development and the first six months even more important than the second.[11] He reported that the first noticeable effect of institutionalization was a progressive loss of weight. If weight loss got beyond a certain point, no change in the amount of food intake or environmental change could save the child. Dryness of skin, loss of hair, and dehydration accompanied this condition. The predominant cause of death was not starvation but pneumonia.

Chapin became convinced that infants were at a great risk for developmental difficulties and a quick death when placed in institutions. In the early 1890s, he opened the first hospital social service in the United States. He believed it was essential that infants only be institutionalized briefly, if at all. Acting on this belief, Chapin began a boarding-out or fostering system in 1902, where hospitalized infants were placed in the homes of private families. This was one of the forerunners of the foster care movement in the U.S.

Society took note: humanitarian changes were made in the U. S. system of institutions. Still, despite serious improvements in hygienic conditions and sanitary practices, increased knowledge of infection control, and better food, the mortality rate of infants in institutions did not substantially decline. The single most important factor, Chapin felt, was a lack of proper individual attention, care and stimulation; that which, under normal circumstances, were provided by maternal love and care.[12] He also concluded that it was not the length of time spent in an institution, but the age at which the child was initially placed: the younger the child, the more serious the effects and greater the risk of negative effects.

Once the family foster system was properly established, the high infant mortality rate declined. Photos and data from Chapin's research clearly show how children looked on the day they were removed from institutions and then how they looked six months after they entered a foster home. The most drastic change was weight gain. By 1917, Chapin had concluded that this effect was a consequence of close individual care, especially the *holding* of infants when they were fed (as opposed to just holding the bottle in an upward position and feeding the infant in its crib without any physical contact).[13]

Subsequent to Chapin, several researchers did seminal work in the areas of the effects of institutions on early growth and development. There is ample evidence that early institutionalization can result in severe emotional and behavioral problems as well as fundamental problems with learning, reading ability, and basic intellectual functions.[14] Behavioral problems included aggressive or antisocial behavior, and difficulty in forming close, intimate relationships. Still, such results have had no absolutes; there have been many cases of remediation or the reversibility of early trauma. For example, in one of the earliest studies conducted, Professor Goldfarb in England[15] concluded that some children adjust well socially and emotionally despite their negative experiences of institutional deprivation in early childhood. Other researchers also found that prolonged institutionalization does not necessarily lead to emotional problems or character defects in all children.[16] This suggests that there will always be some children who fare well, who are resilient, regardless of their experiences in early childhood. However, these earlier studies should be viewed with caution. The institutions in these studies were not prototypical of Romanian institutions. Children in these studies who had been institutionalized had access to individual space, good nutrition, education programs, and adequate child-to-staff ratios.

Still, this work leads to certain conclusions. It certainly is a fact that, while children can be positively affected by moving from institutions to families, the effects of the past do not necessarily disappear over time.[17] Just as is the case with typical families, beyond issues of economic well-being, environment and social class, one comes to a clear conclusion that most of us already know instinctively: a lot depends on parental willingness to devote a great deal of time and attention to their children to help them recover.

A helpful set of studies, for the sake of perspective, is one involving twins done by Jarmila Koluchova in 1972 and 1976.[18] These twins, born and raised in a conventional family setting with the appropriate care up until the age of eighteen months, had then been institutionalized, isolated and neglected until the age of seven. Despite initial diagnoses that were pessimistic, by age eleven the children had made amazing progress. These children ultimately performed at average levels in school. Within four years, they attached strongly with a mother figure and a carefully trained, networked team of multi-disciplinary professionals. Koluchova found that, with good stimulation and care over the first two years of life, children can recover from subsequent bouts of neglect and isolation. A unanimous opinion of experts involved in these early studies is that the children who adjust the least well of all when it comes to coping with separation are the ones who are institutionalized before the age of one.

A specific problem, of concern to parents and professionals, is the effects of institutionalization on attachment. Attachment is a term you'll hear a lot. It applies to a durable, lasting relationship between a child and one or more persons with whom he or she interacts regularly: ideally a family and other siblings. Attachment serves a variety of functions, such as basic nurturing, interaction, discipline and affection. Attachment is the connection that allows parents to teach values and expectations, and for children to accept these values and expectations.

Attachment develops over time; it is not a static process, but a continuum from weak to strong, influenced by life's experiences, that has to be labored at and developed. So, it changes over time. The impact of institutionalization on long-term attachment patterns is not well known. It is clear that institutionalization places children at-risk for attachment problems, and this contributes to fear and anxiety among parents and professionals.

> When we walked into the room, about a dozen children, ages two and three, were sitting on the floor. About half of them immediately got up and ran to us with outstretched arms to be picked up. They were persistent, trying to climb up our bodies if we were not quick enough to pick them up. Some of the bigger or stronger ones would push the smaller ones away. They would touch our face, look at us and say *Mama* or *Tata* (father). They were indiscriminately affectionate. There were a few children who just looked at us blankly and continued to sit on the floor. They would avoid our attention if we looked at them. They made no attempt to move towards or away from us. But a few children looked at us, screamed, and ran to their nurses for protection and comfort. The reactions of these children, all in the same setting with the same experiences, represent different patterns of attachment. What we could not tell potential families is which of these patterns would change.

John Bowlby, who worked for the World Health Organization early in his career, provided the basis for most of attachment theory and practice. He argued that institutions fail to provide children with the intimate, warm, and continuous relationships that primary caregivers (usually mothers) can give. According to Bowlby, such a relationship is an absolutely necessary condition for successful human development. If a child is institutionalized for long enough, he or she may become incapable of forming the breadth and depth of human relationships necessary for survival and development. Attachment also provides the foundation of a conscience. In a "normal" home, attachment to parents results in the child wanting to act in ways that please the parent. If early connections are weakened or problematic, there is a decrease in the desire to please the people important to us—because people are just not that important to us. Related research has identified children with histories of early childhood abuse or neglect as being at greater risk for experiencing attachment difficulties.[19]

> We were told that the Institutions for the Irrecoverables were the training ground for Securitate. It was the perfect place to raise children into mindless, guiltless puppets who would rob, torture or kill for a reward. As an example, one of the children in the institution was considered educable, even though he had some retardation. While we were there, he had been taken to a farm for training. The farmers taught him how to string up and butcher a pig. The next night, he put his skills into action. All night long we had been kept awake by the pitiful howls and moans of a dog. When we asked one of the guards, he said it had been a dog in labor all night. One of the nurses told us, outside the hearing range of the guard, that he was a liar. The boy who had been taken to the farm had taken a dog, strung it up, and tortured it—using the butchering of the pig as his guide. He did this to the jeers and encouragement of the guards. What we heard that night was the suffering of the dog, who after hours of torture was left to die on her own. The next day the boy was beaming as he was praised by the guards, and relished the fear shown by the nurses.

Adults who formed healthy attachments during early childhood will have the capacity to experience healthy adult life. Children who were emotionally deprived, however, will continue to remain emotionally isolated as adults, have difficulty with relationships, and may act in deviant or delinquent ways. They are all too often manipulative in their behavior, using others for their emotional support without reciprocating or letting anyone get close to them emotionally. Some are haunted by loneliness. As adults they often cannot hold on to either jobs or relationships.

These studies clearly have many implications concerning the health and development of children from Romanian institutions. These children can be considered at risk for health and developmental problems. Families adopting them need to be prepared for their special needs. We are still learning to identify the trauma that is reversible and the trauma that is manageable, since the effects of some trauma are long term and unlikely to change.

A Description of Romanian Institutions

A more formal description of these institutions is necessary to gain an understanding of the devastating impact these orphanages and institutions had on some of the children adopted from Romania, as well as the continued risk that they pose for children still surviving in them. In must be mentioned that there were differences among the various institutions—some had bigger budgets and better qualified personnel. Still, in layman's terms—it was a case of bad to worse, the rock in competition with the hard place, the devil doing a doggie paddle to prevent drowning in the deep blue sea.

> We pushed the buzzer and waited to be escorted into the building. We were immediately swarmed by children, some half-dressed, many with obvious physical handicaps, coming to see the *straine* (strangers). They were shooed away by the guards and we were ushered into the Director's office. Since this was our first meeting, after introductions we were all served *tzuica* with selzer water. Of course, it was 10 AM but this is the hospitality of Romanians. Besides, the staff were more interested in Americans than the children under their care. We were then left alone and our escorts left the premises. We were told to make our report to the Ministry for the Handicapped when we completed our work. The Director left his office and said he would return. With nothing else left to do, we waited. This is what you do a lot in Romania, you wait. Often, you wait for nothing. Several hours later we were shown to our rooms—two rooms on the ground floor that were big enough to be a classroom for 20 children—joined by a smaller room with a sink, toilet and shower. The walls were painted mustard-brown. The water, when it ran, was brown. On one side was a pig farm; on the other side the sewer drained on to the playground, and in the back were large garbage dumpsters. Surrounded by sewage, garbage and pigs—a clear metaphor, if this was the "wrapping," you can only begin to imagine what was inside.

The orphanages were colorless, shockingly quiet and devoid of any of the usual visual or auditory stimulation that children usually receive from bright colors, pictures, and displays. Walls were painted in dark browns, to hide the dirt. The paint absorbed any light—when there were working light switches and light bulbs—making halls and bedrooms darker. It seemed as if the entire building was sucking the souls of the children, and perhaps the staff that worked there. There were no toys. There was no exercise or exposure to the outside.[20] Most of the time, the children did not have enough to eat or drink. Consequently, most children were below the twentieth percentile for height and weight compared to normally developing children.[21] One consequence of low height and weight is greater susceptibility to diseases. While official data were not available, some staff said that mortality rates in the winter could reach 40%. Recent information suggests that 50% died within the first 24 months.[22]

> In the back behind the dumpster was a small field with a fence all around it. In a farm village, all land is used. But this small area was speckled with little mounds that were grown over with grasses, weeds and wildflowers. We asked the staff about the little field. They said it was nothing, just unused land. Then, one of the children, an "irrecoverable" with spina bifida who had learned to speak English, said that it was the field of the dead children. After speaking to some of the volunteers and the local school teacher who taught English, we learned that when children died, they were buried in this field in unmarked graves. These children had no families, so there was no sponsor to have them baptized. If they had no families and were not baptised, they could not be buried in holy ground. Besides, even if the families knew the children were here, they couldn't afford a burial. So, the little mounds were graves. It was as the bitter Romanian saying: lucky for the dead, their ordeals are over.

In addition, children in orphanages were exposed to stunningly inadequate child-to-staff ratios ranging from 8:1 to 35:1. This allowed for an absolute minimum of personal interaction.[23] Crying was ignored, both as policy and as a natural reaction to so few staff caring for so many children. The staff provided minimum touching and handling of the children; the children who were left lying in cribs were not changed in position or stimulated for most of the day.[24]

> The first day that we were to conduct assessments, the Director had set us up in a room at the end of the hallway on the first floor of the institution. The first floor housed all the children ages 3 to 6, our target group for assessment. We were on time for our program and waited for the translators to arrive. They were an hour late. We went with the translators to the first room, which had 8 beds and 12 children. The nurse was directed to bring the first child, a little boy of 5 named Florin, with her for the assessment. She picked up the child; he pushed her away. As she got to the door to go down the hall, he started crying. By the time we had walked about 100 feet to the office, he was inconsolable—screaming, crying and trying to get out of her arms. We were shocked—we asked the translator to explain to us. First, the nurse said it was because we were strangers. However, we pointed out that we had been in the bedroom with him and he had been curious about our presence, not upset. After going in circles for almost an hour, what we discovered was that this child had

never before been out of the room. Can you imagine? Five-years-old and only to have known the same four walls! Children only distinguish between what is familiar and unfamiliar to them. This child was frightened and distressed by the unfamiliar surroundings. Since most of the children had never left their rooms, we changed our protocol and conducted the other assessments in the rooms where the children had lived most of their lives.

However, on a bizarrely positive note, jobs are hard to find in Romania, thus staffing was and remains very stable. The same people were involved with children over time, and, one can surmise, that, even if the quality of care was extremely poor, the children were familiar with the staff who "took care of them."

It was never clear if there were expectations for the staff to do something with the children. We would see them standing together at the end of the hall, smoking cigarettes and drinking coffee, once the Director left the premises. The children were put in bed after dinner and just lay there. If the television was on, it was usually for the staff, although sometimes the older girls were allowed in the staff's room to watch TV. At night, while we sat in the room, we could hear children crying, followed by a slap, and silence. It wasn't unusual the next morning for us to see a bruised child, reportedly caused by one child hitting another child.

The only time the children were allowed out of bed or outside was when the foreign volunteers came. But the volunteers (from Ireland) did everything while the Romanian staff just stood by and watched. Did they just watch because they didn't care? Did they watch because it didn't matter what they did, they would have the same job at the same wage for life? Or, did they just watch because they felt no ownership in what was going on? A disempowerment from strangers who did not know the Romanian reality, strangers who would leave and go back to the comfort of their rich countries while nothing really changed here? With so many children, who belonged to no family, and a guaranteed job regardless of what you did-as long as you showed up-why do anything?

With so many children and so few staff, the children received minimal routine care. Educational and recreational programming was virtually nonexistent—no activities for children to stimulate them or for fun, no school or specialized programs designed to help them grow and develop. Children were left to their own devices for stimulation. Many would become autistic-like—having a blank stare, rocking back and forth, and looking constantly at their hands. Those children who were too active in exploring their environments were restrained—either physically with straps or chemically through tranquilizers.[25] Proper hygiene often could not be practiced due to a lack of hot water, soap, washing machines, clean bed linen, and an inadequate number of cots and beds. It was not uncommon for children to lay in their feces or urine. Having two children in the same bed was typical. In addition to a lack of running water, sewer systems were often inoperative.

What I remember is the smell. Having had nasal surgery a decade before I went to Romania, I suffered some damage. If I could smell it, I couldn't imagine how others were experiencing the smell. The staff would start to wash clothes, then the water would cut off. So, they would take the half washed clothes—most of which were covered with feces or soaked with urine—and leave them in the tubs until the water came back on. Sometimes, they stayed in their watery trough for days and a fetid film would develop. At times, when they ran out of bed clothes, they would put them in the dryer regardless of where they were in the wash cycle. The heat from the dyer would spread the smell throughout the whole building and the sheets would return with huge stains as well as the dried-in smell. So, our experience was open sewer on one side, pig farm on the other, pools of fetid water in the basement, and the hot air of human excrement. Some days we would have to walk to town. We could escape. The children could not.

The physical structure of these institutions was also a problem. Most windows had neither screens nor glass. In the summer, flies would swarm the rooms and rainstorms would flood the floors. In the winter, children suffered frostbite due to a lack of heat and an inability to keep cold out of the wards and rooms.

Problems with administrative records added to the horrifying physical conditions. Birth records, medical histories, and information about biological parents would obviously have been invaluable to such children and their care; but, because so many children had been abandoned at the hospital, this was an impossibility. Most charts in Romanian institutions were found to only have two lines, created by the institution itself.[26] When children were moved from institution to institution, which was a common practice, their charts rarely followed them. In many cases, if parents wanted to find their children again, it became an impossibility; they were lost to the system. Even more diabolical was the fact that, after Iliescu took power and the adoption chaos began in 1990, the law insisted that no adoption could take place without parental consent. So, you had children with no records and parents who didn't know where to find their children, often having no contact with them for several years.

We spent one day just reviewing children's records with our translators. You have to keep in mind that these children were between the ages of three and five. Typically, there was a one-page record. We did get some information, however, from these records: about 60% of the children were there because of poverty—the parents couldn't afford to keep them. But, then there were all these diagnosis that we had never heard of—nor had the translators, both who were college educated in Romania. It seemed that under communism an entire nomenclature of diagnosis had been established that had no relevance to western treatment and made little sense to the Romanians. Even if the Romanians understood the "diagnosis," there was no treatment or plan for treating the diagnosis given. The saddest thing is that we found almost nothing in most of the files about the families of these children.

Staff hired to work in the orphanages and institutions were not required to possess any special qualifications that might improve their interactions with these children. Job descriptions, rewards for excelling, and organizational charts were not available. Penalties for failing to perform tasks were not enforced, which only served to enable incompetent staff members.

> It was obvious that the only person in charge was the director. So, when he was in his office for a break or left the building, the children were ignored. The staff, who were mostly unskilled peasant women, would congregate around the television to drink coffee, smoke and laugh with each other. Usually, one of the older children was left to oversee the other children, or else the door to the room was shut and the children would not dare open the door. One day, when we came back from doing our daily shopping at the *piata* (market place) in town, we found all the children on one floor huddled under the steps of one of the landings with one of the boys standing over them. They cowered silently while he glared at them. If they moved, he would grunt and lunge at them—forcing them to cower back under the stairs. One of the children obviously had challenged his authority and was left bruised and bleeding. It seemed that the Director had left the grounds for the day, so the one child was rewarded with cigarettes and candy to "watch" over the other children.

Since the closing of social work programs in the 1960's, there were no social workers to conduct permanency planning, crisis intervention, extended family foster care services, domestic adoption, or home-based care. When abandoned children became ill, despite socialist propaganda claims, hospitals would oftentimes refuse them based upon insufficient means of official family identities. These children had no advocates, so it was common for them to remain in institutions and receive little or no medical care for their illnesses. It was no wonder they had to have a burial field for the children whose only escape was through death.

Studies of Romanian Institutions

> *A whole people, not yet born*
> *Is condemned to be born.*
> GABRIELA ADAMSTEANU, 1990

The veracity of Ms. Adamasteanu's verse cannot be doubted. There are more children institutionalized in Romania than ever before. The Romanian government, despite the elections that set "democracy" in motion, still plays shell games when it comes to information access for visiting foreign social workers and the media. Nevertheless, the anecdotal evidence gleaned from scores of interviews and off-the-record conversations with English, Irish, French, German, Canadian and American social workers, nurses, physicians, lawyers and adoption consultants—many of whom have been regularly in and out of Romania for the past seven years—and accounts such as the United Nations Report on Children in Eastern and Central Europe,[27] shows that, although conditions are slightly better in some institutions, the number of incarcerated children has risen. The much publicized Orphanage Number One—patronized and filled with toys by the pop music icon Michael Jackson—may look great in the thousands of sound-byte broadcasts put out around the world, but it's all cosmetic. Help is still desperately needed.

Several studies were conducted in various institutions and orphanages in Romania. Studies were conducted prior to and in the immediate aftermath of the "revolution," and over the past seven years since. The findings of these researchers are remarkably similar to those first published by Henry Dwight Chapin at the turn of the century.

Olimpia Macovei,[28] a Romanian scientist, assessed the developmental delays of institutionalized children in the district of Iasi from 1976 to 1986. The delays she noted included less physical growth, decreased social and motor skills, and lags in psychological and intellectual functioning. These findings were corroborated by Dr. Dana Johnson and colleagues[29] when a group of 65 adopted children from Romania were examined at a clinic in Minnesota. Dr. Johnson and colleagues reported that only 15% appeared to be developmentally normal and in good health; head circumference, weight and height had all been negatively affected by institutionalization.

Two other problems of institutionalized Romanian children, reported as early as 1990 by the Center for Disease Control, were the predominance of the human immune deficiency virus (HIV) and hepatitis (HBV) infections. As of 1990, the incidence of pediatric AIDS ran second only to the number of cases reported in the U.S.

Consequently, because of the lack of knowledge about infection control and a denial of the existence of the virus by the Romanian government, universal precautions were not practiced. It appears that the infections children acquired, along with those passed on by blood transfusions, came from syringes that weren't properly sterilized and were used repeatedly on as many patients as possible. As early as February 1990, two months after the revolution, families adopting children from Romania were encouraged to have their children tested for HIV/AIDS[30].

As the world's attention focused on the orphaned and abandoned children in Romania, many organizations and individual volunteers entered the institutions. From these efforts, several reports were generated about the children from these institutions. Some researchers suggested that the children in the orphanage displayed clear deficits in social and cognitive functioning compared to same age children attending kindergarten.[31] On the basis of these differences, researchers predicted that these children would have learning difficulties in the future. Yet, the way in which these children utilized one another during testing—constantly adapting to each other as "friends" even though they were deliberately rotated from room to room and, sometimes, from facility to facility—showed major coping skills and strengths. Also, once international groups arrived, the vast majority of children made tremendous positive changes in their growth and development. Some promising results have been reported that offset many of the harsh effects. Programs that involved changing the institution and training community volunteers to stimulate children can improve children's functioning, even if they continue to reside in institutions.[32]

Summary: An Institution Is No Place to Call Home!

"Please, sir. I want some more."

CHARLES DICKENS: *Oliver Twist*

Institutions, regardless of the quality of care, have profound negative effects on children that may well last a lifetime. At a minimum, the regimentation of institutional life does not provide children with the type or quality of experiences they need to be healthy, happy, fully functioning adults. In group care, the needs of any individual child are secondary to the requirements of group routine. Relationships between adults and children are superficial and brief, with little or no warmth or affection. Institutional staff do not connect emotionally or physically in nearly the same way families connect with children. In developing countries like Romania, early institutional care will likely lead to institutional care for the rest of a child's life. Prevention of institutionalization should be emphasized because some children may not ever be able to completely overcome the negative effects of institutionalization.

Hope is there, however. Some children are just plain ol' resilient, regardless of the sticky experiences and circumstances of their early lives. Children leaving institutions can be positively affected by the quality of the family life they enter. The effects of institutionalization are very much influenced by the age of the child when they enter and the length of time spent incarcerated. While this evidence has been accumulating for many years, the children of Romania offer us a unique opportunity to review what we know and further examine until we know for a certainty which trauma is reversible and which is at least manageable.

Notes from Chapter 3

[1] Johnson, A. K., Edwards, R. L., & Puwak, H. C. (1993). Foster care and adoption policy in Romania: Suggestions for international intervention. Child Welfare, 72(5), 489-506.

Stephenson, P. A., Anghelescu, C., Bobe, N., Ciomartan, T., Gaistenau, M., Fumarel, S., Goldis, C., Georgescu, A., Ionescu, M., Iorgulescu, D., Lupu, R., McCreery, R., McKay, S., Manescu, V., Mihai, B., Moldovanu, F., Moldovan, Z., Morosam, I., Nanu, R.,

Nicolau, A., Palikari, G., Pascu, C., Popa, S., Popescu, P., Raican, A., Stanescu, A., Stativa, E., & Stoica, M. (1994). The causes of childrens' institutionalization in Romania. Child Care Health and Development, 20(2), 77-88.

[2] UNICEF. (1997). Children at risk in Central and Eastern Europe: Perils and promises. Florence, Italy: United Nations Children's Fund, International Child Development Centre.

[3] Romanian Monitor News, August 7, 1997.

[4] See also Johnson, A., & Groze, V. (1993). The orphaned and institutionalized children of Romania. Journal of Emotional and Behavioral Problems, 2(4), 49-52.

[5] Johnson, A., & Groze, V. (1993). The orphaned and institutionalized children of Romania. Journal of Emotional and Behavioral Problems, 2(4), 49-52.

[6] Sloutsky. V. M. (1997). Institutional care and developmental outcomes of 6- and 7-year old children: A contextualist perspective. International Journal of Behavior Development, 20(1), 131-151.

[7] Harrison, L, Rubeiz, G., & Kochubey, A. (1996). Lapsele Oma Kodu (bringing abandoned children home): A project from Tallinn, Estonia to reunite institutionalized children with families. Scandanavian Journal of Social Welfare, 5, 35-44.

[8] Hetherington, M. E., & Park, R. D. (1986). Child psychology: A contemporary viewpoint. New York: McGraw-Hill.

[9] Bowlby, J. (1951). Maternal care and mental health. World Health Organization Monograph No. 2. Geneva: WHO.

Bowlby, J. (1969). Attachment and loss: Attachment. New York: Basic Books.

Bowlby, J.(1973). Attachment and loss: Separation, anxiety and anger. New York: Basic Books.

Bowlby, J. (1988). A secure base: Clinical applications of attachment theory. Routledge, London: A Tavistock Professional Book.

Frank, D. A., Klass, P. E., Earls, F., & Eisenberg, L. (1996). Infants and young children in orphanages: One view from pediatrics and child psychiatry. Pediatrics, 47(4), 569-578.

Freud, A., & Burlingham, D. T. (1944). Infants without families. New York: International University Press.

Goldfarb, W. (1943b). Effects of early institutional care on adolescent personality. Journal of Experimental Education, 12, 106-129.

Goldfarb, W. (1955). Emotional and intellectual consequences of psychologic deprivation in infancy: A re-evaluation. In P. Hoch & J. Zubin (Eds.), Psychopathology of childhood (pp. 105-119). New York: Grune & Stratton.

Provence, S. A., & Lipton, R. C. (1962). Infants in institutions. New York: International Universities Press.

Spitz, R. A. (1945). Hospitalism: An inquiry into the genesis of psychiatric conditions in early childhood. Psychoanalytic Study of the Child, 1, 53-74.

Tizard, B., & Joseph, A. (1970). Cognitive development of young children in residential care: The study of children aged 24 months. Journal of Child Psychology and Psychiatry, 11, 177-186.

Tizard, B., & Rees, J. (1974). A comparison of the effects of adoption, restoration to the natural mother, and continued institutionalization on the cognitive development of four year old children. Child Development, 45, 92-99.

Tizard, B., & Rees, J. (1975). The effect of early institutional rearing on the behaviour problems and affectional relationships of four-year-old children. Journal of Child Psychology and Psychiatry, 75, 61-73

Tizard, B., Hodges, J. (1977). The effect of early institutional rearing on the development of eight-year-old children. Journal of Child Psychology and Psychiatry, 19, 99-118.

[10] Chapin, H. D. (1911). The proper management of foundings and neglected infants. Medical Record, 79, 283-288.

Chapin, H.D. (1916). A scheme of state control for dependent infants. Medical Record, 84, 1081-1084.

Chapin, H. D. (1917). Systematized boarding out vs. institutional care for infants and young children. New York Medical Journal, 105, 1009-1011.

[11] Gray, P. H. (1989). Henry Dwight Chapin: Pioneer in the study of institutionalized infants. Bulletin of the Psychonomic Society, 27(1), 85-87.

[12] Gray, P. H. (1989). Henry Dwight Chapin: Pioneer in the study of institutionalized infants. Bulletin of the Psychonomic Society, 27(1), 85-87.

[13] Chapin, H. D. (1917). Systematized boarding out vs. institutional care for infants and young children. New York Medical Journal, 105, 1009-1011.

[14] Freud, A., & Burlingham, D. T. (1944). Infants without families. New York: International University Press.

Goldfarb, W. (1943b). Effects of early institutional care on adolescent personality. Journal of Experimental Education, 12, 106-129.

Goldfarb, W. (1955). Emotional and intellectual consequences of psychologic deprivation in infancy: A re-evaluation. In P. Hoch & J. Zubin (Eds.), Psychopathology of childhood (pp. 105-119). New York: Grune & Stratton.

Provence, S. A., & Lipton, R. C. (1962). Infants in institutions. New York: International Universities Press.

Spitz, R. A. (1945). Hospitalism: An inquiry into the genesis of psychiatric conditions in early childhood. Psychoanalytic Study of the Child, 1, 53-74.

Tizard, B., & Joseph, A. (1970). Cognitive development of young children in residential care: The study of children aged 24 months. Journal of Child Psychology and Psychiatry, 11, 177-186.

Tizard, B., & Rees, J. (1974). A comparison of the effects of adoption, restoration to the natural mother, and continued institutionalization on the cognitive development of four year old children. Child Development, 45, 92-99.

Tizard, B., & Rees, J. (1975). The effect of early institutional rearing on the behaviour problems and affectional relationships of four-year-old children. Journal of Child Psychology and Psychiatry, 75, 61-73

Tizard, B., Hodges, J. (1977). The effect of early institutional rearing on the development of eight-year-old children. Journal of Child Psychology and Psychiatry, 19, 99-118.

[15] Goldfarb, W. (1955). Emotional and intellectual consequences of psychologic deprivation in infancy: A Re-evaluation. In P. Hoch & J. Zubin (Eds.), Psychopathology of Childhood (pp. 105-119). NY: Grune & Stratton.

[16] Pringel, M. L., & Bossio, V. (1960). Early, prolonged separation and emotional adjustment. Journal of Child Psychology and Psychiatry, 37-48.

Wolkind, S. N. (1974). The components of "affectionless psychopathy" in institutionalized children. Journal of Child Psychology and Psychiatry, 15, 215-220.

[17] Wolkind, S., & Rutter, M. (1973). Children who have been "in care"—an epidemiological study. Journal of Child Psychology and Psychiatry, 14, 97-105.

Tizard, B., Hodges, J. (1977). The effect of early institutional rearing on the development of eight-year-old children. Journal of Child Psychology and Psychiatry, 19, 99-118.

[18] Koluchova, J. (1972). Severe deprivation in twins: A case study. Journal of Child Psychology and Psychiatry, 13, 107-114.

Koluchova, J. (1976). The further development of twins after severe and prolonged deprivation: A second report. Journal of Child Psychology and Psychiatry, 17, 181-188.

[19] Bowlby, J. (1951). Maternal care and mental health. World Health Organization Monograph No. 2. Geneva: WHO.

Bowlby, J. (1969). Attachment and loss: Attachment. New York: Basic Books.

Bowlby, J.(1973). Attachment and loss: Separation, anxiety and anger. New York: Basic Books.

Bowlby, J. (1988). A secure base: Clinical applications of attachment theory. Routledge, London: A Tavistock Professional Book.

[20] Ames, E. W., & Carter, M. (1992). Development of Romanian orphanage children adopted to Canada. Canadian Psychology, 33(2), 503.

[21] Johnson, A., & Groze, V. (1993). The orphaned and institutionalized children of Romania. Journal of Emotional and Behavioral Problems, 2(4), 49-52.

[22] Bascom, B. B., McKelvey, C. A. (1997). The complete guide to foreign adoption: What to expect and how to prepare for your new child. New York: Pocket Books

[23] McMullan, S. J., & Fisher, L. (1992). Developmental progress of Romanian orphanage children in Canada. Canadian Psychology, 33(2), 504.

[24] Sweeney, J. K. & Bascom, B. B. (1995). Motor development and self-stimulatory movement in institutionalized Romanian children. Pediatric Physical Therapy, 7, 124-132.

[25] Ames, E. W., & Carter, M. (1992). Development of Romanian orphanage children adopted to Canada. Canadian Psychology, 33(2), 503.

[26] Johnson, A., & Groze, V. (1993). The orphaned and institutionalized children of Romania. Journal of Emotional and Behavioral Problems, 2(4), 49-52.

[27] Wolkind, S. N. (1974). The components of "affectionless psychopathy" in institutionalized children. Journal of Child Psychology and Psychiatry, 15, 215-220.

[28] Macovei, O. (1986). The medical and social problems of the handicapped in children's institutions in Iasi. Bucharest, Romania: Pediatrie-Ed. Didactica si Ped, Institutul de Igiena si Sanatate Publica.

[29] Johnson, D. E., Miller, L. C., Iverson, S., Thomas, W., Franchino, B., Dole, K., Kiernan, M. T., Georgieff, M. K., & Hostetter, M. K. (1992, December 23/30). The health of children adopted from Romania. Journal of the American Medical Association, 268(24), 3446-3451.

Johnson, D. E., Miller, L. C., Iverson, S., Thomas, W., Franchino, B., Dole, K., Kiernan, M. T., Georgieff, M. K., & Hostetter, M. K. (1993, April 28). The health of children adopted from Romania. Journal of the American Medical Association, 269(16): 2084-5.

[30] Judy Siegel. (1990, February 9). Health Ministry Recommends Testing Adopted Romanian Children for AIDS. The Jerusalem Post.

[31] Kaler, S. R., & Freeman, B. J. (1994). An analysis of environmental deprivation: Cognitive and social development in Romanian orphans. Journal of Child Psychology and Psychiatry and Allied Disciplines. 35(4), 769-81.

[32] Sweeney, J. K. & Bascom, B. B. (1995). Motor development and self-stimulatory movement in institutionalized Romanian children. Pediatric Physical Therapy, 7, 124-132.

Chapter 4

Ivan and Ciprian: A Child Lost and Found

Although I had spent a few days in Romania back in the 1970s, the first visit I made there with the intent of adoption was in March, 1990, shortly after the news stories in the West began appearing concerning the overcrowded orphanages. Aside from the news articles themselves, the only additional information I secured was from a *New York Times* reporter who had written one of the orphanage stories. I talked with him in Sofia, Bulgaria, en route overland from Istanbul to Bucharest; and, while his article may have been accurate concerning the situation in Iasi, nearly all of the information he gave me—which was uniformly discouraging concerning the prospects of a non-Romanian single person being able to do an adoption—was inaccurate. This is not an indictment of his competence, it's just that he had not researched the rapidly changing adoption procedures himself and his conjectures proved to be wrong.

According to the U.S. Embassy in Bucharest, at the time of my visit, there had been only ten American adoptions approved, all from the Bucharest orphanages. Because the American Embassy did not have information concerning orphanages in other towns, I went to the health ministry and got a list of towns having orphanages, along with an estimate of their size and capacity. The orphanage locations I visited were in Timosoara, Arad, Sibiu, Brasov and Babadag. I found a two-year-four-month-old ethnic Russian boy (his family had immigrated many years ago) at the Babadag orphanage who I decided to adopt because of his exceptional intelligence and freedom from any physical or health problems. The major difficulty at all of these locations—and throughout Romania—was that few of the institutionalized children truly were orphans, and, without parental consent, which was usually lacking and unobtainable, they were not adoptable.

I returned to the U.S. in April, 1990, to begin the process of getting a home study completed and the INS forms processed. During this time, the local Commission for Minors was making an effort to convince the child's father to sign a consent form for adoption (which he had previously refused to do), which they were successful in securing by May, 1990. I approached this process backwards, by completing the Home Study and paperwork second. It made sense to me to find an adoptable child first and then do the paperwork later to effect the adoption, rather than doing the paperwork first with no idea as to whether it would lead to a successful adoption. Also, at the time the news stories about the overcrowded orphanage situation came to light, there appeared to me to be an issue of timeliness involved in getting over there fast, before the most easily and ideally adoptable children were spoken for. I hope this does not sound humanly insensitive, but, being unemployed and lacking health insurance at the time, I knew that I did not have either the financial or emotional resources to cope with the expenses and emotional drain of adequately treating and trying to raise a child having serious physical or mental problems. The timeliness perception issue proved to be correct. At nearly all of the orphanages I visited, I was the first American to have come there, and, in several cases, the first foreigner to have arrived expressing the intent to adopt. Had I waited and done the appropriate paperwork in the U.S. first, I know I would not have been able to find a child as intelligent and as in good health as I did without encountering the ethical dilemmas later facing so many other adoptive parents. These parents had to deal with the corruption issues of child buying and bribery that became rampant.

In early 1990, there were *no* adoption agencies in the U.S. that had experience in foreign adoptions in the Romanian environment—at least none that I was aware of. I found Ciprian (Chip) in early 1990. Due to the amount of time it took me to write an autobiographical history for the agency doing the Home Study, and the amount of time it took them and the INS to issue the Home Study and approval papers, it wasn't until fall that I was able to return to Romania to get the process moving again. After a brief sojourn in the United States, I was finally able to return in early November to actually complete the adoption process.

I find it unthinkable for someone to pay an adoption agency a huge sum of money to locate a child and do all the preliminaries of the process so that all the adoptive parents have to do is put in a token appearance in court to finalize the adoption and walk home with their child in the same way they might purchase an animal in a pet store. To pose another analogy, although I am aware that arranged marriages are made through marriage brokers in some parts of the world, the concept of doing this is so offensive in Western culture that most Americans shudder and laugh at the idea of it. And, aside from the newborn infant whom no one has cared for at all, any child, no matter what age, is going to have at least a few personality characteristics that can be discerned by a caregiver, and which can best be expressed directly between the caregiver and a prospective adoptive parent without being filtered through an adoption agency or broker. For example, the orphanage pediatrician, who had known Chip for only about three months since he turned two years of age, told me that he was a very headstrong child, and she was right. Although Chip and I sometimes intellectually lock horns over his stubbornness, I respect someone with the intellectual conviction to go to the mat for what he believes in and have approached the issue by always trying to explain the rationale behind my decision-making so that he can formulate decisions in his own mind, based on sound reasoning rather than emotion. As a probable consequence, his schoolteachers tell me that he has a very logical mind and is exceptionally good at conceptual and abstract reasoning.

My son was at home with his birth family until approximately seven months of age when (according to the orphanage pediatrician) he took sick with diarrhea and was taken to the hospital, where his parents simply didn't reclaim him. Afterwards, he was transferred to the orphanage where his parents didn't bother to visit him. The real story, at least according to first-hand information furnished by my son's biological father, was that Chip had not been sick, but the village doctor just came one day and took him away, apparently out of a perception that

Chip's mother was unable to take care of him. His mother, it seems, had developed a lingering and then increasingly severe case of postpartum depression, manifesting itself in sporadic violent reactions, which the social report from the local Commission for Minors refers to as *oligrophenia*. This is a condition which is not recognized by American psychiatry; it is a non-specific Romanian term for people who are half-crazy. Traceable to its Greek roots, it literally means "few brains." This was so sad because, at an earlier stage in her life, the woman was known to be highly intelligent. Meanwhile, the father had made repeated attempts to secure the child's return but was always rebuffed by the court system. Other relatives in the family corroborated this story, but they also explained that two other children of the family had died, and they were surprised that Chip's older brother and sister—aged sixteen and eleven respectively—survived, given the extremely impoverished circumstances in which they were raised. Chip's father explained that the reason he didn't visit him at the orphanage was that he was simply too saddened and embarrassed to do so.

Starting in Spring 1992, Chip and I visited his birth family, bringing them food, clothing and tools. So far, we have made five return visits and intend to keep returning. The first visit was met with some emotional strain on the part of Chip's birth mother, despite the fact that it was an extremely brief visit. However, the absolute delight of his brother and sister in seeing him again, after probably thinking they'd never encounter him again, as well as the happiness of his father, convinced me that this was something to continue. We have gotten to know his extended family and now Chip always asks me when we can go back, especially because he's developed a particularly close relationship with his cousin, who is a little closer to his own age than are his older brother and sister. While I obviously cannot predict the ultimate effect it will have on Chip as he grows older, I can only say that, based on the last four years' experience, the re-establishment of ties with his family has been overwhelmingly positive and I would certainly recommend it to other adoptive parents.

Based on my own experiences, as well as those related to me by other parents of Romanian adoptees, there are probably a host of problems and minor idiosyncratic behavior characteristics that are attributable to these children's early experiences in orphanages. However, I'd conjecture that results may be the same for children who experience neglect at their homes in the case of privately-arranged adoptions. There is already an adequate body of knowledge developing right here in the U.S.A. Concerning this assertion, research should identify and determine how common the characteristics are and track these children into maturity to see what effect, if any, these social and biological antecedents will create in their future lives.

Everything was fine for my son in pre-school and kindergarten. Unfortunately, troubles of a serious nature began at the bilingual English/French school in which I initially had enrolled him. According to Chip's teachers in school, he has difficulty in transitioning from one activity to another when the teacher wants to change the class' patterns of activity. I am unsure, however, as to whether this may be due to his headstrong nature and a reflection of the fact that I generally allow him to decide which activities he wants to do without forcing him to change from one thing to another. They also say he is overly sensitive to the actions or comments of his peers, or those of the teacher. For example, two or three weeks ago, in the morning, a classmate of his broke apart a Lego model Chip had constructed. His teacher indicated that it upset him so much that the rest of the morning he was unable to do any of the work in which the class was participating.

Enrolling Ciprian at a French International School, although it has done wonders for his French fluency skills, has revealed some problems I had not anticipated. In talking with native French people, I've learned that verbal teasing seems to be ingrained in the French culture from childhood to adulthood—to a much greater extent than here in the U.S. At the previous school, the teachers did much better at teaching socialization. Chip had closer friends there and seemed to make friends more easily. As a combined result of his early childhood experiences, as well as with the tendency I have of always discussing things with him as an equal rather than at a 'baby talk' level, his speech patterns in English are more adult-like than his classmates. Chip (at least in his own mind) believes he is being teased on the playground. He also has a tough time with the European school's systematic emphasis on the cursive system of handwriting, probably because of a slight lag in motor skills due to his early institutionalization. I, too, have the typically American lackadaisical attitude toward penmanship; despite the fact that he already knows more about history, geography, the social sciences, etc., than most of his classmates, his handwriting assignments seem to bother his teachers quite a bit. There has been discussion of his repeating a grade because of this problem, and, as a safety net, should the school not promote him next year, we have applied at one of the city's better English schools.

Having never raised a child before, it is impossible for me to tell how out-of-the-ordinary his behavior is. On the rare occasions I've had to leave him with others for a few days, I've received a variety of feedback responses, ranging from his being extremely well behaved, to his being angry, to his just being different than most kids. Because of my unemployment since before the adoption, he has had virtually my full attention for the last four years in terms of reading to him (for which he has developed a remarkably long attention span) as well as nearly always being there when he needs me. Since I speak to him as an adult and have never tried to talk down to him as a child, his vocabulary and cognitive skills probably far exceed those of most native-born English speaking children his own age. Last year, his schoolteachers told me that he frequently came up with ideas and concepts that completely blew the minds of his classmates.

When he is in a completely adult setting, his behavior generally impresses the adults; they often comment favorably upon his maturity. Nevertheless, there have been a few times when his behavior was the critical issue in his not being able to attend something or another because, previously, he became so disruptive that he completely blew his chances. His social skills with his peers often leave much to be desired. When he's in a mixed child/adult environment, especially if he becomes jealous that some other person has my attention, he is capable of some disturbingly anti-social behavior. I can only attribute this to the fact that, at the orphanage, he was unquestionably the master of his environment. It was a place in which he was very much able to control or orchestrate the play activities of all the twelve to fifteen other kids in his age group because of his superior intelligence.

Because Chip was happier, more responsive and attentive to the adult orphanage staff, they devoted much more time to him than they did the other children. Consequently, he learned to manipulate both the adults and children at the orphanage to his advantage. When he came to live with me there were no other children generally present, so, when he started school and attempted to execute the same tactics of trying to control the other children and teachers (because his peers at school in America were much smarter than his peers at the orphanage and the teachers, understandably, divide their time up more equitably among all the members of the class than did the staff at the orphanage), he found that it didn't work anymore. Therefore, sometimes he becomes so frustrated that he vents it in anti-social behavior.

How to overcome these problems is an issue I'm currently struggling with. I don't want to dampen his innate enthusiasm, but it's worrying that he'll take on virtually any challenge based on the assumption that he is always the best or the smartest. I'm trying to moderate his getting too big an ego because there has to be a realization that the competition is much stiffer now, and he must rely on hard work to compete with his classmates rather than his relying on having a natural superiority in ability.

Recently, Chip had an appointment with a speech therapist. He had never had a diagnosis before, and, after being advised to do so by his teachers, I went ahead and scheduled it, since it was free and there was nothing to lose. It turns out that, at the time he came to the U.S., although he *understood* Romanian, the staff at the Romanian Embassy in Washington with whom we visited could not understand him. My assumption, then and now, was that the orphanage teacher had never taught the children how to speak correctly, assuming, I guess, that they would just pick it up by listening to the adults speaking. I never ascribed much importance to his speech patterns because they seemed to be in a continually improving mode—i.e., people who had talked with him a long time ago, and again more recently, would comment on how much clearer his pronunciation was—so I made the assumption that he was going through a development or maturation process that only got underway for him at around age three rather than earlier for children whose speech patterns were taught from birth.

The sounds Chip has trouble with are the 'th', 'ch', 'sh' group—which are somewhat like an inverted or reverse lisp. I've seen in the relevant literature that these are frequently the most difficult for children to clearly enunciate, often not developing well for even a child in a normal situation until five or six years of age. Even I have some difficulty differentiating Chip's pronunciation of thirty from forty, or thirteen from fourteen. After about an hour-and-a-half's-worth of tests, the diagnosis of the speech therapist was that there was nothing physically wrong with his mouth or speech organs, but that he was not being precise enough about his articulation. This general 'sloppiness' of articulating certain sounds can largely be made up if I tell him to repeat it and where to place his tongue and lips, which he generally can do. However, he easily reverts back to a more lazy pattern if I don't correct him.

The speech therapist felt it was not particularly serious—she felt he may or may not outgrow it—but having some speech therapy practice would be a good idea to assure that it would be most easily corrected. The speech therapist also said that there was no lag in his vocabulary development, which was something I had no doubt of anyway. Hearing the vocabulary of most kids his age, I'm convinced he's got a much broader and mature vocabulary than his peers. Since some people don't differentiate between vocabulary development and pronunciation, I'd say it's definitely worthwhile having a professional diagnosis in one's hip pocket that says he's not behind in his vocabulary skills.

I've found networking with other adoptive families to be most valuable. For example, I talked by phone with a woman in Virginia who had adopted a boy about the same age as Chip, but from a different orphanage. Both of us were shocked that the unusual behavior characteristics of both children were virtually identical: a preoccupation with sweeping and clean-up activities, a tendency to move toys around from place to place, always arranging them in ordered rows—never playing with them in the sense of fantasizing and duplicating real world activities they could emulate through play; a preoccupation with the whereabouts of one's shoes, and other matching idiosyncrasies. Upon reflecting upon how these orphanages were run, the reasons for this behavior became apparent: At Babadag, for almost an hour each day, a big plastic bag full of 'toys' (really the most shoddy, broken and indestructible forms of toys) were dumped out. It turned into a free-for-all of everybody grabbing whatever they could and doing with it whatever came to mind. The better toys were kept out of reach or out of sight for fear they would be broken by the children. About the only adult activities the children would have observed were the staff sweeping and swabbing the floor to pick up pieces of food thrown there by the kids. No child was permitted to have a toy they called their own or to keep something for themselves throughout the day. Of all clothing items, shoes were in shortest supply and, thus, having possession of a pair of shoes probably conferred a sense of power, status and freedom to the child. What a treat to tread the corridors outside the room in which they were confined, or even to make an illicit trip outside!

As Chip's knowledge and exposure to the outside world broadened, it didn't take long for his play activities to keep pace in terms of fantasies that more closely correlate with reality. Stories that he had heard, or completely imaginative situations that had a sophisticated line of reasoning behind them were, in his view, far superior to more primitive play like 'putting all the ducks in one row.' He still enjoys doing clean-up activities, though our cramped, gridlocked apartment offers little opportunity to clean anything up when there isn't enough space to organize things. And, because he was the only child at the orphanage who the staff allowed to help them out, being able to help out an adult in whatever activities they're engaged remains an important aspect in his life.

I've spent a lot of time reading to Chip. My reading to him seems to have developed into his main form of entertainment, and, in the typical list of jobs that he wants to engage in when he grows up (which includes doctor, policeman, etc.), there is, with an ever-increasing frequency, an expressed desire for some atypical occupations such as a writer and inventor. His ability to verbalize completely original and interesting stories, which often include the option of listener-participation, produces a variety of levels of excitement, plots, and endings. This amazes and far exceeds anything I was capable of doing when I was his age.

When I went to Romania in March, 1990, I had a mental image of what I was looking for—a child not more than a year old, because I was convinced from what I had read that so much intellectual development occurs that early. Therefore, any child who had been institutionalized at over a year old would have suffered such an intellectual deficit that he would never catch up with other children raised in a more stimulating environment. When I first saw Chip it took less than one day to reorient my thinking and realize that my preconceptions could be seriously challenged. I have later come to realize that all my preconceptions were completely wrong. I assume that at least some other adoptive parents have had similar experiences, too. I challenge a lot of the preconceptions concerning a child's intellectual development. Do not give up on a child's progress just because they've had a disadvantaged background in terms of a lack of intellectual stimulation at all the right times since they were born. They can "catch-up."

Chapter 5

The International Adoption Circus

The Crisis Response: Save the Children!

In 1990, the attention of the world focused on the difficulties that thousands of children faced living in Romania. Images of hundreds of starving and neglected children, treated worse than animals, haunted the pages of magazines and the television programs. At the same time that adoption developed and proliferated, there was massive attention paid to the institutionalized children. Hundred of agencies and individuals went to Romania to help the orphaned and institutionalized children. From 1990 to 1992, approximately 391 nongovernmental organizations (otherwise known as private, nonprofit agencies) providing humanitarian assistance (helping care for children), supplies (diapers, toys, medicines, etc), infrastructure repair (fixing roofs, water systems, heaters, etc.), personnel (increasing the number of people caring for children) with occasional training (how to care for children with disabilities), and technical assistance (how to develop programs for children with special needs), were registered in Romania[1]. By the end of 1992, almost every institution had some association with a foreign aid group[2]. However, many groups, especially volunteer groups or individuals, never registered with the government. With so many international organizations providing aid, the Romanian government had no accurate idea of how many organizations were in the country, what the purpose of each organization was, or how to coordinate these multiple efforts[3]. With no official endorsement, these individuals and groups worked in institutions all over the country and it wasn't unusual for groups from several countries to set up different programs within the same facility.

Most of this help was crisis-oriented; it was reactive and emotionally driven. These efforts had a child rescue or save the children approach. The response grew from a belief that moral decadence and inherent inferiority resulted in the institutional problem, and it was the responsibility of industrial nations to "rescue" the children. In the foreign public's mind, the humanitarian thing to do was to remove children from terrible institutions and place them in other countries. There was tremendous external and some internal pressure on the Romanian government to allow children to go to foreign countries and enter nice, middle-class homes where they have all the "material advantages" they did not have in Romania. In reality, of course, even if we could provide such homes for all these children (and we know we can't), this may not be the best thing for them or their country anyway.

As many foreign aid groups established themselves in the institutions to improve the physical structure, they conducted their own analysis of the needs and made plans to correct the problem. Sometimes they informed the Director or Tutelary (public child welfare) authority of their plans before making the needed repairs; most often they did not do so but worked with the verbal agreement of the institution's director. Other groups focused on providing routine, daily care and programming to the children, but often this care was implicitly or explicitly critical of the women who had previously been the sole caregivers for the institutionalized children. In addition to ignoring the feelings of the workers, many of whom feared that their jobs were being taken by the international volunteers, the needs and potential capacity of the local community to solve its problems were virtually ignored. Foreign criticism of the quality of institutional care also overshadowed any gratitude that was due to these caregivers for the help they did provide for many years when few resources were available.

Moreover, while generously focusing their energy and resources on the needs of the institutionalized children, these international organizations often failed to recognize that these institutions mirrored the general poverty of their local communities. Romanian staff in these facilities often grew resentful when clothes, food, medicines and the like were continually devoted to abandoned and disabled children while their own children suffered. As a result, medicines, cleaning supplies, clothes and shoes were stolen. Of course, this made the international groups think that all Romanians were thieves and not to be trusted.

Finally, few training and staff development activities were directed to the Romanian employees. Of those few staff who received training, most were bilingual and were able to communicate with the groups providing assistance. However, since the vast majority of staff at the institutions were not bilingual, only a select few were given the opportunity to benefit from training. Often, once the bilingual staff were trained, they could find other, better paying jobs and left the institution.

Even with the chaos, confusion, criticism and short-sightedness of foreign groups, the institutions improved briefly from 1989 to 1992. However, since 1989, the quality of life for many Romanians has not improved. In fact, it is worse. In the country's move to a market economy, state subsidies have been removed from food, housing, and utilities (gas, water, electricity); prices have gone up to their "real" market value. For example, bread in one day went from 2 leu to 10 leu (leu is the Romania currency). Wages, however, have not been increased enough to keep up with over 300% yearly inflation!

As the attention of the world has changed focus from the crisis in Romania to other parts of the world, resources previously going to Romania have been reduced or eliminated. Relief agencies began leaving in 1991 and by 1994 few remained. As an example of the change, in 1991 a French organization named Equilibre had 1200 people in country; by 1993 they had 200 people working in Romania. As relief organizations have left, many have failed to leave behind Romanian staff trained and empowered to continue to make progress with handicapped and developmentally delayed children. Even those organizations that trained staff have not achieved cooperation with local and national authorities to secure a funding base to continue the programs that were developed with international aid, nor did they get a philosophical commitment from local and national authorities to continue the programs.

While international agencies have left, during the period 1991-1993 many indigenous Romanian organizations have formed to help institutionalized children as well as the disabled and impoverished children living in their homes[4]. There are many progressive Romania leaders in the Human Service field who recognize that family life is superior to group care. There are leaders encouraging and developing legislation that will promote family preservation, family reunification, foster care and domestic adoption. There are elements of a contemporary child welfare system developing that include a developing private (nongovernmental or nonprofit) sector. But, the country has a long way to go to implement a modern child welfare system. And, the children keep rolling into the institutions.

The Opening of Romania to International Adoption

One accomplishment of the "Revolution" of December 1989 was the opening of Romania's borders to international adoption. As early as January 1990, a month after the Ceausescus were shot, media reports brought the world's attention to the thousands of abandoned children residing in institutions and the ease in adopting[5]. Romanian adoption laws[6] made international adoption relatively easy to process through the Romanian court system. Prior to changes in the legislative framework for adoption, all adoptions by foreign citizens had always required presidential authorization. There were rumors of baby selling under Ceausescu—with babies going to France and Israel and money going to the family's personal fortune. The change in law, which took effect August 1, 1990, eliminated presidential approval, created the Romanian Adoption Committee (RAC), and independent (private) adoptions quickly developed. Initially, someone wishing to adopt could go to an orphanage and view a child or several children, depending on the policy and practice of the orphanage. In some orphanages, every child was presented. In other orphanages, after a bribe was paid, a child was presented. After the presentation of a child or children, the person adopting could chose a child to adopt or reject the one presented and another child was presented. A fee was usually paid to the orphanage director, although some administrators refused to accept money. An attorney was then hired to process the adoption in Romania. The process usually included securing parents' signatures for relinquishment, approving the foreign family as adoptive parents in Romania, obtaining a passport for the child from the Romanian government, and obtaining an emigration visa for the child from the American Embassy. The Embassy had clear criteria about the type of child who could be adopted and issued a visa, but it was also clear that lawyers and officials would manipulate the facts of a child's abandonment to fit U.S. emigration policies.

At first, in 1990 and early 1991, this was an easy process that cost very little; an adoption would cost between $2,000 and $5,000[7]. However, in a relatively short time the "system" became out-of-control[8] and both gray and black markets developed in adoption. The black market consisted of out-right baby selling and buying, with babies going to the highest bidder. In the black market, instead of children in the institutions being adopted, children were adopted from their families. In a few instances, the exploitation was obvious. As one mother wrote:

> Romanian friends in the U. S. arranged for the birth of a child for me under the direction of a
> leading OB-GYN in Bucharest. The birth mother was *carefully* selected. The baby was essentially
> mine before she was even born.

One-fourth of the children adopted between August 1990 and February 1991 were adopted under the age of six months from poor families rather than institutions.[9] The Defense for Children International, an international child advocacy organization, stated that these parents had been pressured to give up their children in exchange for cash—in essence, children became commodities or goods, purchased much like an animal in a pet store or some other product.

The gray market was more complicated. Some children were removed from hospitals, orphanages or institutions by parents and traded for goods or the parents were given money as a part of the children being adopted by foreign families. In some instances, families went to Romania to adopt from an orphanage, only to have the door closed to them. As one parent commented:

> I expected to find a child in an orphanage. The orphanages were essentially closed to foreigners
> [when I got there]. I hadn't thought of taking a child from a family…

For other families, the circumstances were unclear. Some children were identified by "middle men" as abandoned and procured for eager families waiting to adopt, always for a fee. Usually, these middle men were found by families wanting to adopt through word-of-mouth or, if you went to the Intercontinental Hotel in Bucharest, they would approach you about whether you wanted a child for adoption. Of course, the reason most Americans were in Romania at that moment was to adopt, so the Hotel became the "storefront" for the "gray baby market."

These middle men found children in hospitals, orphanages or institutions. Already knowing the Byzantine process of Romanian business, they would locate the birth parents and arrange to have the appropriate forms signed and for the parents to appear at the court hearings. True to the capitalist fever, it was a process of buy-sell-bargain-trade.

The market economy quickly caught on, but the system became exploitative of Romania's children. This led to worldwide criticism and more negative media attention. Reacting to the criticism as well as recommendations made by child advocacy groups such as the Defense for Children International, the Romanian Committee on Adoption suspended inter-country adoption in June, 1991.[10] A moratorium was placed on adoptions so that

Parliament could draft appropriate legislation to deal with the problems generated by the "baby market." Between August 1, 1990 and July 17, 1991, about 10,000 Romanian children were sent abroad[11]. The moratorium, enacted in the summer of 1991, specified that if the adoption of a Romanian child by foreigners was not in process via the filing of court documents, all processing of adoption applications were suspended. While the moratorium was only supposed to last about six months, it wasn't until June of 1993 that Romania passed a new law, the Judicial Declaration of Child Abandonment.[12] The Romanian Committee on Adoption (RAC) was redefined by the Parliament. A new central registry of children available for adoption was designated, and a procedure for identifying children as abandoned was developed. The new legislation strengthened government control over adoptions by making it illegal for parent(s) to select a child to adopt and requiring that all adoptions be processed through adoption agencies approved by RAC. While initially only four or five licensed international adoption agencies were selected to work with the Romanian government, by 1995 over 15 agencies had approval to work in Romania, and by 1997 there were over 100 agencies from around the world.

Romania Regulates Adoption

As mentioned, Romania closed its border to international adoption in July, 1991, after receiving much criticism from abroad. At that time its parliament was struggling with developing policies to guide and regulate many aspects of the child welfare system. Although it took two years and not six months, the Romanian Adoption Committee (RAC) was indeed refined and new policies were put in place. Between 1991 and 1993, virtually no children were placed for inter-country adoption, and the population of children in institutions rose.[13]

In the chaos of 1990 and early 1991, although the RAC tried to coordinate adoption activities, it was overwhelmed and understaffed. It was similar to trying to stop a raging river by putting a sand bag in front of it. The RAC had been designed to be the central government agency for processing adoption applications and abandoned children. The mission was for the RAC to certify that all children available for international adoption were truly abandoned and to obtain all the appropriate paperwork (using the new laws enacted in 1993), verifying in each particular case that a Romanian family could not be found to adopt the child. They would then approve adoptive families offered by agencies approved for international adoption from Romania and match them with children.

None of these tasks were easily accomplished, however. While initially having capable leadership, the office remained under-funded and had too few personnel. To get all the necessary documentation gathered to have a child verified as an abandoned child required full-time personnel with training and expertise in domestic child welfare, which was lacking. The catch-22 though, was that if birth mothers left the maternity hospital without completing all the necessary paperwork, their children could not move through the system to be processed for adoption. Theoretically, the birth mother had to be found by a member of the RAC, had to complete the necessary forms, and in some locales had to go to court three times to declare that she was abandoning the child. Locating the birth mothers and walking them through the process required more time, skill and expertise than was immediately available to the RAC, however. In addition, birth fathers had to be located to sign all the necessary forms. There was also an assumption that maternity hospital directors and the directors of the various orphanages and institutions would identify and refer children to the RAC. Nothing could have been further from the truth. First, many people had strong, nationalistic feelings and felt that adopting the children out of the country was cultural genocide and bankrupting the future of Romania. Second, institutional budgets were tied to the number of children they served—moving a child out of the institution meant a decrease in funds for the next month. If the abandoned child was not replaced by a new child, the facility would have a reduction in resources. This was perhaps the biggest barrier to getting children identified for adoption. Third, there was still the old mentality that the state would provide, and many Romanian believed the children were fine in the institutions.

Eventually, when it became apparent that the RAC would have difficulty fulfilling their mission to make sure children were clearly abandoned, they began to rely on the international adoption agencies to identify abandoned children, secure the necessary documentation, and obtain the permission to adopt by the parents. However, there was no guarantee that any child referred to the committee as "abandoned" would subsequently be referred back to the same adoption agency for placement with a foreign adoptive family. The RAC was by now very concerned about appearances of impropriety. The process then got bogged down with the steady stream of children entering the child welfare system, the general inertia of government agencies, and the lack of training and technical assistance that the RAC members needed to function well. While, eventually, the adoption agencies took a major role in RAC activities, this caused some strain in the relationships of institutional directors with adoption agency personnel.

(From Victor's notes and diary): Sandy, an adoption worker employed by an American adoption agency, was trying to find a way to make the situation work. The Director at the Leagan refused to sign the paperwork to release any of the children for adoption. The new law allowed Directors to declare children as abandoned to begin the process of legally freeing the children for international adoption. Both Sandy and the Director had discussed how sad it was that in the 18 months they were waiting for the new legislation, not one parent or other relative had visited any of the 120 children. At first the Director said that Romanian children needed to be raised by Romanian families. Who could argue? The fact-of-the-matter was that no families were willing to adopt these children and there were no programs targeting the recruitment of Romanian families for adoption. The Director knew this. It was only when Sandy has spent a few months building a relationship with the Director that she was told the budget would decrease as children would leave. Sandy and the Director worked out an arrangement that her agency would pay the salary of staff

members who would work jointly with the agency and the orphanage. That way, as the money decreased because there were fewer children, the number of staff would remain the same because they were supported by an outside source. Sandy also agreed to help with medicines, food and supplies for the children, which prompted the Director to begin to forward the names of abandoned children to the RAC.

As indicated in the above story, a related problem was that Romania lacked an organized domestic adoption program. While adoption has occurred throughout Romanian history and Romania law had historically emphasized the best interest of the child,[14] with the elimination of social work programs under the Ceausescus in the early 1960s, there were no trained adoption workers to promote domestic adoption. Thus, only a few international adoption agencies played a role in establishing domestic adoption. This has included generating new federal policies and procedures to regulate adoption practice as well as training Romanian social workers in contemporary adoption practice. At the same time, several of the international adoption agencies were also instrumental in establishing foster family care in Romania to try to prevent institutional care of abandoned infants. Unfortunately, foster family care had not been widely endorsed by the government as a solution to the problem of children who could not remain with their biological parents. In fact, it wasn't until 1997 that plans for establishing domestic adoption and foster care and decreasing the use of institutionalization was developed by the Constantinescu government. However, the future of both the domestic adoption programs and foster family care programs are uncertain. These programs still lack funding, trained staff, and support from the government and the community.

While it is not able to carry out the mandate as initially conceptualized, the areas where the RAC exerts influence and final authority is over the matching process of children with families, and approval of families for international adoption of Romania children. However, this process has also developed some problems. In 1995 there was a change in the leadership of the RAC. The new director declared that single parents were unsuitable for Romanian children and immediately halted all current and future adoptions by single adoptive parents. Part of the problem, once again being caused by various media stories—usually with a negative spin—are accounts of gays and lesbians who have adopted from Belarus, Romania and the Ukraine. Gays and lesbians pursue adoption as single parents, mostly due to the lack of a legal framework for two unmarried individuals to adopt the same child. Fearing that at least some of the singles adopting from Romania were gay or lesbian, the new Director banned adoption by single parents. Of course, this policy contradicts research, which has consistently demonstrated that adoption outcomes are very positive for single-parent families.[15] Nevertheless, single-parent adoptions in Romania virtually stopped by the summer of 1995. However, by 1998, the policy was getting less enforcement and singles were trickling in for adoption again.

What this incident highlights is how one individual can have a major influence in the way a system functions (or does not function). Possessing little experience in contemporary child welfare practice and lacking current, relevant information, government policies and procedures hinder the placement of children in families at a time when the number of children entering institutions is increasing. An agency designed to regulate a problem that developed during the chaos of 1989 and the subsequent exploitation of children and families until 1991, has begun to develop into a bureaucracy. The bureaucracy, in effect, slows down the process of adoption it was designed to promote and regulate. The result will be an ever-expanding group of children entering institutions, hurting both children and Romania's image abroad.

The U. S. Role in Promoting International Adoption

The U. S. government has played a role in promoting international adoption. Prior to the closing of adoptions in 1991, the U. S. embassy ran weekly groups for parents who came to Romania to adopt and assisted many American families with their adoptions. The role of the U.S. after 1991 was more veiled, however.

In 1991, the United States Agency for International Development (USAID) sent out requests for proposals for federal demonstration projects to develop the child welfare system in Romania. These projects were to demonstrate models of permanency planning for children. The proposals, which had been funded, were given to agencies with little experience or expertise in international child welfare, but who had a vested interest in promoting international adoption. In essence, the U. S. government funded "demonstration" projects that built an infrastructure for these international adoption agencies in Romania to develop programs that they could use to place children with American families. The result was that when the project ended, the adoption agency would have personnel, foster homes, government contacts and relationships with local judges and lawyers that would make it easy for the agency to arrange international adoptions.

A specific example will demonstrate this point. One agency with a long and credible history of international adoption was awarded a grant to prevent the abandonment of children at maternity hospitals. Whenever possible, children were to go from hospitals into foster care when they were abandoned, including placing some children from orphanages. The agency was also asked to develop a domestic adoption program. To accomplish these goals, the agency had to develop a relationship with local maternity hospitals, local orphanages, personnel for the tutelary authority (which are similar to personnel in local departments of human services), members of the RAC, lawyers, and judges. These projects also trained their staff and employees from the tutelary authorities as well as staff from other nongovernmental organizations (NGOs) in basic social work interviewing and assessment skills, foster care skills, and adoption practice skills. As these projects ended, the international adoption agencies were left with trained staff and local relationships to support their continued efforts at international adoption. The changes in the ways that Romania conducted its child welfare programs were minimal. As federal funds ran out to support the project staff, and USAID did not fund new projects because they did not believe the Romanian government was committed to reform, fees charged for international adoption funded the programs. In essence, the federal government provided the seed money for selected international adoption agencies to firmly establish themselves in this developing country. It has played both an overt and covert role in promoting the adoption of Romania's children.

This support raises some important questions. Should the federal government play a role in international adoption? If the federal government supports international adoption, is there an obligation to provide support to families who adopt these children, some of which have special needs and need many services once they come to the U. S? How are decisions made to fund adoption agencies with little social development experience compared to other agencies? It is not our intent to answer these questions, but to raise the issues that need to considered as the U. S. enters other countries and tax dollars are invested in programs of this type in other countries. At a minimum, if the U. S. indirectly provides funds to promote international adoption, they must also support families when they return and if they have difficulties.

Notes from Chapter 5

[1] Romanian Information Clearing House (R. I. C. H.). (1992). Index (Directory) Oganizatii Neguvernamentale (Nongovermental Organizations): National and international organizations providing humanitarian assistance to Romania. Bucharest, Romania: Ministry of Health.

[2] Bascom, B. B., & McKelvey, C. A. (1997). The complete guide to foreign adoption: What to expect and how to prepare for your new child. New York: Pocket Books

[3] Johnson, A. K. (1995, April 26). Homeless persons in Romania: The context of institutional care. Paper presented at, Social Work and Disabilities Conference, Co-sponsored by NASW and the Social Work Division of the American Association of Mental Retardation, New York, NY.

[4] Johnson, A. K., Ourvan, L., & Young, D. (1995). The emergence of nongovernmental organizations in Romania: International support and the third sector role. Social Development Issues, 17(2/3), 38-56.

[5] Hodges, Anthony. (January 5, 1990). Orphans may come to Britain. The Times. Australia seeks Romania orphans. (January 5, 1990). Chicago Tribune. North Sports Final Edition News; Pg. 6; ZONE: C. 61 Adopted Romanian children met by new families in France. (January 7, 1990). Los Angeles Times. Home Edition, SECTION: Part A; Page 7; Column 1; Foreign Desk. Carlin, John. (January 18, 1990). South African couples on orphan spree. The Independent (London). Page 11. Upheaval in the East; Romania Is Prohibiting Adoption by Foreigners. (February 9, 1990). New York Times. Late Edition—Final. Section A; Page 11, Column 1; Foreign Desk

[6] Zugravescu, A., & Iacovescu, A. (1994). The adoption of children in Romania." In E. D. Jaffe (Ed.), Intercountry adoptions: Laws and perspectives of 'sending' countries. New York: Gefen Publishing House Ltd.

[7] Bohlen, C. (November 15, 1990). The Hurdles Are Many, but the Reward Is a Child. The New York Times. Late Edition - Final, Section A; Page 4; Column 3; Foreign Desk.

[8] Johnson, A., & Groze, V. (1993). The orphaned and institutionalized children of Romania. Journal of Emotional and Behavioral Problems, 2(4), 49-52.

[9] Defense for Children International. (1991). Romania: The adoption of Romanian children by foreigners: Report of a group of experts on the implementation of the Convention on the Rights of the Child regarding inter-country adoption. Geneva (Swtizerland): Defense for Children International.

[10] Defense for Children International. (1991). Romania: The adoption of Romanian children by foreigners: Report of a group of experts on the implementation of the Convention on the Rights of the Child regarding inter-country adoption. Geneva (Swtizerland): Defense for Children International..

[11] Zugravescu, A., & Iacovescu, A. (1994). The adoption of children in Romania. In E. D. Jaffe (Ed.), Intercountry adoptions: Laws and perspectives of 'sending' countries. New York: Gefen Publishing House Ltd.

[12] Verona, S. (1994). Romanian policy regarding adoptions. Washington, DC: Congressional Research Service.

[13] The rate per 100,000 children ages 0-3 in infant homes (i.e., orphanages) went from 753.0 in 1989 to 582.7 in 1990 and 595.4 in 1991. By 1992, this rose to 654.0, rising again in 1993 to 749.7. Even with adoption increasing in 1993, it was not at the levels that were occurring in 1990 and 1991. Thus, in 1994 the rate increased to 1093.5, falling only slightly in 1995 to 1031.9. See UNICEF. (1997). Children at risk in Central and Eastern Europe: Perils and promises. Florence, Italy: United Nations Children's Fund, International Child Development Centre.

[14] Zugravescu, A., & Iacovescu, A. (1994). The adoption of children in Romania. In E. D. Jaffe (Ed.), Intercountry adoptions: Laws and perspectives of 'sending' countries. New York: Gefen Publishing House Ltd.

[15] Shireman, J., & Johnson, P. (1976). Single persons as adoptive parents. Social Service Review, 50, 103-116.

Shireman, J., & Johnson, P. (1985). Single-parent adoptions: A longitudinal study. Children and Youth Services Review, 7, 321-334.

Shireman, J., & Johnson, P. (1986). A longitudinal study of Black adoptions: Single parent, transracial, and traditional. Social Work, May-June, 172-176.

Shireman, J. F. (1988). Growing up adopted: An examination of some major issues. Chicago: Chicago Child Care Society.

Rosenthal, J., & Groze, V. (1992). Special needs adoption: A study of intact families. New York: Praeger.

Groze, V. (1991). Adoption and single parents: A review. Child Welfare, 70 (3), 321-332.

Chapter 6

Adoption Stories During and After the Chaos

Bryan: A Journal of Searching and Discovery

Saturday March 9, 1991

My dear child, this is the first entry in the journal of how we joined together as a family.

Right now I am sitting in an airplane over the Atlantic Ocean, flying to Romania to see you for the first time. We don't know you yet, what you look like, or even whether you are a boy or a girl. We do know one thing. Your mother and I love you very much!

Let's start at the beginning, when your mother and I met. We met at a car fire; she was in the ambulance, I was a firefighter. Your mother is a very beautiful woman and I knew then that she was the one for me. We dated for a year and then got married. From the very start, we knew we wanted to have a child, but we also knew it would not be easy. Your mother knew there would be some problems giving birth to you, so right from the start we went to the doctors to see what could be done. There we found out that both of us could not give birth to you naturally.

We tried for almost five years to find a way for you to come to us and had almost given up hope of ever seeing you. Then it happened. In 1989, in Romania, a very bad man was the leader of the country. He did many bad things to Romania; one of them was to force all the women to have many, many children. In time, there were so many children that the country could not take care of all of them.

When your mother and I saw what was happening, we wanted to help. We also knew that God had shown us a way to find you so that we could be together!

So with the help of a lot of friends, we started on our way to Romania to find you. We started in January of 1991, by talking to a lady named Rose. She was a lawyer who felt like we did and went to Romania. She and her husband Bill adopted a baby named Alexander. Rose and Bill helped us do all the paperwork to allow us to adopt you, and for that we are grateful to them. They also introduced us to John and Susan. They were a couple just like us; they wanted to adopt a child. Because they had already completed all the things they needed to do, John went to Romania first.

One day I was at home when the phone rang. It was John. He said that a little four-week-old baby boy was available for adoption if we wished to do it. Your mother and I said yes, and that is where we are right now. I am going to keep a journal of all that happens on this, the most important trip of my life! I think I will close now but I will write more later! I love you!

A PEACOCK OR A CROW

Sunday, March 10, 1991

This has been a very busy day. It is 8:30 p.m. here in Romania. Yes, I finally made it. When we landed in Vienna, I noticed a couple that were carrying an empty infant carrier. I talked with them. Sandy and Don are from New Hampshire.

They are a very sweet couple and have come to adopt a fifteen-month-old boy. They hope to get it done in two weeks. On the flight to Bucharest, we all sat in the same row.   When we landed the first thing that shocked me was the anti-aircraft guns all around the airport. You could tell they were manned, too. The military was everywhere.

When we got off the plane, we stood in line in an unheated airport terminal for about a half-hour to forty-five minutes until they started checking our passports.   After that, everyone was patted down—I guess to search for weapons. We then stood in line for almost half an hour, waiting to get our passports validated. The guard had to write down where we were to stay while we are here. Being totally lost as I was, I had no idea what to say. I finally cleared that, and then had to open my bags and boxes for customs inspection. That was when I saw John standing outside the terminal waving at me. It sure felt great knowing that I was not alone! John introduced me to Dan. Dan is a shorter man, about 5'5", about 130 lbs., wears glasses, has dark hair and a broken nose. He and his girlfriend, Mary, are students at the university. We spent the day talking, getting to know a little about each other. Dan seems like a nice guy but somehow I can't shake the feeling that I'm talking to a used car sales person.

Dan and John took me to the place where I am staying. Maria is an older lady who lives alone in a two-bedroom flat. Maria is about 65-years-old, frail, and makes you think you could break her bones just by shouting at them. That is until you see her eyes. When she speaks (almost no English, also) you can see the fire lighting up in her eyes!!

Dan, John and I sat down and talked about the whole thing they call the "Romanian Experience."   After talking with them, I have to admit that my spirits are down. It looks worse than I thought with the four-week-old boy. It appears he is not in an orphanage. The Mom can't be found and she has not signed the child for adoption. All this makes for a bleak picture. To top this off, John's deal fell through and he and Susan have no prospect for a baby. Needless to say, I'm a little discouraged, but tomorrow is another day.

Monday, March 11, 1991

Looking over last night's entry, I am embarrassed. The combination of a long flight, hectic day, and Romanian Tsuica really took its toll. Tsuica is like vodka. It is home brewed by everyone. I had a total of three small shot glasses in about five hours, but it really affected me. Lorrie, you would hate it here. Everyone smokes and everyone drinks. The whole city is dirty with the smoke from factories. Even the evergreen types of plants are grayish-green at best. There is mud everywhere.

The culture here is totally alien. The overall attitude seems to be, if you can't be bribed, you can't be trusted. If you take bribes, you are seen as an honest person. I am learning slowly how to cope with Romanian life. Last night I slept from 22:00 to about 4:30. I had some trouble getting back to sleep, but when I did, I slept till 8:30. This was my first mistake. The hot water was turned off at 8:00. My first shower here was a sponge bath with icy water. When I finished washing I was afraid my hair would freeze. My scalp was actually numb.

This a.m., John went to Brailla to the orphanage to tell them he will not adopt the three-month-old. They found out a few days ago that it also has a deformed skull and right ear from lying on its side for so long.

Lorrie, I am so afraid here; not for myself, but for our child and for all the children. I have never experienced such poverty. Sure, I see it all the time in our city, but then I drive away about two or three miles and I'm in a beautiful area. Here it is everywhere with no end.

I went with Dan today into the town. I tried to register at the Embassy, but they were too crowded. The place is a mad house! Everywhere you look there are people with children waiting for exit visas. I tried to talk with one couple but got the cold shoulder. Well, enough of that! Went across the street to the Intercontinental Hotel to check things out. Found where Don and Sandy (from NH) were roomed. Called them and met them in the lobby. They were on their way to Arad. Traded phone numbers then said goodbye and met up with Dan again.

We spent the day taking in the shopping around town. There are two types of stores here, private and state. The private stores can have anything. I saw tires sold right next to candy, which was right next to women's clothing. Very strange! The state stores are a different thing. Like Dan said, they are full—full of air, and very little else. One store was completely empty of merchandise on the first floor, and the second had only a few men's sweats and shirts.

This was about 1:00 p.m. By 6:30, I was completely bored. When John got back from Brailla, we went to Dan's apartment for more Tsuica and Dan said that his friend, Alis, found a few children we might be interested in adopting, but one is eleven months old and the other is the three-month-old I told you about earlier. All in all, this was another depressing day.

Tuesday, March 12, 1991

This a.m. it was so good hearing your voice. It made me want to forget the whole thing and come home right now.

This a.m. I had my first warm bath in Romania. It wasn't warm enough. You know how I am. Dan was to take my paperwork to be translated, and go with Alis to check up on things. I took a cab to the Embassy. The cabbie looked just like Walter Matthau. I couldn't help but laugh. I met John at 11:30. We found Pat. She had adopted the two-week-old baby girl that Rose turned down. Lorrie, that was the hairiest baby I've ever seen. She was beautiful, though. We all traded addresses and phone numbers. By now you should have received a phone call from her. I hope so! John and I split for lunch and then went walking. Would you believe of all the stores we went into, not one had a book on English-Romanian/Romanian-English translations at all! Unbelievable! Dan said that tomorrow was a "free day" but Thursday was the day I went to the orphanage to see the children. This confused me because earlier I was told that we would go to the orphanages tomorrow. Sometimes I feel like I'm spinning my wheels, but I have to realize that I am not in control here. Dan and Alis are, and even then not fully. I'll pray for guidance tonight.

Thursday, March 14, 1991

An incredible day! It's hard to believe that I have just met my son. This morning did not start out very eventfully. After a small breakfast, John called and said he is coming to Brailla with us. Dan also told him it looked like there were no children for me to look at. They picked me up and went to pick up Alis. She is about 30 with blonde hair, gray/green eyes—a nice girl. We drove to Brailla. This town is about a hundred miles from Bucharest and about fifteen-twenty miles from the Soviet Union. On the banks of the Danube River, Brailla is almost a seaport. The trip was about two-and-a-half hours through land that would look like South Dakota if it wasn't so smoky. The haze was everywhere from fires in the fields. When we got to Brailla, we went downtown. I don't know what I really expected to see, but it wasn't this. All in all, the orphanage was not bad looking from the outside. I never went inside any orphanage, so I don't know what conditions are like. The main orphanage sits on one of the downtown streets with a stone wall around it and wrought iron trim. The wall is about eight to ten feet high. Beyond the wall I could see the structure of the orphanage. More ornate than the other, younger, buildings in this area, it stood out. The vast amount of East European trimming and the faded green slate roof of Mansard construction only enhanced its visibility. It had the look of a French castle.

John and I waited while Alis and Dan, both decked out in nice business suits and cologne, went to talk to the main directress. They returned in about five minutes and asked if we could squeeze one more in the back. The Romanian social worker would be coming to show me where the child they had for me was located. I was stunned. Thinking I was only going along for the ride, I wasn't truly prepared for this. In retrospect, are you ever ready for something like this?

On the way over, Alis told me about the story. The child's name is Madeleine, a boy. He was born February 2, 1991 at 5 lbs, 8 oz. He is almost six weeks old. The mother is single, 24-years-old, and has two other children. She says the man she is living with is the father of all three children but refuses to accept the third child. The mother is now living with a friend, can barely support two children, and when Madeleine was born was left on her own. At least this is what I have been told so far.

We parked on the street beside a complex of apartment buildings which, although they look new, were in various states of disrepair. We went to one and then began the long march up the stairs to the top floor of an eight-story building. The paramedics law of buildings was in effect here too: The place you need to go to is on the top floor at the end of the hall. We knocked on the door and the mom greeted us. She was a very pretty woman with dark hair, medium complexion, brown eyes. She was about Lorrie's weight and height and was dressed in a bathrobe. The apartment seemed well taken care of, though sparsely furnished with only a daybed, chair and dresser drawers. Lying on the daybed was a little package wrapped in blankets tied with a string and with a tiny face poking out. He looked so tiny! The poor guy was frightened. I don't think he had ever seen so many people before. I bent down to see him and he looked straight at me. Such a beautiful face! I picked him up and could tell immediately that the wrap was soaking. I unwrapped him and saw his whole body was beet-red and blotchy, very warm and moist. So many things went through my mind to check, but I could do nothing but look at him and stroke his cheek. He spit up a little and I sat him up. Then he did something I swore would never happen. He peed on my leg! I had to laugh. I cleaned him up as best as I could, and looked a little closer at him. Ten fingers, ten toes. Okay. Bottom had a little diaper rash, but otherwise not bad. His face was angelic, but I'll tell you one thing: Romanians are hairy! He has dark brown hair, even on his forehead! He had a slight rash on the right side of his neck, but not bad. A closer look in his eyes showed he had a small hematoma on the left eye, just distal to the corner. Other than that he looked to be a pudgy but perfectly healthy baby boy. I decided to try for the adoption.

Would you believe I had to draw the blood to test? We took the blood from the mother. For some reason, the court won't accept blood tests from infants less than three months. They need the mom's blood. We did not have any alcohol, so we had to improvise. I had to use (would you believe?) English Leather cologne? I scrubbed pretty hard to make sure what alcohol there was did the job. After I drew her blood (no problem!), we left. I was a little giddy, as you can imagine. The whole way home, Alis kept asking me if I was alright. No, I was not. I was stunned at the suddenness of it all. I felt very guilty also. John has been here for over two weeks and still has no child. The only possible child was the three-month-old child, but she has a deformed skull. After talking it over, he and Susan decided to pass. It must have been agonizing for them both. Since then it has been one disappointment after another. They told John Tuesday that there will be another trip to Barilla to look at another possible newborn. I hope and pray it works for them. They deserve it.

A PEACOCK OR A CROW

Friday, March 15, 1991

John and I walked to the Embassy to clear some things up about adoptions. This was the most informative visit yet. The duty officer explained that "unequivocally abandoned" meant having something in writing, not just the Romanian Home Study, but also the mother's statement as well. Here's the catch, though: proof of abandonment must come before the adoption process begins. Hopefully, we will be able to get the papers done in the proper order. In our case, with the child I saw yesterday, the mother had already decided to abandon the child, so legally everything is okay.

We also talked with a couple of Mormon women. One had already adopted a beautiful six-week-old baby girl and wished to adopt a second one. The other woman still had not found a child. A pretty tall order! They stated that *60 Minutes* had just been through before we got there and had interviewed them. I hope you tape it if it shows before we get back. Before leaving, I bought a *Time* and a *Newsweek* magazine just to read up on the world. I have seen a total of maybe one hour of news since coming here.

Dan took us to a nightclub called Melody. It was like all the cheap discos you've ever been into rolled into one. The food was bad, the service was lousy. They had a show that consisted of dancing girls dressed like Las Vegas girls, some singers, and a comedian that had a routine in five or six different languages. In between these acts they had two or three striptease girls do their thing. No, Lorrie, I promise I didn't look…much (ha! ha!)!

Monday, March 18, 1991

Dan called this a.m. and asked if I wished to go with him to run errands. Needing to get out of the house, and wanting to speak English to anyone, I agreed. We drove first to an auto shop to see about a fan for his engine. Then we waited 30 minutes to have the car washed. It was an automatic car wash but long in a state of disrepair. This car wash consisted of two old women standing under the brushes of the broken machine using old sponges and a water hose. This gives you a good idea of how dirty the air is here. We drove a total of ten to fifteen minutes to the stores. When I got out, I looked at the surface of the car. It was still dripping wet from the car wash, but the water drops were now gray with soot from the air.

We then went to pick up paperwork for the adoption that had never been translated into Romanian. When we got there they told Dan it was not there, but was taken to be notarized. They said it would be returned momentarily. We went to a bar and ordered coffee. There Dan suddenly became in a bad mood. We went back to check on the papers but they still had not been returned. We went back to the car, and on the way back Dan told me why he was in a bad mood.

That morning when he came to pick me up, he told me he would need some of the fee required for the adoption. This would be the necessary "bribe money" for the official paperwork fees and other things. I gave him $1,000 in $100 bills. Well, somewhere today Dan lost one of $100 bills I had given him.

I hope I am wrong but I have a sneaking suspicion he will bill me an extra $100 one way or another. He keeps track of all the transactions in a book and John says he has seen it and trusts it, but I will have to see. On the way back, as luck would have it, Alis was coming down the street in a taxi. She brought my translated papers.

Alis and Dan then told me that all was ready for the adoption court proceeding, except two things. One was the medical report on the child, the other a paper requesting power of attorney for Dan or Alis to act as translator for me in court. This was to be obtained at the Embassy by me. I have to talk to them about what the paper requires, so we'll see about that in the morning.

Tuesday, March 19, 1991

Dan stopped here this a.m. to pick up some gifts to give, and also told me that there is a chance of a one-month-old baby girl being available for John. I pray he is right. Poor John is going stir crazy now. After he left I called John and he said he had already tried to get the Power of Attorney there but they said no way! We will have to use a Romanian notary, they told him. John and I also went to the Embassy to see about the Power of Attorney, but it was too late. They did say "yes" they can do it, but (a) the Romanian courts will accept a Romanian Power of Attorney before an American Power of Attorney, and, (b) the notary was not there. Good news. I got word from the Embassy. Our visa cable is in—we're o.k.'d by the U.S. Embassy to adopt a child. More good news! Alis called a little while ago and said the blood tests are in. Everything is fine. No hepatitis, no AIDS, no nothing! Next stop, Barilla to get a court date (I hope)!

Later that day.

Well, I finally got the Romanian crud. Diarrhea is the benign name for it. I have been running back and forth to the toilet for one hour now. I guess I'm lucky I didn't get it sooner. I hope it passes quickly!

One quick note. I just finished packing a special bag. It seems that Dan called and said I *might* be bringing home a special package a little earlier than I thought. Might is a very big word. One part of me is overjoyed that tomorrow will be the first day of the rest of our lives. The other part of me is terrified, though. There are so many big "ifs." If I brought David home tomorrow, I have no idea when the official court date would be. It could be one or two days, but it could also be late next week. I have 120 diapers with me, and twelve cloth diapers that, according to what I've read, will last me ten days, maybe less. The baby food is no problem. But what of clothes? Maria is sweet—she does wash my clothes for me, but I don't know about the baby clothes, or worse yet, the diapers.

Wednesday, March 20, 1991

I HAVE A BABY! Life, as we know it, ceased to exist. My way of life has changed for ever. I have a baby!

We went to Brailla this a.m. We got to the orphanage. Good news for John: a one- or two-week-old girl is in the maternity hospital and all that is needed is to transfer her to the orphanage. We will learn more tomorrow. We then went to the mother's place where our child was. Alis and the social worker went in, originally just to square away some of the finer points of the adoption. They were gone over 45 minutes. The longer they were gone, the more sure I was that the mother had changed her mind. Actually, she never changed her mind, but the family was very angry at her. I admired the woman for standing up to the family and fighting for what she believes is right. In the end, that was what decided it, because Alis came out of the house, followed by the mother, holding a little wrapped package. She came to me and handed me our soon-to-be son. She kissed him lightly on the cheek, looked once more at him, then turned and walked away. I looked at him. He was so beautiful! He then hiccuped. Alis said he was just breast fed for the last time. She also said that we will have a little problem getting him used to baby food. A slight understatement. He began to cry, so I unwrapped him to check him and he had pooped, so I changed him (the first!). He never stopped crying until we got on the road, and even then he cried most of the two-hour trip back to Bucharest! We got back at about 6:00. It is now 10:30, and he has been crying for all but about thirty minutes. Thank God for Maria! She has mostly taken care of him since I got him here. Already my nerves are shot, I have a splitting headache, and I am dead on my feet. You know what? I can't think of anything else I'd rather do! This poor child is very frightened. In the space of six hours everything that was familiar and comforting to him has been torn away. He has new clothes, sees new faces, has a new environment, even his food has been replaced with something else. I'm sure he will grow accustomed to it, but until then, I hope to give him all the love he can handle.

Tomorrow morning I'm leaving for Brailla to set the court date for the Romanian adoption. Once that is done, I will call Lorrie and let her hear her son for the first time. I can't wait. I want to do it now, but I will wait until we are 90% sure that everything is okay.

John has been a Godsend with the baby. He let me use some of his baby clothes and gave me some diapers and formula for the trip back to Bucharest. I only hope I can repay the favor to him. He is also going back to look for a pediatrician to see our child, if anything, just for my own peace of mind. He seems very alert, very attentive, and he sure knows we are not his mother! So far, so good! I have to close for now, we leave for Brailla at 6:30, and I don't think I'll get much sleep tonight! What a fantastic day!

Thursday, March 21, 1991

Right now it is 10:30 p.m., the baby is asleep with Maria—hopefully for the night. I just finished telling Lorrie about her new son. I know she was crying and I had a tear or two also. I love and miss her so much!

This morning started early. At 4:30 a.m. Maria came to ask me for help changing the baby. She is a wonderful babysitter but has no idea how to work with a disposable diaper. I changed him and fed him. It was a very emotional time for me because he didn't cry. He just kept looking up at me with those saucer eyes, studying my face while he was feeding. When he fell asleep, Maria came back and lay down with him. I covered them both with a blanket and then got ready for Brailla.

Dan came to get me around seven, and we picked up Alis and left. Lorrie, everyone, including me, loves the Townhouse crackers. We have been feasting on them on the way to Brailla, along with chocolate and Certs and sugar-free gum (Alis' favorite; how did you know?).

We went to Brailla and right away ran into problems. The social worker was to meet us at the orphanage to give us some paperwork for the courts. She was not there, and was nowhere to be found. We drove around for about half an hour looking for her, but could not find her. We even went to the child's mother's place; partly to find the social worker, but also because Alis was worried about the mother's family. To help the mother with the medical costs and everything, we gave her $500. That more than covers everything in Romanian Lei, and helps her get on her feet again. Here, $500 is worth two to three times what a doctor is paid per year! Well, the family seems to be very unscrupulous. They want to hold out for a better offer and are pressuring the mother to cancel the adoption. So far, so good, though. This is where Dan excels. Alis is the emotional one about this business, but Dan does all the negotiations. He is the business man. If the family wants to treat this as a money deal, they have to talk to Dan.

We ended up going to court and talking the judge into a date without the medical report on the child. During the judicial interview, though, we found out I was missing another piece of paperwork—the Embassy letter stating we are approved to adopt. I have the same thing in the INS approval, but not in Romanian. Alis did some sweet talking and talked the judge into okaying our court date anyway with the stipulation that we bring the necessary court papers in Monday. I promised him come hell or high water it would be there. I think he liked that. I hope so.

By this time it was 3:00, and I still haven't eaten a meal (just crackers and a little sausage), so we went to dinner at the hotel in Brailla. A man was waiting for us. He happened to be the Mayor of Brailla. We all sat down for lunch and had a very fascinating conversation about communism and its relationship to U.S.-Romanian-Soviet affairs. What I didn't realize until this lunch was that we needed the Mayor's approval for the adoption. Needless to say, it flew through! After this, we found the social worker. She said she could not find the pediatrician, and when she finally did, he would not complete the report until either he saw the baby or talked to the adoptive parent. We figured we'd kill two birds with one stone on Monday.

Friday, March 22, 1991

This has been a very good day. I got some sleep. Poor Maria stayed up the second night in a row with the baby. She is very tired, but always insists on doing everything. After breakfast, I called John. I told him about the letter from the Embassy, and he didn't have it either. John had to go to town to pick up his passport anyway. He had to have his visa extended. For some reason, we paid the same for our visas, got them at the same place, yet mine was for sixty days and his was for only thirty.

We took a cab to the Embassy, where we talked to the duty officer about the letter. No problems, just made sure we were on the approved list, put our names on a letter, stamped it, and we were on our way. We went from there to pick up John's passport. I think it's the same place we'll get the baby's Romanian passport. From there we walked around, taking in the sights and waiting till noon to get to the hotel to eat.

After lunch we were walking away from the hotel to get a taxi (it's cheaper the farther away you get). A man came up to us, flashing a $100 bill and asking for change. We told him no, but he was very persistent. The next thing I knew, John was pushing another man away from him with such force, I thought the man would fall to the ground. He had his coat over one arm. John and I both saw this was a scam. The first guy came at us with a $100 bill to get our attention, and the next guy comes in to pick one of us clean using his coat for cover. Well, the coat man came back like he was going to fight while John was walking away. I stepped in front of him and made sure he understood the game was over. All in all, that was a real barrel of fun. We hailed a taxi, and were halfway home before either of us was calm enough to discuss it. The adrenaline really flows in situations like that.

When I got home, Maria told me that the doctor I talked to last night had called and I was to call her. She asked if 4:00 was okay for him to come over. Can you believe it? A pediatrician who makes house calls? When she came she had a friend with her from Washington state, affiliated with an adoption agency there. The doctor, Doina, examined the baby from head to toe. She did a very thorough exam, short of blood tests and x-rays. Besides a small fungus problem in the mouth (a common problem here in babies), he was a perfectly healthy baby. She then asked how I was feeding him. I said I wish I was, but Maria wouldn't let me. She insisted on doing everything. I showed the doctor the bottle and nipple Maria was feeding him with and the doctor asked if we had the Playtex bottles. I told her how I couldn't be around when formula time came around, but I would mix the formula, place it in a Playtex bottle, and Maria would switch it to the old green beer bottle with a nipple that the mother gave us. She said this would not do, and I said "Hallelujah!" The good doctor talked with Maria, told her the finer points of feeding and clothing, which were new and improved over the Romanian style. This was like a great weight lifted off my shoulders, as I have tried to explain to Maria before, but there is only so much you can do when you can't speak the same language. The doctor left and came back with some medicine for the fungus and that was that. Not bad for $40, eh?

This evening was very pleasant. After his first really big meal in two days, he slept from 5:30 till about 10:30. Maria and I had a nice, easy dinner and even communicated very well. I told her that I need to learn how to take care of the baby and she was very tired. I would take care of him for this night and the next night. She went to bed about 9:00 this p.m. and it's been me and the baby ever since. I'm feeding him whenever he's awake and wants it, which so far seems to be every three hours. The Playtex liners won't last long if I go at this rate for the next week, so I have to reuse each one a few times. I will have to rinse them out with boiling water and I don't think it will be any worse than what he has been having for the last two months. Things look good.

Sunday, March 24, 1991

Captain's Log, Stardate 032491. Boy, am I tired! I am writing this entry early because not much more will happen today. I came home from the party. Maria left for church so I had the baby from 7:00 to about 1:00 this afternoon. He has been ravenous today. He finished 8 oz. of formula at 6:00 a.m., slept till 10:30, ate 8 oz. more, and had another 4 oz. 'snack' at 1:00. I went to sleep at 1:30, and slept non-stop until 6:30. I really needed it. I am learning rapidly that you catch sleep when you can when you have an infant.

Dan just called. He said the trip to Brailla on Monday is changed to Tuesday because Alis has some other paperwork to do. I don't know what that means, but he assured me that it won't make any difference to my court date. It had better not! I am going to take over as primary caregiver for the baby until I go to Brailla. Maria has had him for three or four nights, but not by my own choice. Now she will get a break and I can start trying to wean him from the Romanian way of baby care.

Monday, March 25, 1991

Let me out of here! The baby has been crying non-stop since this a.m. He has not slept all day, and it takes the most intense walking and jiggling and rocking just to keep him to slow down his crying. I think that it is from overstimulation, but Maria won't let him alone. I just want to let him cry it out alone for ten minutes or so, but she won't even let him cry for one minute without picking him up.

As you can see, this is a bad day. Not only with the baby, but about the baby. John called this a.m. with bad news. Dan told him that an Italian couple have been in contact with the mother and they are, in essence, trumping me. They will pay more. The mother told Dan she wants $1,000 more for the baby. The thought of the mother selling her baby to the highest bidder turns my stomach, but what can I do? I'm in an impossible situation. If I say no way, the baby goes back to her, and I'm out $500 and two weeks of work. I spent the day figuring expenses, and if I say yes and give her $1,000, I will in two weeks leave with a baby (maybe) and have $18. The money is so tight, I don't know.

We go to Brailla tomorrow morning, and Dan says to bring the child. We are going to try to negotiate with the family. I think they are the ones who are really greedy anyway. I told Dan, if we have to, go ahead with the $1,000. It's a lot of money, but we have gone too far to quit now. I've spent six days with a baby, possibly my son, and now I'm going to give him back? This is just too much. I feel so empty, so desperate to go home. I know that, after all this is over, when the years have softened some of the pains, maybe I'll look back and say it was all worthwhile. Right now, though, I feel like I can't give any more, and I can't take any more. I just want to go home to Lorrie and hug her until I fall asleep. Just thinking that I can't do that for another two weeks brings me physical pain.

I pray every day to God to lighten some of this load, and it helps, but I can't even read the Bible here. I forgot it!

Tuesday, March 26, 1991

Well, a lot happened last night. I blew my stack during one of the baby's crying spells. I had to leave the room and scream in my own. I think I have a right to. I'm stuck in a place with no heat, hot water very infrequently, I have a baby to take care of that won't stop crying, the only one helping me can't speak my language, and to top it all off, I don't even know if I'll have to give this baby to an Italian couple because they're richer than I am!

Anyway, I guess I really blew my stack because the neighbor came over to see if she could help. She had a teenage son who could speak a little English. He acted as a crude interpreter. It really helped being able to communicate with someone. We all figured out he was constipated. He had not had a BM in over thirty-six hours. The poor thing would cry, then grunt, then cry, then grunt. We fed him some tea and I felt something happen "down there." He visibly eased up after that, but still would not stop crying.

Dan came by about 8:30 last night. The baby was fierce. He was exercising his lungs like never before. I must have really looked beaten, because Dan took one look at me and said I will not be going to Brailla. He said he would take the money and the rest of whatever gifts I had and do all the talking. That was just fine by me. He said he would call me when they got back.

This morning has been great. The baby has been beautiful. He ate some formula and after that some tea at 7:00 a.m. and slept till 10:30. He was a little fussy this afternoon, but fell asleep at 2:00 and is still sleeping now at 4:30.

It is now 10:30 and the baby is finally asleep. I learned a valuable lesson. Never let the baby sleep more than a few hours during the day. He will be impossible at night if you do. This evening John and David visited after they came back from Brailla. Good news! The Mother has accepted $1,000 total for the baby. She already has $400, and will get the rest when the papers are signed on Friday. I'll believe it when I see it. By then, I'll be too busy taking care of the rest of things that I won't have time to celebrate.

Wednesday, March 27, 1991

The baby had his first outing this afternoon. We went to have him photographed for his passport and immigration visa. I was a little nervous about taking him outside. For one thing it was cold and rainy, though it did not rain this afternoon. The baby did fantastic. I kept a blanket wrapped around him the whole time, and he never got cold, in spite of the fact you could see your breath. I did dress him in three layers of clothing, too, so that helped.

John just saw a child at Brailla, and everything looks good for an adoption. He says the boy is only three months old but seems very heavy for his age. It is being held in a good home right now so there is no need to get him out of an orphanage, but I think he will get the child soon, anyway.

Words cannot express my need to leave this place. I know there is a lot of good here, but I can only see the bad now. The baby is wailing right now. I can't help it, I feel numb. There have been times when the baby cries so awful that I actually want to take my frustrations out on him. I feel ashamed even writing this down. I hope what I'm feeling is normal but I just can't stand myself when I feel this way. I just want this all over so I can go home.

Thursday, March 28, 1991

This evening the baby started with his crying routine again. He seemed to have a lot of trouble passing stool. He grunts, all doubled over, then screams, then grunts again, and on and on. Last night I took his temperature rectally; I didn't know what else to do. This seemed to help because he passed his stool as I pulled the thermometer out. I tried it again tonight and it worked again. I hate to think that this kid is going to have to go through the first month of a new life with a thermometer up the butt!

A PEACOCK OR A CROW

Dan and I went into another room and settled the score financially. It somehow made me feel more like the end is in sight. I now just have the Polyclinic, the Romanian passport, the visas (American and Austrian), and the airline ticket to pay for.

John got some bad news. The baby he is to adopt has both parents on the birth certificate and the father is nowhere to be found. It looks like he won't be able to even think about adoption until April 18th. I have to feel sorry for John. I know that if I had to wait here that long, I would very seriously have to think about calling it quits. I have to admire his stick-to-it-iveness. I'll pray for him tonight.

Friday, March 29, 1991

Today is Good Friday and Good Friday it is. After five long years of searching, Lorrie and I have a son. The adoption became final in court proceedings today.

I left for Brailla at 6 a.m. I wore my suit. I figure, I dragged the thing halfway around the world, might as well use it! We got to the court house at 9:15 and waited. The Mom never showed up so Dan left to see where she was. That was the scariest part. If she bolted we would have to schedule another court date. He found her waiting to be picked up at home. We all walked in and sat down: the mayor, Alis, the mother, myself, a prosecutor, a court typist and the Judge of the court. A lot of talking ensued. I will never know what all happened, but I do know that, even though there were some discrepancies in the Romanian Home Study and the medical reports, the prosecutor stood up for me and said, "Hey, let's give the child a break. It's obvious the mom cannot nor is willing to support the child, and this couple can." The Judge then looked at me, and through Alis asked me if I planned to take care of, include him in my will, love, educate and provide for the child. I said "da" to all of these questions. This got a chuckle out of the court. Then the Judge said I'd have to teach him how to play the guitar (It says in our Home Study that I like to play). Then he said: "Congratulations, Daddy!"

After the court proceedings, we went to finish the rest of the paperwork, but ran into some snags. We ate lunch, picked up the court decree and came home. I just talked to Lorrie. It sure feels good to know I'm on the downward slide to this great adventure, soon to be with the woman I love.

Monday, April 1, 1991

It was a Monday, a day like any other day. Just another day here. One day closer to the day I leave this hole. I spoke with a nice couple from Wisconsin while waiting at the Embassy. They were going to Tulcea to look at a two-year-old boy, but they also wanted to adopt another child. I told them a few other things about some other children I'd heard about. It's pretty strange giving others here advice.

I am waiting to hear from Dan or Alis on their return from Brailla. I hope they have good news. If they don't have everything they went for, I might just wring one of their necks. Lately, they have been models of ineptitude—the paperwork after the court date, constantly patronizing me with "No problem"s—they even lost the orphanage abandonment statement somewhere between coming from Brailla and here!

God has been watching over me. I just got the rest of my papers! Alis stopped by just now to drop off birth certificates, the orphanage abandonment statement (of course, it was in Dan's car), and John has the baby's medical records. Tomorrow Alis is sending a translator over to help guide me through the day. Things are being done slowly, but surely. If the translations get done on time, I might really get a Friday appointment with the Embassy for his immigrant visa. I hope so.

Wednesday, April 3, 1991

At the Polyclinica, the baby was surprisingly good. The doctor took a real good look at him and did find one thing wrong. I noticed this earlier but thought it was normal. The flap of skin under his tongue extends too far forward. It really isn't much, but, if we let it go he will have a very bad lisp. When we get back (sometimes I think if!) we have to discuss this with a doctor.

I need to talk to someone before I start really going berserk. Sometimes I feel so frustrated here I have to destroy something. The other night I blew up and threw a plastic baby bottle against the floor. It didn't break, but that only pissed me off more. So I threw it again. This time only the plastic retaining ring broke. So I threw it away and spent the next five minutes throwing a bottle (the cap) against anything I thought would break it, and I didn't break anything else either, but I felt (and still do) so much rage that I know I need to see someone. Tonight I broke a chair. It's still usable, I only broke off a few pieces of wicker, but I still broke it out of rage. I need to go home! I fear for my sanity sometimes.

Thursday, April 4, 1991

Today has been slow so far but I have been able to check off one more item on the list. I picked up the baby's Romanian passport this morning. I got back at 10:30, and Maria was in the kitchen with the baby. He seemed to be in a good mood when I played with him, so I decided to experiment. The baby had a bad case of cradle cap: a dry, caked-on layer of dead skin that won't flake off. I took some baby oil and massaged his scalp for about ten minutes with lots of oil. Then I noticed some of it coming off, so I kept this up, sometimes scraping it off with my finger or a comb. He didn't seem to mind. I even shampooed his hair and scalp and he didn't cry. His scalp looks ten times better now. There's still some cradle cap left, but I'll take care of that either tonight or tomorrow.

A PEACOCK OR A CROW

I went to the Embassy this afternoon to see if I could get scheduled for an interview. The lady asked me to come see her when I get his birth certificate. She said the earliest interview was Tuesday. An American heard her and pulled me aside, telling me to come tomorrow anyway, because they usually can do some extra interviews. I hope so. After that I went to the Austrian Airlines office and asked when the flight leaves. She said daily, at 4:25 p.m. That will give me enough time to leave the Embassy, get the tickets, go to the Austrian Embassy for his transit visa, get my things and go! I will pray tonight like I never prayed before!

Friday, April 5, 1991

Morning came like most other mornings. Met Alis at the Embassy—she gave me the birth certificates and orphanage statement. I stood in line. No questions were asked. She took what she needed and gave me a visa application and an appointment for the ninth. I pleaded with her, but she said no way to expedite. To make things worse, the baby started crying. Try filling out a form with one hand and keeping a crying baby quiet with another. It's impossible! I then let a consulate employee see the baby (a requirement for the visa) so that I would not have to bring him back. On the way home, I made reservations on Austrian Airlines for Tuesday afternoon. Here is where the incredible began happening. A demonstration had been taking place in front of the Embassy, something about Iraq, so they closed from 11:00 to 1:30. When we came, there was no one in the Embassy. I went straight to the window. The woman gave me my document. I then asked her if the visa could be done today. She said, hold on, just have a seat and they would work on it! Those next forty-five minutes were the longest of my life. John ended up taking my passport and the baby's to the Austrian Embassy to see about his transit visa, but they closed at noon. The American Embassy pulled through, and at 4:04 p.m., the baby got his exit visa to America.

Sunday, April 7, 1991

Today was fantastic! Last night the baby slept very little and so did I, but in the morning I ate some breakfast with Maria. Today was Easter for the Orthodox religion. Last night Maria went to church at 10:00 and didn't return until 4:30 this morning. Maria ate a hard-boiled egg, cheese and even drank a tiny glass of cognac, all things she gave up for Lent. After breakfast, I went out, took a taxi and rode through the streets of Bucharest one more time. I just wanted to look at this city. I pray that the next time I see it the city will be revitalized and alive. The Romanians have a long way to go!

John came over at 11:00 and we ate lunch. The driver came to pick us up at 1:45, and after some pictures with Maria and a final tearful goodbye, we left. Then we picked up Alis and went to the airport. At 2:30 they accompanied us to the airport checkpoint. We said our goodbyes and John gave me a hand carrying the baggage through. I finally cleared customs and said, "Until we meet again," to John.

We were then on our own. I found an empty bench and laid David down on it so he could take a break from the carrier. We played a few games until a lady came up to us with a two-year-old and a four-week-old. I thought I had it bad! She said she was going to Alaska. We talked for awhile until the announcement came for our flight. I helped carry one of her bags, and we went downstairs to go through another search.

When we took off, the relief was almost physical. The whole flight David was a doll! He would make a little fuss, and I'd give him a bottle and he would instantly quiet down. One time he really kicked and screamed—of course, at meal time—but I couldn't blame him. He had the biggest load of ca-ca in his diaper I had seen yet! Changing him up in the toilet of a DC-9 was almost impossible.

After the plane landed, I went to customs, to the visa application office. I had to lie a little (whoops!) but they bent the rules a little and gave David a visa for 150 schillings (about $14). I knew it was free in Bucharest, but I would have had to wait till next Tuesday to get it. A visa usually costs three times as much—I got off easy. Someone has been watching over me the past three weeks! Thank you, Jesus!

We took a bus ride to downtown Vienna to the Hotel *Erzerhog Rainer* (what a name!). It is a hotel in the old style, very quaint, old world. Our room is a very small one. Here was where David turned werewolf. He wouldn't stop crying from about 7:00 to 9:00 p.m. He then fell asleep out of sheer exhaustion. While he slept, I finally called room service for my complimentary dinner. I have to say that it was some of the finest restaurant food that I've ever eaten. I just ordered the first thing on the menu. In about twenty minutes came a tray with a plate of tossed salad (Fantastic, fresh vegetables)—the dressing was out of this world. The main entrée was a steak on a slice of black bread and, on top of it all, a fried egg with grilled onions cooked into it. The sauce was like I'd never tasted before. I drank a little white wine with dinner and washed it all down with a coke. Fantastic! After four weeks of Romanian food, this dinner was almost orgasmic. All in all, our first day out of Romania has been a fantastic day. One to remember! I only hope tomorrow goes as smoothly.

Monday, April 8, 1991

I am a little worried about David. He slept from 9:00 last night till 3:30, ate, then slept again from 5 a.m. on. It is now 8:30 and he is still asleep. I hope he does okay on the flight and doesn't cry.

Later that day:

Well, here we are now at 35,000 feet, almost halfway between Vienna and New York. So far, so good! On board they found a place for me in business class. I am sitting in two seats and David is mounted on the wall in a very ingenious cradle. He fell asleep shortly after taking off, and has been asleep for over three hours.

The Final Chapter of the Beginning of Our Lives as a Family:

This is the final entry of the most important part of our lives. I don't even know how to do this. I'm ending this journal, but this is only the beginning. The rest of the plane ride to New York was busy, but uneventful until our descent. The baby started crying because of his ears equalizing under pressure. I tried to feed him, but he refused to eat. This started a vicious cycle of no eating, increased pain, no eating. We landed in New York. I thanked the whole crew for an incredibly easy flight and ran to customs. My first step was to a customs officer. I told him all that I had to declare from Romania: a bottle of wine, a loaf of bread and a baby! He waved me through and I went to immigration. They hurried me up. The lady was a very sweet one. She took his color pictures to make his green card. I'm glad we didn't have to wait for it. She said it would take four months.

At about 5:30 they announced boarding for passengers with small children. We had to shove just to get there, but we made it on board. David had been a dream until then, but the airport was very hot and humid and had no air conditioning. We got on board and he began crying. Nothing I did helped any and he began wailing. To make matters worse, the aircraft was stuck in dock for another half hour and there was no ventilation. Poor David was sweating buckets and nothing would help. We finally got moving and had air, but that only slowed him down a little.

We were still stuck in taxiing traffic and did not take off until after 6:30. After we were flying, a young lady named Leslie was seated behind me. She leaned up and asked if she could hold him and give me a break. David fell in love with her in about ten minutes. He was cooing to her. She walked him up and down the length of the aircraft and he finally quieted down. On the descent into Washington, I took him back, but it was too late, his ears started popping and the crying began again. I couldn't slow him down till we landed. I'll tell you, I was never so relieved as when that plane touched down.

I waited till everyone got off, then we left. I got into the terminal and started the long walk down the tunnel. As I got closer to the end, I heard someone say: "There he is!" I looked and saw a large group of people start waving, yelling, and holding up signs. They were all friends from church, the fire department, the hospital and Lorrie's office. I wish I could name them all here, but I was too much in shock to count and remember them all. I will say, though, it was a tearful reunion. Out of the crowd came Lorrie, looking so beautiful. She came up to me and we held each other close for two or three minutes. I leaned back, showed her David and introduced them. It was almost impossible for me to talk. We came close to the rest of the crowd and they pelted us with confetti, which I still found in my hair the next day.

I have one thing to say. I have had the opportunity to have many joyous occasions, but in my whole life, if I live to be a hundred, I will never feel a more happy time full of love, friendship and fellowship as I did that

Monday night. It was the happiest night of my life and I will always feel a special love for the people who came to celebrate this moment with our newly formed family.

This ends the first chapter of our lives together as a family. I look back now and I am sure that the Lord was watching over us all. It was the hardest thing I've ever had to do, going to Romania. As David grows older, I am going to raise him to learn that it is really true that with God, with your faith in Him, all things truly are possible. David, as you read this, I hope you understand what it was like to go through this experience. Now that it is done, I feel so much love for you my heart swells with pride in you, and in us as a family. Thank God for you!

Cindy, Jerry and Crina: Adoption after Regulation

Friday, March 1, 1996

When we landed at the Bucharest airport I was surprised not to see military personnel everywhere. The customs officer was very nice and we went through rather quickly. We got our bags and were bombarded by lots of men at the door offering taxis. They start grabbing your bags before you can give them an answer. Thank God, Rodica and her stepson, Liviu, were there to meet us. Knowing they were family and friends from our adoption agency made us feel calm and relaxed about the whole situation.

We got into Liviu's little Dacia automobile and headed for Rodica's flat, where we would be spending our first night. The sky was clear, the weather cold. It reminded me of a typical winter day in Michigan. The area around the airport seemed to be run down and in disrepair. Getting closer to Bucharest, we noticed a whole city in need of repair. A lot of buildings, it was explained, were started under the dictatorship but never finished, or else built so poorly that people refused to live in them. Even the cranes were still sitting at some of the sites. There are some parts of Bucharest with very nice houses in the old style, but it appears they are few and far between.

Liviu dropped us off at the flat. I gave some gifts to the owners. Their flat was small and cozy. They were very gracious and warm. They made us a dinner of pork cutlets, salads, mashed potatoes, vegetables, bread, cheese and homemade wine. Before leaving we had bought Berlitz tapes and tried to learn a little Romanian, but we still needed to often refer to the pocket dictionary/phrase book. Nicholas, the husband, spoke very little, if any, English. Rodica, the wife, wasn't too bad, but our conversations were very cryptic. During dinner we watched an American movie with Romanian subtitles. That night, Jerry and I went to bed about 10:00 p.m.. We were very tired from traveling and drinking too much homemade wine. As tired as I was, I found it hard to fall asleep. I think the excitement and anticipation was too much for me. I tried listening to my Walkman radio and found a station that played American music. Later, I found a station that was airing a drama in English about a husband and wife who were trying to flee the country. I still couldn't sleep. Eventually, I put on the Romanian conversation tapes and fell asleep.

Saturday, March 2, 1996

Nicholas made us a breakfast of fried pork, fried sausages the size of knackwurst, fried eggs, salad, bread, fried potatoes and homemade wine. I also drank coke and seltzer water from the kind of old-fashioned bottle I hadn't seen in years. Needless to say, I tasted that meal several times during the course of the day. Rodica and Nick's flat has one bedroom, one bath. They gave us their bedroom and slept on the sofa bed. It's nice and clean inside, although the outside and hallways are somewhat dark, run down and unkempt with just a bare light bulb hanging down for light. The elevator is barely big enough for two people. The kitchen is small and the refrigerator so tiny that they keep their beverages outside on the balcony to keep cool. I wonder where they keep them in the summer.

After breakfast we walked over to Liviu and Rodica's house. She wanted to meet us again before we went to Braila, the town we were going to for the adoption, northeast of Bucharest. After all, we'll be staying with them when we return to Bucharest next week. Their apartment is a two bedroom flat in one of those institutional block-style housing complexes. It's considered nice by Bucharest standards, but the apartment is on the fifth floor and there's no elevator. Then we packed our belongings at Rodica and Nick's. We were told that we would have to carry whatever suitcases we took and to be sure to store them in an overhead shelf wherever we sat because Gypsies snatch things. We took two suitcases and headed for the station. It was interesting to watch the people at the station. I felt like I was in some old movie.

We went "First Class," staying in a compartment that sits about four people comfortably but usually contains six plus luggage on overhead racks. The train was comfortable. When we first got there, a homeless-looking man with both legs amputated below the knee was sitting there. When two other people came to the compartment they shooed him away. Pulling out of the city, I noticed that this part of Bucharest is very drab, even for winter. I feel for these people whose treasury and way of life was raped by their dictator. The city has had some snow lately and it doesn't look like they have snowplows or salt to keep the streets clean. It makes for hazardous walking and driving.

There seems to be no rhyme or reason to the layout of the streets. Many of the streets are narrow and I saw very few traffic lights outside their downtown. You drive at your own risk. I also noticed a lot of stray dogs around. Everywhere you look you see laundry hanging out to dry on the balconies of their flats or their backyards if they have a house. Very few people have dryers. The people dress in very dark colors and it seems everyone smokes cigarettes (mostly American) and walk around with fur hats. The toilet paper they use is rougher than paper towel, but you get used to it.

The train ride for the first hour goes through a mostly barren, flat landscape and then farmland. We made occasional stops at some towns and passed by manufacturing plants that seemed vacant. At one stop, a dirty poor boy came by our carriage looking for a handout but was shooed away. We saw no signs showing what city we were pulling into and got a little concerned. How are you supposed to know when to get off if you don't know the country or the language? Still, Rodica had told us exactly how long the trip would take. When that amount of time had elapsed, we asked the young people sharing our compartment if we were pulling into Braila. They said yes and we got off at a small station. We saw a few dirty and obviously poor and/or homeless young boys running around. We were met by Rodica's sister, Florica, one of her sons, Florin, his friend, and a girl who spoke pretty good English. We were escorted to Florica's flat, which was within walking distance of the station. It was another communist institutional flat, run down on the outside. Inside it was clean and quite homey. We were given Florin's bedroom; fortunately he was away attending college. The room had little room to move around, especially when you pulled out the sofa, which turns into something between a twin and a full bed. Hot water is only available at certain times on certain days so we were told to bathe accordingly.

Sunday, March 3, 1996

Today is our first full day in Braila. Florica served leftover chicken schnitzel from last night's dinner, assorted cheeses, toast, quince and plum jams, and crepes filled with jam for dessert. Jerry had the instant oatmeal and raisins he had brought from home. Florica has taken off time from her job as a math teacher. We were paying her $50 a day for room and board.

We then went to the orphanage to see our daughter for the first time. I was so excited, worrying whether or not she'd be healthy. The orphanage was number four out of five in Braila. Crina was born on April 2, 1995, and has been institutionalized since birth. The building was very institutional-looking, which I had expected. When we entered, I noticed it was clean and somewhat quiet but also as hot as a sauna. No wonder the babies are always sick. In this kind of heat germs will have a field day. We went up to the second floor to a common area between two wards. They had a few toys hanging on the wall and one table in the middle of the room where a brand-new television they told me they'd just acquired was playing.

When they brought Crina (her given name) out, I felt like I wanted to break down and cry. A few tears managed to trickle down my cheek. She was beautiful, even though her complexion was somewhat grayish and she was still getting over an upper respiratory congestion condition that had sent her temporarily to the hospital. It was obvious that Crina had been held by very few people in her young life. She seemed to like the toys we had brought with us, especially a little yellow rattle, which became her favorite. She checked out both our facial features with her tiny hands and especially liked to grab at my glasses and bangs. It was love at first sight. Even though she was sick, she had a cute personality and was very friendly. The clothing she had on was worn and torn and didn't fit. It was a one-piece outfit with feet that tied around the back of the neck. None of the children wore diapers. They are expensive and time-consuming. When a child soils itself, the clothing is taken off, then they are washed and another outfit is taken out and put on—not necessarily the right size.

Crina had four teeth—two up, two down. She tried several times to put her hand in my mouth. She actually got hold of one of Jerry's hands and gave it a good chomp. She also bounced a lot to the music from the television and wiggled her fingers a lot. We were only there for about one hour because we'd decided we wanted her to get used to us gradually. My only concern was about Crina's hearing. She didn't seem to respond too well to noises out of her eyesight. There was a chance she might be deaf. We went back to Florica's flat and had lunch, which seems to be the main meal of the day. We had soup, bread, chicken, shredded carrot salad, mashed potatoes and crepes filled with jam for dessert. The food might be basic but is very good. After lunch we went for a walk. The city was bleak-looking and grungy. I noticed several mangy street dogs roaming about. Still, some old buildings are ornate in the old-world fashion and the main part of town has a tree-lined boulevard. Jerry said that Braila must have been beautiful prior to the communists. Later that afternoon, Florin returned for a visit. He's the younger of Florica's two sons, is a computer student at the University of Galati, and speaks very good English. Florin says that many of the people in power are holdovers from the dictatorship. He calls the new government "Neo-Communism" and feels that the voters do not know any better. He believes things will get more democratic, but will take time, maybe fifteen years. Gabriel, our translator, said it will take more than fifty years. Anyway, it is apparent that life here is very hard and people go without many things we take for granted. The condition of the apartment buildings is very sad. They are in great disrepair and very grungy. Florica does the best she can with the interior of her flat. If you want to get anything done in a decent amount of time here you have to pay a little money under the table or give them a token present. Everyone seems to expect it.

Monday, March 4, 1996

It seems that Florica only gets hot water from seven to nine in the mornings, except for Fridays and weekends. If they bathe on weekends, she boils water and fills the tub. The bathtub was deep and rather old-looking with a hand-held shower head. I decided I would wait and only take showers in the morning, if possible. Florica told us that, as bad as conditions are in these apartments (flats as they call them), the people who have one (no matter what condition they're in) consider themselves lucky. Florica's flat is heated by a boiler/radiator. Jerry thinks that's why they keep the windows open, even in the dead of winter

At 9 a.m., Rodica and Gabriela arrived. Everyone who drives has a Dacia—the national car. They are sparsely outfitted and have doubled in price in one year. Gabriela's Dacia, which she purchased for seven million Lei, costs fourteen million this year. Anyway, we all drove to the orphanage to see our daughter and talk to the doctor. The doctor was at a meeting, so we talked to the nurses. One of the nurses wrapped Crina up and came with us to the hospital to have Crina's hearing checked out. The children are rarely taken out of the orphanage, and the fresh air put her to sleep quickly. It seems that many of the children from the orphanage are apathetic and do not really know how to respond to people or play with toys. They seem to just want to tune out the noise of other children. The hospital (which is the one Crina was born in) is about fifty years old, pretty seedy and run down. Most of the patients were lying on army-looking cots and many lined the hallways. Crina was examined by a doctor who looked in her ears and used a tuning fork. She didn't respond. The doctor said the inside of her ears looked normal, but he could not tell us for sure if she could hear. I talked to Jerry for a short period of time. I felt in my heart that her lack of response was mostly institutional. If it wasn't, and she was deaf, we could deal with that. We decided to take her, regardless. I just could not imagine leaving her there in those conditions. When we returned to the orphanage, Crina seemed to respond a little better because of the familiar surroundings. We talked to the nurse in charge of Crina. She said that children get desensitized to noises on either side of their crib and usually focus straight ahead, which is usually their only line of vision.

We saw the ward where Crina was kept and the condition of some of these children would rip your heart out. Two of the children directly across from Crina had very bad harelip conditions and were desperately in need of surgery—which they will probably not receive. The child next to her was a head banger. I felt so sorry for the children. I wish I could have taken them all. As we left, a very cute and cheerful boy, about four years of age, came up to us and called out to us in Romanian, "Mama and Dada, I can be adopted!" Another small boy did the same thing, but this time Jerry and the boy exchanged facial rasberries through the door.

On the way to the courthouse, we saw several carts pulled by horses and people fixing (or else clearing) the street with pickaxes and old ladies sweeping the streets with old-fashioned whisk brooms. We got to the courthouse a little early. Gabriela, Jerry and myself walked down to take a look at the Danube River. Rodica went inside the courthouse. When we finally hooked up with her again she told us there was a problem. My heart sank. The birth parents had not shown up. The Judge of the Tribunal was willing to wait and see if Rodica and Gabriela could go to the village where they live and bring them back. The Judge also said that, if we did not get them to sign off on the paperwork, we would have to wait until next Monday for our hearing. After Rodica talked to him privately, however, the Judge said he would accept the signed paperwork today.

Jerry and I took a taxi back to Florica's flat. I ate and took a nap. At about three o' clock, Gabriela came and got us and told us they had found the birth parents. The birth father's name is Ionel and he was born in 1971. The birth mother's name is Vasilica; she was born in 1975. The birth father is employed as a milker on a livestock farm in a village and earns 200,000 Lei (3,000 Lei per $1 U.S.). The birth mother does not work, as far as I know. They live in the stable, which is dirty, and have no furniture. They had gotten notice of the hearing, but the foreman would not let them leave the farm. They signed the papers and Rodica gave them some of the money we had given her for that purpose. Gabriela said that they are very poor and that one of their kids had already been adopted by another American family. Additionally, their two-year-old son, Marian, was born 2/3/94 and had been given to someone else to look after. Then, that person could no longer do so and the child was sent to an orphanage—a different one from the one Crina was in. They also had a four-year-old named Nicolae, whom they kept. The mother is only twenty-one. I felt sorry for Crina's parents for everything they had gone through and their current living conditions, as described by Gabriela. I hope some day that Crina (soon to become Emma) will appreciate what we have done for her. I hope that we will be good parents and help her grow to be a self-confident, intelligent and caring person. I would have loved to meet the birth parents, but Gabriela thought it was a good thing that we did not see the conditions the parents live in because it was beyond description.

We went back to the courthouse and had our hearing before the tribunal. It was short and sweet. The Judge made small talk, asked us a few questions, and then it was over. He also told us that we were taking a little part of Romania with us. When it was over, I breathed a sigh of relief. Tomorrow, Rodica will return to the courthouse to give the Judge some gifts on our behalf. The gifts I have given have been very much appreciated. I wish I had brought more, especially clothing.

I have been dying for a little salad. Tomorrow, Gabriela is going to bring us some lettuce and tomatoes from Galati because they cannot be found in Braila. I haven't noticed many fresh fruits either.

Tomorrow we get to spend two full hours with Crina. I can't wait to get her out of the orphanage and take her home. I can't stop thinking about what I saw at the orphanage today. Gabriela says conditions are not much better than they were under the dictator and funds are scarce.

Tuesday, March 5, 1996

Slept well and love the down bedding. Since I've been here I have had the weirdest dreams, sometimes nightmarish and sometimes disturbing. I wonder why, since I'm so happy and excited about our daughter. I woke up about 7:30 and took a shower. I got hot water by only turning the hot knob—didn't use the cold knob at all. I still have a sore throat, chest congestion and runny nose, which I've had for several days. My right ankle is throbbing. Florica is serving us too much food. At this rate I'm going to gain weight. I got a second dose of tea to help with my constipation. No luck.

I keep thinking about Crina and her poor physical and probably emotional condition. I can't see how anyone can thrive under such conditions. The smell of the orphanage makes me ill, although Jerry didn't smell anything (but he doesn't have that good a sense of smell). One of the first things I'm going to do with Crina is give her a bath and give her back that baby smell.

Rodica and Gabriela came and we went to get certain papers signed, giving Crina our last name and preparing to pick up her passport. We went to the orphanage to meet the head doctor. We spent more time with Crina. She seemed to be in better spirits today and was more playful. She said "La! La!" to the music of one of the toys we brought. While we were there Crina had to be changed twice. She teethed for a while on the small yellow rattle on the mirror. One of the nurses mentioned that Crina was her favorite little girl—I can see why—and that she wished a Romanian family had adopted her.

Lunch—more tea, with lemon this time to help my condition, but to no avail. I asked about going to a restaurant but was told it was not a good idea. The quality is questionable, they say. Good news. Florica informed us that we would have hot water in the mornings and evenings until we leave, except on one day. It's just a matter of remembering what time. This evening I'm going to try washing my hair for the first time since arriving here. After dinner there's *E.R.* (in English with Romanian subtitles) and Bugs Bunny in German.

Wednesday, March 6, 1996

We filled out police forms for Crina's passport. The visit to the passport office was a breeze. It will be ready on Friday (I hope). I noticed that they remove ice from the streets by banging it with shovels and pickaxes. There are many stray dogs roaming the city. One has been lying in the same position under the same tree for days now. We figure it must be dead. The city has little money to spare and definitely no money for dogcatchers. We bought fruit for the orphanage at the public market; also a case of bananas and some tomatoes for Florica. Tomatoes are hard to come by in these parts. It was also hard finding good bananas and even harder to find good looking apples.

I asked Rodica about Crina's heritage. I want to be able to tell my little girl everything about being Romanian. Rodica was concerned that I thought Crina might have Gypsy blood in her. The thought never crossed my mind. To put everyone's mind at ease, she is going to take us to the village to meet Crina's birth parents tomorrow. Gypsy women here are easy to spot because of the bright colored clothing they wear. Apparently, they do not want to work and would rather beg or steal. At least that's what the Romanians tell us. Regardless of the reason, I am glad we will have a chance to meet her birth parents.

They let me feed Crina with some chicken soup mush. Afterward we played with her for a while. I didn't want to leave. On the way home I saw homeless people begging on the street. The older, pre-communist buildings in Braila are very nice but in dire need of repair. Florica's flat building has pieces of cement that have fallen off, open wiring in the hallway; nevertheless, they still feel lucky to have a flat.

I can't say enough good things about Rodica. What a woman! She truly is a wonder woman and, although not young, possesses a lot of energy. I can't imagine anyone coming to adopt a child without the help of such a woman. We don't speak the language and things are done differently here. No hot water on Wednesdays, for example, so I washed my upper body with baby wipes (One of the first things I want to do when I get home is take the longest, hottest shower I can). You really need to have someone here who knows the ropes, people and language.

Thursday, March 7, 1997

The drive out of town was interesting. We saw a part of town I hadn't seen before. Lots of blocks of flats in the same condition as others I've seen. We also saw a subdivision that had been under construction but never finished—another failed communist project. We passed a paper mill, a chemical plant and several horse-drawn carts.

Crina's parents were not expecting us. When we arrived at the village, we pulled up to the entrance of a livestock farm. Rodica got out, approached someone and asked where Ionel could be found. By luck he was walking toward the gate with a horse. Soon afterward his wife, Vasilica, came out as well. They were very nice, good-looking, and pleasant about the whole thing, considering we sprung it upon them without notice. We took a few photos together, although I wish we had taken more in case the ones we did take don't turn out. We gave them the gifts we had brought and told them through Gabriela that we would take good care of their daughter and give her a good home. Vasilica said, "God bless you because I cannot raise her." They were somewhat dirty, dressed in layers of peasant clothing and Ionel wore a fur hat. They kind of reminded me of some character from *Fiddler on the Roof.* I think they would be a nice looking couple, once cleaned up.

Afterwards, we went to the orphanage where Crina's brother, Marian, is staying. On the way we passed by a hospital and the odd sight of people walking out in the cold in their hospital gowns and bathrobes (one guy even had his head bandaged up). The orphanage struck me as identical to Crina's and just as drab—basic institutional white with little color anywhere. The children at this orphanage seemed older. Upstairs we looked into one of the wards where several little children were sitting on small plastic potties, apparently in the midst of toilet training. At first I thought how cute, but then it struck me as sad that there's no privacy.

Marian then came out. He was very shy and cowered behind the nurse. Jerry took his picture. The flash frightened him and he started to cry. My first instinct was to run up and hug him, but I didn't since he had never seen me before. The speech therapist spoke English. She told us he has a shortening of one of his leg muscles.

Then she asked us if we knew of an agency that could help them get a copy machine. They do not have one and have to spend half their time making copies by hand. Jerry wasn't sure if she was asking if we knew of an agency that could help them or wanted us to help them ourselves. We told her we didn't know of any agency.

About 3:30 we went to see Crina. She seemed to be taken with Jerry's nose today. We spent about an hour, then walked back with Florica. We said goodbye to Rodica and Gabriela.

Friday, March 8, 1996

Our last full day in Braila. We went to the police station about ten o' clock to pick up Crina's passport. It wasn't ready, but Rodica gave the head man a box of chocolates and some flowers. We waited in his office and shortly thereafter the passport was ready. The man spoke pretty good English. It turns out his daughter is in Chicago studying Math at Loyola University.

On our way to the orphanage we bought five bags of animal crackers for the children. We also bought a large box of chocolates for the nurses. We played with Crina and gave her some animal crackers. Shortly thereafter, she wet herself and me and had to be changed. Crina hasn't smiled a whole lot. It is not uncommon for orphanage children. Besides, what do they have to smile about? In a couple of months, they say, we won't believe the change in her. She's still coughing quite a bit and so are many of the other children in the orphanage. Crina still falls over from a sitting position. Her development seems to that of a six- or seven-month-old, yet she's eleven months old. Still, a delay in development was expected. I hope she'll catch up once we get home. Her favorite toy so far has been a yellow rattle with a mirror and a teething ring. Tomorrow will be the first day in Crina's life she'll wear a diaper and have a teething ring.

For our last dinner it was food plus apricot champagne and *tzuica* that will knock your socks off. I have put on five pounds since we came here.

Saturday, March 9, 1996

We went to the orphanage to pick up our daughter. The nurses dressed her in the clothing we brought. I brought two different outfits. First, the nurses put the diaper on backwards. Then they put on an undershirt and a one-piece outfit. *Then* the pink sweatshirt and sweatpants. They put on *everything* I brought, which was not my intention. After all that went the snowsuit, hat and scarf; after saying goodbye, we were out of there.

When we got to Florica's, Crina was looking at everything and everyone and seemed the happiest I've seen her so far. She was also the most vocal. We tried to put her down for a nap. I think it was too strange a place and she didn't sleep long. She then fell asleep in my arms at the train station and slept a good amount on the train. Rodica was a big help and thank God she was there. It's good to have the hand of experience when you're a novice. I was very nervous and excited at the same time. I wondered how I'd do at motherhood. The oncoming first night scared me to death.

Putting Crina to sleep after dinner wasn't easy. We grow more attached to her by the minute. All night long we drank *tzuica*. I couldn't sleep. I kept getting up to look at her. About 2:15 she woke me up. I figured it was either time for a diaper change or the herbal tea mixture Rodica gave me for colic. She drank half a bottle of baby tea and I rocked her to sleep. Sitting there in the half dark, rocking my baby, I know what maternal bliss is. I was truly happy with my new family. Jerry seems to be as smitten as I am, although he hasn't fed or changed her yet. That's just as well at this point because her eating habits are iffy at best. Every time I have to remove her clothes she cries something awful. If you saw the way some of the nurses handle the babies to change their clothing, you'd know why she was screaming.

Sunday, March 10, 1996

Crina slept past 8 a.m. Just before breakfast was ready I gave her medicine and a bottle of milk. It was one that Florica had made before we left. Crina didn't like the contents and I emptied it out. What I didn't know was that Florica had cut the opening of the nipple. When I refilled the bottle and gave it to Crina, the liquid came out too fast and she threw it up over herself, the blanket and me. The episode tired Crina out and I put her down for a nap. She wouldn't go down, though, except if she could lay on my stomach. So I lay down with her on my stomach for an hour. How sweet she looks.

Later, Crina ate three-quarters of a mashed banana and some baby tea and, again, would only sleep on my stomach while I cradled her in my arms. I don't know if she was cranky because she was sleepy, or because she needed a diaper change. It turned out to be a little of both. When I began changing her, she screamed bloody murder. Just as I started to put on a clean diaper, she urinated all over the place and soiled her clothes. Then she slept for an hour. When Jerry came in the bedroom he stood over and looked down at Crina and the biggest smile I'd ever seen came over his face. Tomorrow, we will go to the police to put in the application for Crina's formal birth certificate listing us as parents.

Monday, March 11, 1996

Rodica watched Crina while I took a shower and washed my hair. I'd done neither since arriving back in Bucharest. After putting a second dose of shampoo in my hair the cold water went and I almost got scalded. Then the hot water went and there I was with a head full of shampoo lather. The bad part was that I hadn't started washing my body yet. When Crina awoke, we went to change her diaper, which had a very small deposit. She had finally made a nice bowel movement: her first bowel movement in Bucharest.

The child on the right is 3 months old and the child on the left is 18 months old. The child on the left was institutionalized for the first part of her life. This photo was taken during the first month of adoptive placement.

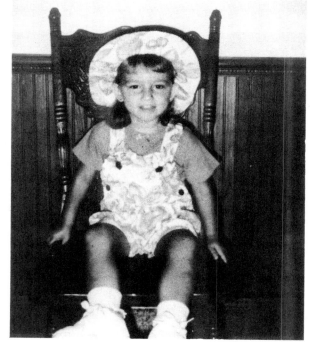

The same child 2 years later, at age 3 ½ years. A "wounded wonder" who made a tremendous recovery from her early trauma.

Victor Groza holding a child from an Institution for the Irrecoverable (circa 1996) in Hirlau, Romania. The child is 10 years old but was light enough to be carried as a toddler. The developmental problems the child had at birth were exacerbated in the institution.

Daniela Ileana in a renovated Casa de Copii (orphanage) in Bucharest (1994). There was much improvement in the institutions between 1990 and 1994.

Older children who become lost in the system. Orphaned at birth and not receiving the medical, psychiatric, educational, spiritual or physical stimulation they need, they are a lost generation of children. Photo is from a Camin Spital (special hospital) in Suceava, 1992.

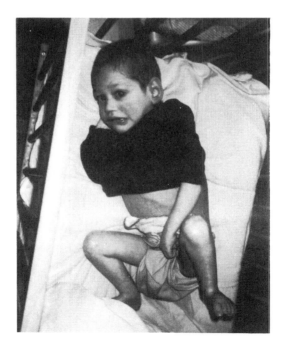

Physical deformity of legs in a child due to inappropriate diapering and the lack of physical stimulation.

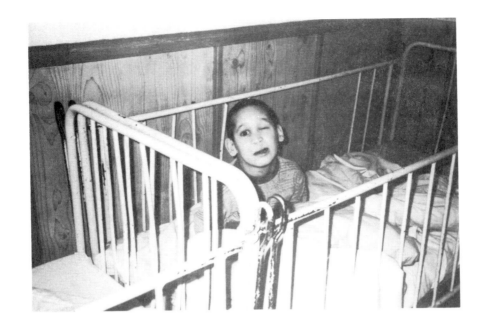

Child who was blinded and brain damaged after an unsuccessful abortion, abandoned at birth.

Ivor in Bucharest in 1976.

Tuesday, March 12, 1996

We couldn't give Crina anything to eat or drink because we had to take her to the hospital for the physical exam and T.B. test required by the American Embassy. To get to the hospital, we went through the downtown area. There was a McDonald's and a Pizza Hut. We ate carry-out pizza for lunch in the car.

At the hospital we went into a waiting room with a bunch of other Americans and their adopted children. It was like a cattle-call operation. It was strange being in a room in Bucharest where just about everyone spoke English: people from Boston, New Jersey, Minnesota, and Wisconsin. Only one child was younger than Crina. Her exam went as expected. They didn't weigh her. They checked her all over, used a stethoscope, checked her reflexes, held her up by her hands and forced her to take a couple of steps and checked her hearing. Of course, she was crying so hard, she didn't really care what the doctor was doing. I held her while the doctor drew blood and she screamed her head off. Afterwards, we went to the police station to get the birth certificate. It wasn't ready. We gave the man in charge some cigarettes and he said they'd finish it. While we waited, Crina, all cooped up in the car, her schedule off, got more cranky. That night I put Crina to bed late, about 8:45 p.m. I hoped she'd sleep long, considering she missed her normal afternoon nap. It was not to be. She awoke at 11:45 p.m. I gave her a bottle and rocked her back to sleep.

Wednesday, March 13, 1996

Crina woke at 5:15. I gave her three-quarters of a bottle and rocked her back to sleep. She slept till 7:15 a.m. I picked her up and she was soaking wet. Oh, the joys of motherhood! I cleaned out her runny nose with a Q-tip. When I changed her diaper I used a warm, wet washcloth instead of the usual baby wipe. She didn't cry as hard. I don't think I'd like someone putting cold wet wipes on my behind either. I asked Rodica to look at the diaper and see if it was a normal bowel movement. That might sound like a silly thing to do, but I am a novice and have no frame of reference. I feel sorry for Crina. She's got a novice for a mother who's relatively unsure about what she's doing. Poor Crina was irritable today because of her cold. It's a hacking cough. Every time she coughs she cries. We gave her some expectorant for the coughing. She seems to be a fighter, which is good. This afternoon she was making faces. We checked but she was clean. About fifteen minutes later Crina had a bowel explosion. Another diaper change and, to my dismay, I found diaper rash. Shortly afterward, though, Crina was happy and babbling, to everyone's delight.

I asked Jerry to clip her nails but after two minutes he gave up. He's great at playing with her, yet tentative when it comes to care and feeding. That will change with time—I hope. I also think it will be a while before he changes her diaper. Usually, by the time Jerry gets near Crina, she's been cleaned, fed and is very alert. When she starts getting cranky, it's mommy's turn. Crina seems to really like the Big Bird music box with the blue pop-up knob, which she is always trying to put in her mouth. Jerry can only stand about once through, then he says, "Don't you have something else?" Repetition is something he has to get used to with babies. He hasn't spent enough time with babies to know how, if they like something, they play with it or watch it often. A lot longer than any adult can stand. I'm going to try and have Jerry spend more time with Crina so he can see for himself what babies are really like.

Thursday, March 14, 1996

Last night was the night from Hell. Crina was up almost the entire night—congested and wheezing with a hacking cough. Every time she'd cough, she would cry at the top of her lungs. Any medicine I gave her didn't last very long. She spent the entire night in my arms while I walked the floor. Finally, I sat down with her on the chair in the living room, spending the rest of the night there so we wouldn't disturb anyone. When the sun came up I was overtired and cranky.

At noon, it was on with Crina's snowsuit, which she hates, and off to the Embassy. It was as hot as the orphanage there and I was concerned that she'd cry and cry in front of the Embassy workers. Anyway, there we were, standing on American soil and it felt good. We saw a number of families we'd seen at the hospital on Tuesday and we took the time to all wish each other luck. Then I was told that she passed her TB test. I started tearing up with joy because the end was in sight.

Tonight, I was crabby and needed a good night's sleep. Jerry finally got Crina to sleep, but, after he put her down, she started to cry. We decided to let her cry for as long as it took for her to fall asleep—which she did, although she woke and coughed and cried a few times. We don't want Crina to think that every time she cries we jump. That night, Jerry came in twice to wake me about the baby's crying. Once again, I got the crisis night and Jerry got off relatively easy.

Friday, March 15, 1996

Crina seems better. Her coughing fits are not as bad. Today she actually stood up and held herself up without falling over. Tonight, Jerry put Crina to bed and she slept. We got a call from KLM. We could change our flight because they had open seats for the Sunday morning flight. I have really enjoyed my stay here but it feels good to know the three of us will be on our way home soon.

Saturday, March 16, 1996

Crina woke up in a cheerful mood. We played with her, changed her, fed her and she played in the walker till 11:30 a.m. Later she sat up real well. She likes it when you hold her up by her hands. In fact, she spent a good part of the day in the walker, almost standing. Now you can stand her up on the sofa with her back against the sofa and she'll stand for a couple of minutes at a time.

Rodica brought over a couple from Ohio, Craig and Laura, who've just arrived. They are going to Braila to the same orphanage Crina was in to adopt Toberio. We have already seen him a few times. He's really cute, smiles and laughs a lot. They will be staying with Rodica and Liviu next week. In private, Laura told me how depressed she was by Bucharest's drabness. We answered some questions about the process and traded phone numbers and addresses. It will be interesting to exchange impressions later.

For our last dinner in Romania, Rodica made Mititei—ground pork and beef, shaped into sausage-like patties, and a 'Malaysian' soup with a hint of curry. Rodica thought it was spicy. She has no idea what spice is. The food here is good but basic. Over tzuica, cherry port and toasts with peach champagne we discussed politics and history. I am glad we are going home tomorrow and can start to be a real family. I feel like these people have become family and I am going to miss them. This is one trip I'll never forget. Liviu insisted we'd never be back for a vacation. Jerry and I said we wanted to come back and see different parts of the country or to get another baby.

Chapter 7

The Children Adopted from Romania: Myth and Reality

From 1990 to 1993, according to estimates provided by Adoptive Families of America, of the approximately 10,000 children adopted from Romania, about 2,800 or almost one third of the children were adopted by families in the United States. Several studies and media reports have been circulated about the adopted children from Romania. Most are extremely negative. The media accounts are not to be trusted, given their tendency for sensationalism and exaggeration. In addition, most of the research studies conducted on Romanian children examine children from hospitals or other medical settings. One of the earliest reports concluded that Romanian adoptees are at high risk for medical problems based on a very small group of 65.[1]

Drawing on reports from parents collected through a mailed survey[2], we outline the strengths and difficulties of Romanian adoptions faced by families who are not necessarily getting help from a hospital or medical clinics. This way of gathering gives a different view of adoptive families and the children adopted from Romania and is in stark contrast to many media reports.

At the time the study was initiated, children were under the age of five and had been in their adoptive homes three years. Most had entered families before the age of two. Adoptive mothers were 41 years of age and adoptive fathers were 43 years of age. Most parents had a college or a graduate degree. Families were white and middle to upper middle class.

Development

It is important to note that many of these adopted children came from orphanages, hospitals, or other institutional settings. We have learned several things about these children. The children adopted from institutions can be categorized into three groups[3].

One group of children is the "resilient rascals." These children, regardless of their circumstances, survived well. Some came from horrific conditions, but fared well in orphanages. Some were favored children and received a great deal of attention. Others, who did not receive attention from adults, turned to their peers or even other children in their beds. These "resilient rascals" have adjusted well in their adopted family settings. About one-fifth of the children would fall into this category.[4]

As an example of a "resilient rascal," one mother wrote:

> Our child has done very well. In many cases, Ovidiu[1] is ahead of other children his age. For example, he has very good motor skills—he can hit a baseball, put a basketball in the hoop, and he can write his name well. He does well at memorization of letters, numbers, songs, [and] rhymes. He can stay on task at preschool. My main concern is his "active nature." ...I do think that his active nature might have something to do with his orphanage experience. However, for the most part, he is a very normal child and can function well socially with friends and family.

As another example a parent wrote:

> Irimie came from a very good orphanage in Romania where he was the favorite child. A particular nurse paid extra attention to him and even took him home sometimes to be with her family. I feel that because of this nurse, Irimie is where he is today (and was when he arrived) as far as his development...He is an excellent swimmer, fast runner, and such a good skater that he usually wins roller skate races when his class goes to the rink...If he has anything wrong with him, it isn't very evident. I think he's just a normal child with certain likes and dislikes.

The second group of children is the "wounded wonders." These children demonstrate significant effects from institutionalization. However, families often report, with awe and astonishment, the changes that have occurred after these children have entered the adoptive homes. Initially, they can be a real challenge—marked difficulties in development, nutritional deficiencies, and problems with other life transitions—but over time, these children seem to respond favorably to the home environment. For the most part, the "wounded wonders" do okay in their families and make tremendous gains. This group of children represents the majority of children from institutions (about 60%).[5] Families described these children in the following anecdotes. As one mother wrote:

> When we received Elena from the orphanage she was 21 months old...She did not walk, talk, make eye contact, and would be limp when held. She would take only liquids from a bottle. [After] therapy for two years to help her to eat properly, she still has difficulty chewing and either cannot or will not eat some foods. I feel that she is making good progress in most areas...

As another example of a "wounded wonder," a mother wrote:

> There has been good improvement since [the] age of 2 ½ in [his] ability to tolerate change. When age 1 year or younger, he couldn't even tolerate having his food dish moved from the edge of the table (he would scream over it). He could not tolerate his head being washed but now is able to cope nicely. He is not able to do puzzles—"can't do it, too hard" he states. [He] didn't learn colors until age 3 ¾ years. He still cannot invent games or entertain himself, but likes to play with others and do their games—although sometimes he is unable to follow the games' rules that kids his own age make up. I feel he continues to make improvement...

---

[1] All names are fictitious and have been changed.

A third example:

> Our daughter was abandoned in a filthy Romanian hospital. She was premature, underweight, ill and starving. We were told her 17-year-old mother spent time in a "Home for Irrecoverables" and ran away two hours after giving birth. We knew that the baby would probably have disabilities, but we didn't know to what extent. The first night we had her at the hotel, I didn't expect her to be alive the next morning. She could not cry—she was so weak. [Now] she enjoys perfect physical health. She is speech delayed but comprehends *everything*. She is loving and wonderful.

As another example, a mother wrote:

> When we adopted out son at 18 months of age, he didn't walk, talk, eat or interact with others—except "head-butting." In four months, he learned to eat, speak and walk. After six months, he no longer head-butted and he liked to hug and kiss. At four, almost five, he has developed into a very intelligent and healthy boy. His pediatrician is amazed, and so are we.

A final example:

> Our daughter rocked if not held, would not make eye contact, and showed no facial expressions when we adopted her. She did not walk and had never had solid foods at 18 months of age. Within six months, she reached normal age level abilities and continues at or above age level in all skills—physical, social, and intellectual.

These children make changes, grow, and develop. Although they still have some gaps, overall, parents are able to manage them. Children are able to get their needs met as well as catch up. While they may not be developing the same as other children who did not experience the trauma, they get on a developmental path that is appropriate for them.

The third group of children is the "challenged children." These children are severely affected by their institutionalization. Many have special needs and although the children improve, they continue to have considerable difficulties. Parents have the most difficulty with this group of children and were not adequately prepared to parent these types of children. These children require special services. The families who unknowingly adopted these children remain at-risk for negative adoption outcomes. About one-fifth of the children[6] fall into this category.

The "challenged children" include children with developmental delays, developmental disabilities, emotional and behavior problems, and attachment difficulties. Some children have more than one of these problems. As an example, one parent wrote about her adoptive daughter:

She hates riding in a car and has tried to jump out while traveling numerous times. She has defied cars to hit her by standing in the middle of the street and refusing to move…She hordes garbage and stashes things. She has difficulty going to sleep. She does not value people's belongings….She has carved drawings in our furniture, appliances and cars. She tried to suffocate the cat. She hits and bumps children…She sets up fights.

The "challenged children" are a great stress to families. To not give families the needed support is to risk the break-up of the family. As one mother wrote:

This child has been a heartbreaker. [Her] physical and emotional problems have wiped us out financially and emotionally, and played a big role in the breakup of our marriage.

Some families are able to accept these challenges and manage the stress well. As one parent wrote:

It was obvious to me that our child had…brain damage. We loved him regardless of his condition. I found [our son] in a semi-coma after he had been starved, burned, strangled, and thrown up against a wall. Later, x-rays confirmed 14 broken bones and 2 skull fractures that left severe brain damage. The first prognosis was very grim and it was uncertain that he would ever walk or talk. He was completely blind and very delayed. He rebounded, in some ways, quickly in his new, 'safe' environment. He transformed from an extremely fearful child to a social and loving child… In less than one year [after a specialized treatment program], he has come three years in his ability to process information and have a greater use of functional vision. He now sees form but we are working on detail. He even played T-ball last spring on a "normal" team. I have never known a more loving and cooperative child. He also has great perseverance. When asked, 'Do you give up?' he always yells 'NEVER!'

His adoption is every bit as fulfilling as the birth of our two biological sons and he has been the greatest blessing I could ever imagine.

It is interesting that the same circumstances can result in different outcomes for children; that is, children who came from the same conditions can belong to any of the three groups—Resilient Rascal, Wounded Wonder, or Challenged Child. The reasons why are not clear. However, regardless of the type of child a family adopted, one issue for many parents was the lack of preparation for adopting internationally and not knowing exactly what they were getting into. About half of the families who adopted were not prepared for adoption.[7] They did not know what to expect or where to go for help. One story was very compelling in a parent's frustration with her lack of preparation.

When I first adopted Monica from Romania, I was like many other parents in the belief that a normal family environment with lots of love and healthy influences would be all these children would need to be 'normal.' After six months, we realized we had a hyper 15-month old who couldn't (or so we thought at the time) control her biting or being overly rough about everything…By the time she was three years old, I had turned into an angry, hard-to-be-around person. I was always exhausted! Monica was hyper to the point of ruining our family life…normal parenting was *not* working!

Along these same lines, about half or more of the parents indicated that they did not get enough background information about their adopted children. In some families, the information was clearly a lie. One mother wrote:

I was told [our daughter] was in the second grade and made good grades in school, that she was physically healthy, that she had never been abused, just neglected, etc. When she had been [in our home] a year, I went back to Romania and confronted her family about…this. They admitted they had lied so the child would be adopted. The truth—she was born at seven months after an unsuccessful abortion attempt and not expected to live. She was very slow to learn anything, was sexually abused by her father and was physically abused by her mother …

While it is very clear that most children recover from the trauma, it is also clear that an international adoption is a special needs adoption. Even though only about 20% of the children have pervasive and on-going difficulties, all of the children benefit from early intervention and families benefit from support and guidance.

Health

The most frequent health problems parents mentioned were allergies (19%), ear infections (11%), Hepatitis B (10%), and parasites (6%). The most common allergies reported for these children are the common allergies reported for many children: pollen/ragweed, dairy products, dust, bugs and bees. The problems with Hepatitis were more serious, even if children had no symptoms of liver disease. (Most children who had Hepatitis had no symptoms.) Still, parents had concerns. As examples of comments parents wrote:

[Our daughter] was Hepatitis exposed but the doctors [in the USA] assured us she has not and will not have a problem in the future (something about antibodies).

We had difficulty getting her into the preschool program because of the paranoia about her being a Hepatitis carrier.

We found out about a year after the adoption that she is a Hepatitis carrier. . I worry about when/how to tell her that she is a…carrier and how this will affect her. Also, [I worry whether] she will be able to function in the public schools without being "labeled."

One family's story was particularly sad:

> When we found out about our daughter's Hepatitis B virus, some of our friends asked us not to include our daughter in any family or play group activities. We arranged to have a nurse from the department of public health come to explain the disease, but to no avail; our friends still rejected our adopted daughter from all activities.

Families who have a child with a health difficulty need more information about the problem and support from professionals. Overall, however, relatively few health problems were reported. This is in contrast to research studies conducted at a clinic that suggested that over 80% of the children had health difficulties.[8] It is very clear that children with health problems were more likely to have come from institutions, but the majority of these children did not have health difficulties.

Behavior Problems

Many (48%) families reported that their children had no problems. When problems were reported, the most frequent problem behaviors were wetting the bed (about 20% of children) and being more active than expected for his or her age (about 22% of children). Less than 20% of the families reported children rocking themselves or being over sensitive to touch, sights or sounds. On a positive note, less than 15% of the families reported that their children's disabilities or problems were more serious than reported by social workers, suggesting that most families are given accurate information about their children. It is also very clear that of the children with behavior problems, they were much more likely to have been in institutions prior to adoption. This was particularly true for self-stimulating behaviors such as rocking themselves or hitting themselves; difficulty with response to environmental stimuli (over-reactive or under-reactive to touch, sights and sounds); inappropriate activity levels; and emotional difficulties such as always being scared or anxious and inconsolable when upset.

While families wrote accounts about the types of difficulties they had with their children, one story is indicative of many accounts:

> Our daughter displays all the signs of neglect and institutionalization…She had to learn to chew, swallow, and sit up. She has overcome so many things, and I have chosen to stay home until she recovers and heals. My instincts tell me most of her problems now could be emotional. [When] she is pushed too much, she withdraws. Most of the time she is very well behaved but if frustrated will bite her fingers. So, I will block and redirect this behavior, but it is not always easy…She displays "autistic-like behavior"—a lot of her play is inappropriate; she likes to spin and concentrate for long periods of time on certain activities. She also has several self-stimulating behaviors. Some behaviors cease while others continue. (Child adopted at age three after spending entire life in an institution)

It is very clear that the length of time in an institution and the age of the child when institutionalized have significant effects on behavior and development. In particular, institutionalization between the ages of 7-12 months and for over two years is particularly problematic. Still, as outlined earlier, most children recover. However, the longer they are institutionalized, the more difficult the recovery, and from 10% to 30% have behavior and developmental difficulties long term.

Sensory Problems

Many families discovered that their children seem to suffer from sensory integration disorders.[9] Sensory integration is the process by which individuals organize and interpret information received through their senses in order to successfully meet environmental challenges. When the sensations flow in a well-organized or integrated manner, the brain uses these sensations to form perceptions, behaviors and learning. Children with problems in sensory integration do not have problems with the actual sense organs—the eyes, the ears, or the semicircular canals (the organs of the "balance" sense). Rather, the problem is believed to be in how this information is processed by the brain. Problems in sensory integration include difficulties with sensory discrimination and/or sensory modulation. Sensory discrimination is the ability to identify the information we receive through our senses: hearing, vision, touch, muscles and joints, movement, and gravity. Good discrimination is needed to develop a sense of body awareness, which children need in to order to use sensory information for action.[10] Problems can result in poor skill development. In the young child, this is manifested in problems in play skills— the ability to build with blocks, to cut with scissors, to color, to play ball and to ride a tricycle—and in activities of daily living, such as dressing one's self, including fastening buttons and tying shoelaces. In the school age child, problems include difficulties with handwriting and other fine motor skills, and in gross motor skills and sports.[11].

Sensory modulation deals with the regulation of incoming information. Individuals with problems in sensory modulation may be under-reactive or under-sensitive to sensory stimulation. As such, they may seek intense sensory experiences, such as the child who swings for hours. The child may be over-reactive or over-sensitive to sensory stimulation, responding negatively to stimuli that would not be bothersome to most people. When a child is consistently over- or under-reactive to sensory input, or varies widely in reactions, he/she may be described as having difficulty with sensory modulation. Whereas, some children are typically over-aroused or under-aroused, others have difficulty staying in the middle range, and swing between the two extremes. This may explain the behavior of the child who, one day, may pull away from touch, while the next day, literally "attaches" him/herself to the parent(s), wanting to be held all day. Sensory modulation problems occur within different senses - touch, movement, sound, and vision. Children who are over-sensitive in one sense may be under-sensitive in another sense.[12] Families offered many examples of these types of difficulties. As an example, one mother wrote:

> At first, we felt compelled to hold, hug, dance with, bounce, make contact in any way to keep her from rocking when we put her down. She was frightened to go outside…She had never had solid food and we had to work up to it gradually as well as teach her when she had eaten enough. At first, she would take food as long as I would feed her and never seemed to have a limit. She disliked having a bath…

As another example:

> Our daughter has a keen sense of smell and is easily irritated or wildly pleased, depending on the odor. She can't go through a checkout line without smelling closed candy packages…

In considering treatment of sensory integration disorders, it is critical to rule out medical problems. Evaluation and treatment of children from institutions should be multi-disciplinary. Families should seek services from the occupational therapists and other professionals who specialize in early intervention. Sensory integration and occupational therapy are one piece of the overall plan for intervention for children with sensory problems.

Attachment

Overall, attachment relationships are quite positive. Over 90% of parents are positive about getting along with their children, communication with their children, trust, feeling respected and feeling close to their children. Attachment problems were more likely to be encountered from children who had been institutionalized. Families wrote about the attachment difficulties and issues they have encountered.

> Our child screeched at any attempt of a sibling to touch her…She still prefers not to hug, kiss or cuddle but will tolerate it…She likes to "bump" people with her head, almost like a defense mechanism to keep from other physical contact such as hugging. (Child adopted at age three after spending entire life in an orphanage)

> She hordes garbage and makes stashes…She does not value people's belongings; she takes them and gives them to others to make friends…She has tried to suffocate the cat. She hits…other children…She sets up fights. (Child adopted at age eight after spending entire life in an institution)

One parent described her ordeal.

> Adina threw fits about everything. Especially when you didn't give her what she wanted. I couldn't leave her with my husband to go do anything because the second I was out the door, she started going any place in the house she's not allowed and getting into everything she couldn't

have. Then she'd ask for things she couldn't have (gum, candy, pop, etc.). And then the screaming/whining—the fits would be endless. Nothing we tried for this helped.

I found a book that actually belonged to [a] friend. Adina had 95% of the symptoms of a severely attachment-disordered child. We've been taking her to therapy for two months now. For the first time in three years, someone sat and told us we were okay. We were good parents and it was nothing we did wrong that made normal parenting with Adina impossible. She resisted therapy more than most but we are finally breaking through the walls around her heart. For the first time in her life, we can have harmony in the house, and control over her. For the first time in four years of life, I can hold her like you would a baby—and for the first time ever, she'll actually let me hold her until she falls asleep. She's starting to trust and feel safe. (Child adopted at one year of age after spending over nine months in an institution)

However, this story was typical of an extreme difficulty and generally not reflective of the reality for many families. Most of the adopted children, whether or not they had spent time in an institution, seemed to have typical attachment relations with their families and the families were very satisfied with the relationship.

Getting Help: Navigating Services

Every child will benefit from a thorough assessment some time during the first three months of placement. Many children will benefit from early intervention. As a general rule, parents should obtain complete and accurate information about the child they adopt in order to make informed decisions about early intervention programs. Early intervention may not help a child with severe problems become normal, but there are many positive effects of early intervention. Early intervention can (a) support the family as they try to understand their child and during times of stress, (b) help the family provide the appropriate environment for the child's level of functioning, (c) prevent the worsening of difficulties, and (d) enhance the child's ability to develop to the fullest extent of her or his potential.[13]

Many families wrote and spoke with frustration about trying to find ways to help their children. As one mother wrote:

I did not realize that our son was going to have "special needs."…We needed a specialist on developmental delays. When we realized our son had…delays, we had to search out services ourselves…It was like everything was hidden.

Most parents would start with a pediatrician, often with minimal success. As one mother commented:

Doctors seemed to have a "wait and see" attitude when evaluating these children. Also, it is impossible to compare Romanian adoptees to "normal" American children. There seems to be no blueprint.

Some families stumbled into services or techniques that helped. As one parent wrote:

Our adoption was the best thing we have ever done. Our daughter was eight months old when we returned home and was assessed to be at a one-month development stage by her pediatrician. I went to our local school "early intervention" group and they taught me how to teach her everything she needed to know. At four years she is learning how to read and to do addition (math). So she has caught up and is pulling ahead of her peers. At eight months I also put her in a snuggly carrier and she was "attached" to me for six to eight hours a day. I believe this constant closeness is what helped her overcome the lack of stimulation she had in the orphanage.

Another parent wrote:

We had so many problems with our son—life was hell for the first 18 months. We had very little support because no one had seen these problems before. We did "hit and miss" therapy and finally made great strides…Our needed services change each year.

Many families provide advice on what they would have done differently or what could help them. As one parent wrote:

First of all, we do not have medical or birth information on our son. Over and over I ask myself, "Why? Why does he have delays? Inadequate nutrition in vitro? A traumatic birth? Poor nutrition as a baby? Neglect? Abuse? A high fever?"…I would desperately like to get more information on my son…I wonder if it is too late now to ever get the information and if it really matters now—i. e., the cause of our son's problems may be less important than finding *solutions*.

Another parent comment about what would have been most helpful was:

To have been provided with enough research and medical information in regards to what to expect and how to deal with institutionalized…children and their speech and developmental delays…[also] having a support group available.

As a final word of caution, both parents and professionals need to focus on strengths. Families commented and have written about how professional opinions often are in sharp contrast to their own experiences. As one mother wrote:

Many professionals have been too negative about Romanian children and cannot see the potential the children have…One professional implied our daughter should not have been adopted—"should take her back."...No test...can [adequately] evaluate a Romanian child for several years after arrival.

Successful Adoptive Families

One of the biggest factors that influences successful adoption outcomes is the ability of parents to change their expectations to match their children's capabilities.[14] Families commented on this in different ways. As one mother wrote:

> As time has gone by, Julia's idiosyncracies have diminished to almost nothing. By all comparison, she is a normal kid—although being a mother of three biological children I know there is no such thing. They all have strengths and weaknesses. My job [is] to develop the strengths and uphold them in their weaknesses.

Another parent provided a slightly different perspective:

> As experienced parents, we were aware that birthing a child does not create a clone of the parents. Each of our four children are different. Each required different methods of control or discipline; our rules remain the same for each child.

Both comments are examples about parents who can look at each child as an individual. As adoption research has shown us, such parents can change their hopes and beliefs to match the qualities of their child, both those that will change as well as those that may not change. These parents will experience the most positive outcomes in their adoption.

Even with trials and tribulations, adoptions are successful for the vast majority of families. Most families who were experiencing problems with their children could also easily identify strengths and positive characteristics of their children. As a testament to the stability of these families, over 90% of the families rated their adoptions as having positive effects on their families and reported never thinking of ending their adoptive placements.[15] Given previous research on the effects of institutionalization and the reports on the conditions of Romanian institutions, results are very hopeful. The success of foreign adoptions is extremely high.[16]

Notes from Chapter 7

---

[1] Johnson, D. E., Miller, L. C., Iverson, S., Thomas, W., Franchino, B., Dole, K., Kiernan, M. T., Georgieff, M. K., & Hostetter, M. K. (1993). The health of children adopted from Romania. Journal of the American Medical Association, April 28, 269(16): 2084-5.

[2] In 1994, adoptive families of Romanian children were contacted via 10 support groups from around the country. One thousand nine hundred twenty five surveys were sent to people on the mailing list. Ninety seven percent of the families were successfully located. It was estimated that 5% had not adopted children but were interested in international adoption issues. There was an overlap in the mailing list of

10% to 30%. During the first year, information was collected on 475 children residing in 399 families, representing from 24% to 32% of families contacted (depending on the estimated overlap used). The 475 children represent about 16% of all adoptions from Romania between 1990 and 1993.

In the fall of 1995, families who participated in the first year of the study and gave us their addresses (n=330) were again contacted to collect data for a second time. Additional families who heard about the project also joined the study during the second year (n=10). Surveys were sent to 340 families. Ninety-eight percent of the families were successfully contacted. The second wave of data probed in greater detail the placement history of the children prior to adoption. The changes that occurred in development from the time the children were placed to the time of the study were also examined. Data were collected on 238 children living in 209 families during the second year, representing a response of 63% of successfully contacted families.

From a social science research perspective, there are several problems with the sample. First, it is a convenience sample and results cannot be generalized to other adoptive families. Second, the low response rate for the estimated number of families contacted is a concern. There is no way to ascertain the experiences of families who did not participate in the study. Third, approximately 17% of the families did not give their addresses to participate further in the study, and about one third of families who gave us their address dropped out between the first and second years. Sampling attrition may bias the data. Fourth, the data present parent reports rather than professional assessments of children.

The sample has several strengths. First, this remains the set of information on children adopted internationally. Second, the families are geographically dispersed and not concentrated at a specific site or recruited from specific medical or psychiatric settings. Thus, the sample is quite diverse, and not drawn from locations that biased the sample towards ill or impaired children. Third, while we cannot generalize results, we can be conclusive about the families at the specific point in time they participated in the study. Fourth, parent perceptions are critical components for understanding adoption. Since parents, for the most part, make the decisions about the placements, their perceptions of the children are critical for understanding adoptive family life.

[3] Groze, V. (1997). International adoption. In R. L. Edwards (Ed.). Encyclopedia of Social Work (19th Edition, 1997 Supplement (pp.1-14)). Washington, DC: NASW Press.

[4] Dr. Jenista, a pediatrician from the University of Michigan, suggests that one-third of the children are resilient. See Jenista, J. (1997). Romanian review. Adoption-Medical News, 3(5), 1-6.

[5] As reported in Groza, V. (1997). International adoption. In R.L. Edwards (Ed.). Encyclopedia of Social Work (19th Edition, 1997 Supplement (pp.1-14)). Washington, DC: NASW Press. However, Dr. Jenista in the article referenced above suggests it is only about 30% of the children. Still, Bascom and McKelvey suggest that 90% of families will have the experience of parenting children who heal and grow and 60% to 70% of delays in development are reversible within 2 years after placement. See Bascom, B. B., & McKelvey, C. A. (1997). The complete guide to foreign adoption: What to expect and how to prepare for your new child. New York: Pocket Books.

[6] See also Groza, V. (1997). International adoption. In R. L. Edwards (Ed.). Encyclopedia of Social Work (19th Edition, 1997 Supplement (pp.1-14)). Washington, DC: NASW Press. Dr. Jenista suggests that one-third of the children would fall into this category. See Jenista, J. (1997). Romanian Review. Adoption-Medical News, 3(5):1-6. In an unpublished report by Dr. Michael Rutter and colleagues to the Department of Health in the United Kingdom, they noted that most Romanian adoptees have made spectacular progress in health and development after entering their adoptive families and less that 10% continue to show signs of problems. See Rutter, M., Quinton, D., Hay, D., Dunn, J., O'Connor, T., and Marvin, R. (1995). The social and intellectual development of children adopted into England from Romania. Report prepared for the Department of Health, United Kingdom.

[7] Groze, V. & Ileana, D. (1996). A follow-up study of adopted children from Romania. Child and Adolescent Social Work Journal, 13(6), 541-565.

[8] Johnson, D. E., Miller, L. C., Iverson, S., Thomas, W., Franchino, B., Dole, K., Kiernan, M. T., Georgieff, M. K., & Hostetter, M. K. (1993). The health of children adopted from Romania. Journal of the American Medical Association, April 28, 269(16), 2084-5.

[9] Most of this section is adapted from Cermak, S. & Groza, V. (1998). Sensory processing problems in post-institutionalized children: Implications for social work. Child and Adolescent Social Work Journal, 15(1), 5-37.

[10] Cermak, S. (1991). Somatodyspraxia. In A.G. Fisher, E.A. Murray, and A.C. Bundy (Eds.), Sensory integration: theory and practice (pp. 137-170). Philadelphia: F.A. Davis.

[11] Cermak, S. (1991). Somatodyspraxia. In A.G. Fisher, E.A. Murray, and A.C. Bundy (Eds.), Sensory integration: theory and practice (pp. 137-170). Philadelphia: F.A. Davis.

[12] See Cermak, S. & Groza, V. (1998). Sensory processing problems in post-institutionalized children: Implications for social work. Child and Adolescent Social Work Journal, 15(1), 5-37.

[13] Kenny, T. J. & Culberston, J. L. (1993). Developmental screening for preschoolers. In J. L. Culberston & D.J. Willis (Eds.), Testing young children: A reference guide for developmental, psychoeducational, and psychosocial assessments. (pp. 73-100). Austin, TX: Pro-Ed.

[14] Groze, V. (1996). Successful adoptive families: A longitudinal study of special needs adoption. New York: Praeger.

[15] Groze, V. & Ileana, D. (1996). A follow-up study of adopted children from Romania. Child and Adolescent Social Work Journal, 13(6), 541-565.

[16] See also Bascom, B. B., & McKelvey, C. A. (1997). The complete guide to foreign adoption: What to expect and how to prepare for your new child. New York: Pocket Books

Chapter 8

A Spiritual Calling to Adopt

Carolyn, Fred and Natalie

Fred: I'm an endocrinologist, which is a specialization of internal medicine

Carolyn: I'm a homemaker by choice. I have a degree in Mathematics. I do a lot of community volunteering.

Fred: Carol has been very instrumental in bringing in a lot of Cambodian refugees. She's probably been responsible for at least 185 to 200 lives in that regard.

Carolyn: Not so much bringing them here, but once they're here, we kind of…

Fred: She nurtures them along. We started off with one family in 1980, and we brought in nine people. Then, primarily due to Carolyn's effort, we make sure they get jobs, not welfare. This is all through a very supportive Presbyterian church. So the families that stayed have turned into a nucleus of self-sufficiency—they buy their own homes, buy their own cars, etc. She has touched their lives. She is very much community-minded. She's quick and very diligent in responding to the needs she sees. She's also been president of the church twice in a row.

Carolyn: We're risk-takers. We like adventure. We'd been involved with Cambodians and INS and we knew how to do that. We just seem to get involved in things that are not so easily done. At the time (of adoption) we were 47. Age was a major issue and the adoption process is absolutely ludicrous in Texas. You can get frustrated. I mean really frustrated. There wasn't any other place in Texas anybody would have allowed us to adopt.

Fred: Age limitations—many of the adoption agencies would not even *look* at us as adoptive parents.

Carolyn: And I think it was obvious that these children in Romania needed homes much more than any foster child in America.

Fred: We had three biological kids. It became apparent that there were adoptions going on in Eastern Europe. We considered ourselves experienced parents. And we had a choice. We could either continue parenting, or we could retire to the country club, so to speak, or just bask in our own self-worth or whatever, until Gabriel takes us home. It was then I think Carol and I came to the decision that, if at all possible, we'd like to help a small child.

Carolyn: Then, in December, 1991, there was an article about someone in Texas that adopted. We never called them, but it was something that was in our minds that we were kind of unsure about how far we wanted to go with the thoughts. Does that make sense? We'd think about it tomorrow, because we were older and we did have three children. Then we heard from a lady in our hometown that the Romanians were going to shut it down soon. And as soon as she said 'Shut it down,' my husband went into rapid paperwork acceleration.

Fred: You know, part of the issue, in retrospective, is a naivete I had. I had a misunderstanding of what an orphan was in Romania. I thought an orphan was just that—no parents! I visualized these Romanian children with no parents.

Carolyn: In the book of Luke, when it talks about the birth of Jesus, it says, "Ye shall find the babe, and there will be a sign unto you." Fred did all the paperwork in December. I was busy trying to keep the family together and focusing in on Christmas, and whatever he asked me to do. But I kept telling him that I was hearing that Bible verse over and over again, "It shall be a sign unto you." Later on, I told him that this child would be born on the number nine—the day of the month— mainly because three in our family were born on the number nine. I said, if you say many prayers over the situation, that child will be easily recognized. Anyway, we felt like, throughout the Old Testament, God speaks to people in dreams. Not many and not often, but I felt there was going to be a sign or an easy decision. Anyway, my husband finished all his paperwork, picked a date to travel, and then our friends Tom and Lynn decided they wanted to go at the same time. That put the three of them in Romania while I stayed home to look after the children. This turned out to be a wise decision because the grandparents are older and they wouldn't have been able to watch the children for as long as it took. So, finally, Fred got his INS approval the day he was supposed to leave and they flew to Bucharest, the first of January, 1991.

Fred: You know, January, of course, and I'm going to a communist country taking with me all my own biases. What's it going to be like? How comfortable and secure am I going to be? President Bush and Congress and the United Nations are arguing about going to war with Iraq and we have a buildup going on. I'm thinking of Sputnik and intercontinental missiles. What did I find? I think the most impressive thing was how someone had thrown the economic switch. I had the stark perspective of going to what was probably the premier, most beautiful, and elegant major European city at the turn of the century—now nothing but *dirty, filthy, dark, trashed-out*—like, only two lights turned on in a chandelier! Bucharest!. The Otopeni Airport, of course, was the very first contact I had with Romania, and it was a downer. It was very dark; soldiers with machine guns, the ground was dirty, the snow was stacked up, and it was dirty off the runway. The tarmac lights had an ugly yellow-type glow. It had a surreal effect on me. It was an incredible feeling of, 'Okay, God! You're in control, but I'm not sure I want to be here.' It was this surreal yellow-gold light. And it was cold. *Real cold!* Nothing was warm inside that airport. After that, it was a commotion of taxi drivers wanting your business. It was Tom, Lynn, and myself and we were not met by anybody and we were tired. We got into a taxi and I'm thinking, "what bumpy roads, what horrible roads". And I'm saying, "*This* is a capital?" What came to mind, right off the bat, was that these people couldn't carry on much of a long war; their infrastructure's really kind of crummy. We went to the Intercontinental Hotel and it was just surrounded by people wanting to change money. The lobby was wall to wall with people. The room was at the top of the hotel. The heat was on and it was hot! The door opened up to the balcony where we had a beautiful view of University Square, and rioting against the police. In the background you could see those amber yellow lights making petrified alligators out of all the cranes sitting all over the place. And the next morning we awakened to how dirty it was. No light. A lack of color. If nothing else, advertising in the U.S. adds color to life. There it was—the sameness; everything the same. The buildings, the same. The lines. Dirtiness and no light.

Carolyn: Then Fred was met by a man named Radu. He had already helped this lady from Texas, but they'd had a falling out. That was a major blessing.

Fred: I want to say first that the Romanian people are absolutely marvelous. And Radu is a man I have come to completely love, care for and admire, as well as his family. He is a hulk of a guy, about six-foot-eight and weighs about three hundred pounds; very soft-spoken and articulate. He and his wife had worked this program out together to help these children, and they did it from two perspectives. One, that the children needed homes; and, two, they were building a nest egg, which they ultimately did, hoping to emigrate to the United States. We spent two days in Bucharest and then headed down to the local child welfare department (the Tutelary) to do the adoption. We went to the social worker, who gave us a chart. Then I went to the orphanage, saw the child…and…I asked for a second chart right away then, because I noticed on the chart that the child is Hepatitis B positive. Call this selfish, if you will, but God gives us a brain for a reason and I did not want to bring a sick child into our family. There were too many ramifications. We had three children. I didn't want to deal with that. I told Erica, Radu's wife, "I really need to see a second choice. I can not, in my mind's eye, justify taking home a sick child." And so we went back to the social worker and she gave us a second chart. We went back to the orphanage and that's when I met Ancutza, who became our Natalie. It was incredible. Love at first sight. Big brown eyes. Just saucer-plate sized big brown eyes. Alert. Energetic. She came over to me, got into my lap, grabbed my left thumb in her little hand, looked up into my eyes and gave me a smile. It was almost a command, like, *I'm in charge here* ! And I said, "That's it! This is who we'll go with." The rest of the time would have been the legal process and what not; but that was stalled by the Iraqi war. They shut down all the courts because they had so many Iraqi students in Bucharest. There were armed soldiers everywhere. They told us, as foreigners, not to speak English, to try to look like the crowd, to stay out of the central city area. There's no CNN and you've got to go down to the central post office to a booth if you want to call home.

Carolyn: If the war hadn't stalled everything, Fred would have been home in three weeks. By Tuesday, the first week, he'd already found Natalie. In those days, you had to go meet the biological parents. Natalie had just a mother on her birth certificate. Her husband had abandoned her. The social worker saw the impoverished state of the biological mother and said there was no way they were ever going to return Natalie to that home. The woman had to return to her crippled father's farm. It was like an adobe-type hut—what we'd call adobe—with a grass roof. The place was just crumbling and she already had two children. And once she got established with her father, she went back several times to get her baby, but was told, 'Absolutely never!' By the time Fred met her, she had a new husband and was pregnant with a fourth child.

Fred: That, in itself, was a book. I arrived at the home and they had a small anteroom that had some chickens, and some coal and some wood, and it was ground, just dirt. And the shoes were on a little, tiny step at the door and it was a low door. Instead of being a typical door that we have here, I'll guess it was six feet. I'm six feet tall and I remember I had to stoop down to go in.

Carolyn: The house was probably about ten feet wide and ten feet long, with the blind grandfather, Maria, the new husband and two kids living in it.

Fred: Oh, man, I was taken aback. We meet in front of their twelve-hectare place. They had well water and a privy in the back. She's nine months pregnant, the wind is blowing and it's very, very cold. Erica explains why we're there. She said no, but then her husband comes up and says, 'What's going on? Let's think about it. Come into the house.' We go in. They had a single oil lamp, a tiny table against one wall, a crib that served as a wardrobe for all their clothes, and they had two day beds in an 'L' shape that covered the entire length of the room. I said, 'My Gosh! The people who have control over this country have kept the resources to themselves.' The first thing that came to my mind was: *Someone*'s making lots of money and the people they're sending out to work are getting *nothing*! I sat down there and, first of all, there was immediate denial: 'No, you cannot do this with my child!' But, then the cigarettes come out, the wine is poured and the communication begins. This went on for about three and a half, four hours. Somewhere around an hour-and-a-half into the conversation the tears are flowing. The husband talks to Inella, Natalie's five-and-a-half year-old sister, and she puts on her shoes and goes next door to get the commodore's wife. She works in an emotional sort of way on the mother, but, about half an hour later, I turned to Erica and said, 'I didn't come all this way to take a child out of a family. Let's go!' And, just at that point, Maria gave her consent. At that point, I examined the kids and the commodore's wife with a stethoscope, made some recommendations and gave away some M & Ms to the kids. I want to say one thing. The place was small but the place was clean. Maria did the best she could with the resources she had at hand. I mean, we were a drop-in. They had no idea we were coming. I was impressed by Maria, a reasonable mother. She was clean, and better than a reasonable mother.

Carolyn: Now, at this point, our friends, Tom and Lynn, picked out another little girl, Nina. With Tom and Lynn's little girl, there were two families when they went to the notary at the courthouse to file papers. As they walked out the door, Fred looked up and there was the city square with the city clock, and that clock was the clock in his dream, and there were Tom and Lynn in exactly the position they'd been in, in the dream. Fred was amazed. That's why we told you about the two signs, because they came to pass. As it turned out, Nina had active AIDS and was not adoptable. Lynn went home on a Friday, but by Monday the people at the hospital took pity on Tom and allowed him into the Babadag orphanage where he picked out this scrawny, unhandsome little boy, who grabbed his mustache and started giggling. So, Tom immediately knew this was the child. By Monday afternoon they found the parents, and by Tuesday they had taken out Nina's name and put in the name of the little boy.

Fred: One thing I'd like to be sure you mention. We really feel like we were answering a call from God. We bring Him up and try to center the focus on Him and not on us. We serve Yahweh.

Carolyn: Well, when Natalie arrived, of course, we were all frightened. What do we do now? I was just scared because I'm a henny penny, and it's a woman's job to worry. She came out of the airport doors with Fred. Fred gave her to me, and then my mother gave her a Teddy bear. Natalie hit the Teddy bear's nose and slam-dunked it to the floor, jumped down and started running. And we thought, "Gosh, this is a cute kid, she's got personality." She raged at bathtime, bedtime. She still had her orphanage survival personality. My kids loved her, and it was real useful to have three older children and two parents because she had all the energy in the world. At school, a boy had done a report on AIDS in Romania, and Jeff stands up and says, "I've got a little sister from Romania." My youngest son took her to "show and tell" for a science fair exhibit. He brought her and was just really proud to show her off. But, uhhmm, she loves to go running. At two-years-old, she could run two miles or so. She demanded a lot of swinging. I hung a swing in the garage—rain, shine, heat, cold, we swung every day—and that was meeting her needs. You see, in Romania, they are not rocked. They are kept in baby beds. People here perceive that as evil, but the Romanians didn't. If you put a baby on the floor, the baby can get pneumonia if the floors are cold. They have no antibiotics for the children. They were perceiving it as if they were keeping the children warm and safe. Even the parents who were giving their children to the orphanage perceived that the children were safer and warmer than at home.

Fred :   There's an issue here that most parents are probably totally unaware of. When we become a parent, there's a baby and we hold that child. We think we are bonding, from an emotional standpoint. In reality, we are doing a lot more than that. We are actually programming their little brain stem as to what is actually upright, sideways, what's the good side, what's the bad side, is it a soft sound, is it a loud sound, is it a pretty smile, and so forth. And so all these clues are being delivered to the brain stem and it begins to develop and become infinite, knowing what is both appropriate and inappropriate. With a sensory dysfunctional-type child, if they don't receive that, then any variation on what has been the customary field of perception becomes a very frightening thing. The response to that is rage, as if they were going to fight someone.

Carolyn :   They fight, flight or fright. They do that. Fright, they shut down and become autistic-like; flight, they become a street fighter, or they become very high energy, as in a hyperactive child. Have you ever had an inner- ear infection? It's not the usual ear infection children get—that's outer-ear. With an inner-ear infection you get vertigo and nausea. It's the same principle when you rock a child. In your inner-ear there are hair cells, and when you rock an infant of any age, those hair cells program themselves to gravity. Gravity is really your sixth sense, so that while you're rocking the baby, the baby learns where gravity is. When you pick them up and move them around, they learn where their place in space is. And so when you get a child from an orphanage, one reason that they're doing self-stimulated rocking is that it helps them with that feeling of where they are in space. I was working with a friend who works with foster children. Her husband became blind. She said, once he became sightless, he started rocking himself, saying he just couldn't figure out where his gravity point was. This is a neurological reason why they self-stimulate a lot and rock. It's not an emotional issue; yet, so many children have sensory deficiencies that many people perceive it as an emotional or behavioral issue. Where there is a neurological need, just like my daughter's play-swinging, you give in to it. Another person would say she's demanding way too much of my time, but it's simply a case of neurological need. I know that some kids react to too much lighting because their minds cannot react to the variety or intensity we take for granted. If they go into a restaurant or a mall that has high intensity light, they might get into this defensive visual problem and just go bonkers while you wonder why your child is overreacting. Or maybe it's the noise, or maybe it's something that's just too much to look at. If *you've* been in an orphanage that had bare walls, you understand that they cannot organize the visual input.

As our child got older, we were meeting this need she had for running. Then, when she was two to three years old, we got a rebounder in the house so that we could meet this need—she had to jump eight hundred times in the rebounder without ever stopping. Then her shoes became an issue. She couldn't stand socks. She couldn't stand shoes. She'd rip them off and pull socks up until she would rip a hole in the sock. You know that little seam at the end of the sock—that would just drive me crazy. We had to turn them all inside out. Inside out and about a thousand different brands, different stitching, different fabric. By the time she was in first-grade, all of a sudden her clothes had to be very tight—no movement, no wrinkles. It had to be as if it were her skin. I couldn't *buy* her clothes *that* tight. She'd want her elastics and her hair clipped so tight that it would be painful. But the pain would block out *discomfort*. Natalie couldn't do it by herself, it was as if her neurological system was maturing and she couldn't organize all these impulses from her skin, from her eyes, from her ears.

It just met this *crisis* point by the time she was six. Why did this start at six? Most people would look at my daughter and say she's so-o cute, but she has so-o much energy and she always did. Another person might have taken their child to a pediatrician and put her on ritalin. You know: "Let's just calm this kid *down!*" But, by holy happenstance, we wound up with a therapist who helped us. Sensory dysfunction and associated rage is a terrible problem in the United States. Not many people know about it. Not many doctors are trained in it. Most therapists and most counselors in school have no knowledge of it. Natalie was just trying to control her life and her environment. She was a happy joyful kid, but if something wasn't right with her lifestyle, she would drop back to her orphanage defensive mechanisms and she'd try to control her environment with anger.

Fred :   And, of course, in the orphanage this would work, because kids would scatter. But not here.

Carolyn : We had so many adults trying to parent this new child that screamed in the bathtub and screamed going to bed. Our oldest daughter had an opinion on how to punish her; my mother thought we should do it another way. We had just gone to a family psychologist and she gave us a unified rule of time-out. We finally got the rules from this lady for time-out and it really worked, once everybody got the rules.

Fred : What she really means is...when *I* got the rules, 'cause I really needed to. I was part of the problem.

Carolyn : Well, Fred is taking too much blame. Everybody in the family had a different opinion on how to discipline Natalie. We liked this psychologist. Natalie was probably two at the time—and at about four she was starting to use her anger, not grow out of it. So we went back to this psychologist, Kay, and the lady did a little play therapy. One session Natalie was fine, she was okay. She was immature about handling stress. But, then, by the time she was six, there was the clothing issue. She was in agony. She was irritable from her sensory defensiveness. So Kay started working with Natalie on how to control her anger and Natalie was told why she was seeing Kay. But we could never get it solved until we found Patricia (a sensory therapist) and her way of dealing with sensory defensiveness. I've met other therapists. I've talked with other people with the same problems. Fred, Natalie and I flew up to Denver and met Patricia. She worked with us for two days and taught us just so much, and then we met this other lady, Lisa, who is an active, practicing physical therapist and she helped us even more. All holy happenstance. Patricia had been to Romania in '89 or '90. These women also treat American born children with sensory defensiveness problems. Once you become attuned to it, you can tell why children or adults react the way they do, why they make certain choices, understand the way they dress or what they do—because the sensory defensiveness has never been dealt with. We came back. We did the protocol exactly the way we were supposed to. Eight hours after we began the brushing therapy, Natalie was free from the agony she got from her clothing. You have to repeat it. Slowly, but surely, she hasn't had the rages anymore. Slowly the rages just dropped off. After a few months we were doing it in the morning only. When school was over, we dropped that one. I consider Natalie totally cured after six months. I have presented this to many people with the same predicament and they do not believe it. They think that I am a mere mother by profession. They don't want to get involved. They want somebody else to cure their child. It's a parental activity. *You* have to be with *your* children if you have to have a physical therapist involved. *Excuuuu-se me! This* (she indicates herself) is an occupational therapist ! You know, the fact is, they don't know the real cause. It might be trauma at birth or poor parenting in early childhood. There are multiple reasons and thousands of symptoms, and no two people would have the same symptom. We came back on a Monday from Denver and, on Tuesday, Natalie went to her regular meeting with her friend, Kay, the family therapist, who Natalie adores. Anyway, the traditional game has always been that Natalie goes to her playroom, and the playroom has a multitude of toys, and the child chooses what they want to play with. Every week she would choose the dollhouse, and the parents and children would all run upstairs and hide behind the bed because there was a snake downstairs. And then she'd go find some 'strong men' and the 'strong men' would come and fight the snake away. The Tuesday after we got back from Denver, Natalie played the same game and the children ran upstairs, but, this time, the parents stayed downstairs and *they* fought the snake away. And from then on, she's never wanted to play that game again. So, obviously, the snake was her sensory defensiveness; the fear that no one was meeting her neurological needs. Finally, that weekend, she perceived that the family took control of taking care of Natalie's needs.

Fred :   Let me digress momentarily here. Ya know, Kay told me "I think you need to be more manly and assertive around the house." I thought I was weak as a father. She had me on a guilt trip. Now she says it's a tease.

Carolyn : But it's been a positive experience. All around age two…No! Age three, we had her in a little playschool. No! Wait! Back up. When we first got her, we thought we'd first nurture her at home and let her slowly creep out into the world; but, it became immediately obvious that her environment was a nursery. She thrived on being with children, so I enrolled her two days a week in a mother's day out program. By the time she was three, she was a strong-willed child and I'd probably cried about her more than a few times. Somewhere I read that, if you were having problems with a strong-willed child, put them in daycare or a mother's day out center, but there are major differences between the two. At mother's day out, they didn't care if the kids took their shoes off or ate a cookie before break. Insignificant things, things that drive a mother crazy, they don't worry about that at mother's day out. So there wasn't enough mothering, not enough clashing over my trying to improve her. By the time she was three, she was hitting and biting. Well, she didn't *arrive* hitting and biting, she arrived just hitting. But, umm, *everybody* at her mother's day out was hitting also! So we followed this family therapist's rule on time-out, and, finally, instead of hitting—she went up to the next stage—she learned to say, "Go away! Leave me alone!" She was protecting herself. Neurologically, if she was getting frustrated or overwhelmed by what was going on around her, then she'd go back to the hitting, which she learned in the orphanage.

Then she went to verbal protection of herself, and we'd challenge her to not be so rude in her voice, and then she just evolved into giving dirty looks at people. As she matured, it was no longer verbal attacks, just ugly looks. And then, finally, she outgrew it. When Natalie came at 22 months, she was just barely walking, so I always perceived her as 12 months younger. I just kept thinking, she's 12 months behind and she pretty much was. One subtle difference always was, if Natalie got into a situation where she was frightened, like going to Disneyland—you know, many different people, many sounds—she would instinctively try to protect herself. Our other three children, because they were with us since birth, they instinctively looked upon *us*, the parents, to protect them.

Fred : The difference is that, normally, you would hold and nurture a child that would come to you for protection. With Natalie, if you tried that, she would just rebel.

Carolyn : When you got into frightening situations, she would go back into 'I've-got-to-protect-myself' mode. But people thought she was cute; they thought she was *darling*, and yet, her high energy, at times, embarrassed us. When she'd throw a fork across a restaurant, the kids thought that was fun. You learned to get through church; you held her arms and legs. Twelve months behind, you know. It wasn't a *big* issue. It was just a maturity issue.

Fred : In Natalie's case, 15 minutes was an issue. If she did not get 15 minutes sleep, the next morning, it was the difference between her being in self-control or not, and it was not a negotiable item. You could not talk her out of being in control. It wasn't that you didn't want to, but that she wasn't paying attention. She couldn't. She was operating from her lower brain centers and her cerebral cortex was not in control.

Carolyn : People can misperceive children with sensory defensiveness. They can perceive it as an emotional or control issue, but it's a body need. I mean, sometimes I'm tired because I don't want to *do* something; sometimes I'm tired because I've had *enough*; either way, this is a deep need.

Fred : It's a neurophysiologic need these kids have to have. Structure is imperative.

Carolyn : Many agencies require that, when you adopt, you have to stay home. That's one nice thing, but, these kids are used to orphanages, it's not an issue. I don't think it's a problem that you're employed because the children are happy in a daycare situation. I felt like it was more frustrating to Natalie, at the beginning anyway, staying at home. It was just the two of us. Being a working parent is not an issue here because the children adapt well, although I do think it should be a consistent daycare situation. I think you have to have consistency. I think you have to have structure in your life for these children. *The first thing they need in life is structure.*

Fred :   I'm gonna just ditto that: major, major structure!

Carolyn :   Now, I mean, our other three children, we could skip two hours before eating supper. We could skip an hour at bedtime, but these other kids need structure. You need to do it right on time because they are dealing with a lot of things, even though they can't verbalize it . Things slip. My idea of a working mother versus staying-at-home mother—it has nothing to do with being a Romanian child or birth child or whatever. Women who want to work and parent and be a spouse, they can't do it all. Things slip. My friend, Lynn, who got the little boy at the same time we did, she's a working mother. She travels three nights a week. Her lifestyle to her children is different than mine. I think anyone who wants to adopt should, whether they're old or young, if they have seven kids or no kids. Whether it's a Romanian child or a birth child, a child needs a lot of time. And don't *ever* expect a child to be a small adult. They have childish needs. You can't expect them to sit politely in a restaurant. So, just because you are a perfect human and a perfect parent, that doesn't mean you're gonna have a perfect small person. I think everybody should adopt. Ya know, it's good for the parent, it's good for the child. Nothing is sadder than to be limited as to the type of family you want.

Fred :   Financial stability is a realistic issue also. It's as variable as the kids that are available to adopt, 'cause no one child is gonna be like the other' and, even though there may be some dysfunction among these kids, it may come in different degrees. It requires additional resources. Number one, these kids are not like your (birth) kids, and, number two, they're gonna have special needs and those special needs may mean counseling for therapy, or they may mean occupational therapy. Now a lot of this stuff is covered with health insurance. You may not have a lot of difficulty, except for psychological counseling which often only comes at 50%. They don't necessarily reimburse you at 80%, but it's 50%; though, if you're in an HMO, it may come in differently. The other thing, though, is, one has to choose their therapist carefully, know what and who they're about, and what it is all about, and what kind of needs you have. You need someone, for example, someone who can do diagnostics. Unfortunately, the diagnosticians who work for the school districts are not equipped for this.

Carolyn : No. The United States' professional field, all of them, have had no background information or experience on children coming out of institutions. So, it's overwhelming to people, physicians and therapists. It's a learning process. They don't know exactly what to expect because they've never had this overwhelming amount of children who have such developmental delays, some of which are severe, while others are delays that will work out in time. To adopt in Romania, you can do everything for like $8,000. So, anybody who is not willing to pay eight thousand—and, if you go through certain agencies it can be as much as $20,000 plus travel expenses—forget it. I've had people call me wanting a child, and they'll go, "O-oh! It's gonna cost me something?" And I said—I do have a sarcastic point in my life—"Yes, but it's cheaper than a pick-up truck!" Some people can't even *perceive* paying money. Well, those people won't follow through. Then another person called me, and she said, "Oh, you mean the agency doesn't just bring them home to you?" "No, you have to go get them." Well, that fear factor is going to keep a lot of them back. You have to be a risk taker. You have to be willing to travel in a foreign country and not be in control. And that's a very fearful situation. You are not in control there; you will never be in control over there, and you have to trust somebody else. Those people who are afraid to give up their control—they're not going to be there. You have to have a sense of adventure, let other people work it out. You can't go over there and be the ugly American; you have to do it the Romanian way. What do they expect? These children were caged. Maybe they were benevolently caged, but, at the age of two, are they supposed to say, "Oh, thank you, mother and father. Thank you for giving me a good home." It's not going to work that way.

Fred : I figured that I was going to get a child, come home and that was it. And that evening before we got Natalie, when I was wrestling with God, I said, "Hey, we're getting another family here." And we did. The reality of that poverty situation was that it was just so bad that we had to do something to help that family.

Carolyn : We wound up sending money over there and Maria's house was repaired. A roof was put on it and then two extra rooms were added on, so she had a typical Romanian home with an air of dignity. It's not elegant, it still has an outhouse, but it does have electricity in the main room now, and we have left her with some pride in her existence. I think everybody has feelings. I know we continue writing Maria, maybe once or twice a year. We send photographs that are neutral. Not ones where Natalie is sitting in her bedroom with all her toys. We always send ones where she is standing by a bush or a brick wall. We tell Maria developmental milestones—that

Natalie is a fast runner, that she's a good reader, how she's even better in math—things Maria can have pride in.

Fred : Once a year I go over there and I meet Maria and try to make sure the kids have a nice warm coat for winter and shoes on their feet. Look, the most impressive thing to me is how our relative wealth in the U.S. goes so far. It takes hardly anything to contribute where you can help.

Carolyn : She delights in seeing Fred. Every January, when airfares are cheapest, Fred arrives with thousands of syringes. He takes antibiotics and medicines to the orphanages. Maria has never asked for anything…well, three things. She asked once for money for the plowman, because they had a drought and they have poor crops over there. She also asked for birth control pills and potato bug poison. Those are the only things she's ever asked for.

Fred : I go back every year and note that there are a lot of changes, especially in Bucharest. Bucharest begins to look more and more like New York City every time I go back. More and more people. The stores are full of very expensive items. Obviously, there's money in Bucharest. I'd like to add another thing, which is that you're not going out as an altruistic person to take this child who is going to be eternally grateful for this wonderful opportunity you have given it. This is work and it is sweaty work. It's hard work. It's emotional work. It can be quite traumatic to a marriage. It takes a lot of effort to work through these issues. I had to sit down and rethink and realize that, as a professional, I didn't know what I needed to know. I had to learn that. I had to listen. You know, when you go beyond a certain point in time, you think you know it all and you don't want to listen to anyone. That's hard to do, particularly, I think, for people who live in Ivy-town institutions like Harvard, sit behind a stethoscope and dispense words of wisdom about healing and things of this nature. You have to be humble. I think humility is an important place to begin in the whole process.

Carolyn : You have to realize your personal limitations towards a child. If you're going to get a cerebral palsy child, you have to actually come to the realization that you can handle it. I know my limitations. I couldn't handle a child with that many needs. Each person's level of limitations is different. We got an active, happy child that we could immediately pick up and take to her brother's basketball games, drive to events and do things with, which was good for us. If we'd have had a newborn, it would have been different. You can't conquer every problem and you're not going to get the perfect child.

123

Chapter 9

Saints, Charlatans, Witch Doctors and Good Nails

All the grief of the human heart gathered together

into a bead and given to the crowd to play with.

MARCEL BRESLASU

It became apparent as early as 1991 that some of the children adopted from Romania were having problems—problems largely ignored by the agencies involved in international adoptions, perplexing to professionals trying to help these children and their families, and exaggerated by the media. One of the positive outcomes was the development of parent support groups who sponsored conferences, distributed information, and gave help to each other. In this chapter, Ivor offers a story and reflections on these and related events. While based on interview transcripts and personal experiences, to afford some protection and privacy to participants we used modified names. These stories are offered to provoke and inform. They do not represent all adoptive parents or professionals examining and trying to help with the difficulties in some international adoptions. However, the reflections are accurate for some.

Welcome to the Adoption Conference

Day One

"I've never seen such nice coffee cups. Aren't they nice?" the attractive lady who has just taken the spot next to me says as she methodically lays out her stuff.

I agree. They are indeed very nice. Clear glass. You can see the weak coffee in all its toffee-colored glory. Finished, she individually prods each of the three donuts on her plate, making her thick gold jewelry tinkle, getting powdered sugar on her french-tipped index finger. She takes a quick lizard lick and wiggles her eyelids. "This is nice. Very nice. Well organized."

The lady is ready. She's got her seminar portfolio, a miniature tape recorder, a cell phone, a computer notepad, a dozen pens, a dozen pencils, a pencil sharpener, a calculator, a notebook with an 'Orphan Adoption' label on its cover. I am reminded of the assassin laying out his weaponry in *Day of the Jackal*. She takes a long look at my 'International Adoption Research Team' badge and proceeds to tell me all she wants known about herself: Peggy, a lawyer, divorced, from one of the Heights in the Cleveland burbs; her reproductive system is 'no good'; she desperately wants a child. My turn. I say I'm a writer and her porcupine quills go up. It's a common reaction, so I go out of my way to assure her I'm not a filthy journalist; tell her I teach, what I teach, where I teach, about my novel and the fact that my dear departed grandmother was Romanian. She's in the middle of asking me about Romania when Marty steps up to the podium and tests the microphone. Peggy clicks on her cassette recorder, drains her coffee cup, then leans back in her chair, arms folded, ready.

Marty: What can I say? Heretofore, just an angry voice on the telephone, the plenipotentiary of modern martyrdom, sufferer of sufferers, she wears her stigmata well. A stocky lady with huge framed sea monster spectacles, not tall but way bigger than life, she cuts right to the chase. Rapid fire—rat! tat! tat!—like a freebase-fueled last-ride Sam Kinnison, her arms moving like pistons, she goes into her shtik. Having put this show together, she unequivocally lets us know it. Witty anecdotes about the three musketeers—Mary, Margaret, and herself—the first conference held in a tiny schoolhouse in Maryland; how thirty interested parties became eighty; the size of her phone bills. From teensy little acorns, mighty American oak trees grow. And while I'm throwing out clichés, June Cleaver lives as Mary and Margaret stand there with their hands behind their backs, modestly basking in the praise as the crowd claps. Necessity is the mother of invention and Marty is a Mu-tha.

"I didn't think she'd look like that," Peggy says, playing with the huge emerald ring on her wedding finger. "Somehow I thought she'd be, you know, gray, Mother Jonesy."

"She's something else," I say.

"I hope this isn't going to get too depressing. I've got the vibe that I'm gonna be getting real bummed." I think I know how she feels. I think everyone thinks they know how she feels. Like a lot of people, she's considering adoption options. Amongst other things, it's sort of a sad trade show for barren professionals.

"I'm so glad you're here today. You know I am sincere. I have talked you through crisis and feast and famine." There's an almost demagogic intensity about her. Lest I sound snide, let me reiterate, Marty *is* bona fide. She's candid, frank, angry, unaffected, funny, fanatical, monomaniacal and egocentric all at once. As she enthusiastically introduces Dr. Dominion—"A great big Teddy Bear of a man"—I have to go back to my Kinnison simile. Burning like phosphorus, she irradiates us all with her love for Big D. We should all love him, too. He's just a big, old, sexy, academic pooh bear. Dear God, I think, she could have an aneurysm at any moment and it would seem like part of the show. Peggy's jaw is hanging open. And Marty actually quivers with pleasure as Dr. D steps up next to her. Six-fivish, around two hundred and fifty pounds, when he opens his mouth to speak I'm disappointed. It's not his fault but how could the situation be otherwise? Marty is an act you can't follow.

At this point I have to remind myself of what I'm really there for. The song, not the singer. The book, I've continuously told my colleagues, Victor and Daniela, is interesting but dry as feedbag oatmeal. I need anecdotes. I want people. Thus, here I am at this conference, entitled *International Adoption*. Orphans. Adoptions. Institutions. Legal rights. Adoption agencies. Adoption attorneys. Development delays. Attention deficit hyperactivity. Neuropsychological impairment. Emotional and behavioral disturbances. Language and communication disorders. Anecdotes. Experts. Adopters. The curious. The desperate. The media. They've slowly been trickling in until there are about two hundred or so people gathered together, paying up to $80 per head. A bargain of bargains if you want to adopt yourself a beautiful white baby from abroad.

"Two-thirds of the kids coming in, up to ten years ago, were from Korea," says Dr. D, clicking his remote, bringing up the first of scores of slides, two before and after pie charts, "but in 1990, when Romania opened up, *everything* changed."

The polite crowd is mostly middle class professional couples. They're of all ages but a majority is in their late-thirties. They're all white and include, in my immediate vicinity a German lady, a Greek-American couple, and a Russian. They've come from all over: Toronto, Pittsburgh, Daytona, Milwaukee, Chicago, and Wyoming. Notetaking is the rule. The only movement off the podium comes from the video recording technicians and a nervous man darting in and out who I later learn is, a producer for ABC's *Turning Point*.

Dr. D's lecture veers into the realm of 'worldwide growth patterns'. A little bored, I write VIETNAM and KOREA on my notepad and think of my poet friend John Balaban and how his war and adopted daughter are now just a statistical footnote of history. "In that kind of forgetting," he wrote in his war memoir, *Remembering Heaven's Face*, "there is a sanity, not an amnesia"[1].

"My friends adopted a Korean kid," Peggy whispers, breaking my reverie as Dr. D speaks of the consistency of developmental difficulties in all institutionalized East European orphans. "That kid is smart. Harvard, you know? They're hard to get now."

"It's a different situation," I posit, "a whole other thing."

"You know," she bends and whispers into my ear, "a lot of them are gypsy or part-gypsy. For 15 to 20 thousand bucks I kinda, you know, want to know *exactly* what I'm getting."

"That's why we're here."

My expression must have said it all. "You shouldn't take me wrong, though. I've fostered black kids. I'm not a bigot. But cultures... Umm, like gypsies are heavy into their own culture."

Thank God, right there and then, just like the cavalry, up saunters my colleague, the righteously sharp Daniela. We go outside for a cigarette breather and, after I've vented my spleen, she reminds me of what I'm doing here in the first place. A savvy little social worker is Daniela, cutting straight to the heart of my elitist artist's ire, the Working Class Hero anger that's sometimes a nasty, vengeful hump on my back.

"The kids," she barks at me between drags, those black Romanian saucer eyes glowing, "we're doing this for the kids."

A PEACOCK OR A CROW

Right. Yes. We're doing this book for the kids, but they're the buyers. The customer is always right and we're about to offer a service. Tens of thousands of Romanian children need help. "It's corny to be an altruist, but it's okay," she tells me. And God knows, Daniela should know. A native of Arad in Transylvania, she'd been diagnosed as an epileptic at age 12, then sent to one of the Dictator Ceausescu's homes for "irrecuperables" (which were, for all intents and purposes, children's concentration camps). Having survived that, she is still a forgiver; if she can forgive, so must I.

When we get back, I pick up my stuff and move to a new seat. Dr. D fills me with facts. Scores of slides of pretty children alone in their cribs in drab rooms; the same children squatting together on the potty in neat lines: Stalinist functionalism. It's scary stuff. Buyer beware. According to one survey, 52% of these adopted children carry infectious diseases—Hepatitis B & C, enteric parasites, tuberculosis, meningitis. "When they arrive in institutions, abandoned children have no reliable post-arrival evaluations and certainly no medical history." These are cold hard facts and people visibly wince. "What you have to ask is: Is your child covered? There are federal laws that say adopted children are covered, but insurance companies will fight you tooth and nail."

When he's finished, Dr. D gets a standing ovation. I am drained already. During the break I wander around the lobby; groups gather and chatter nervously and I gaze around. A lot of people congregate around the *Turning Point* crew, watching an interview with a couple. A very old Jewish lady with skin like a brown paper bag that's been crumpled up then smoothed out, looks at my I.D. and grabs at my sleeve. She wants to know if I've been to Albania. I tell her no. She's heard it's opening up there soon, wants to know if I think, having undergone half a century of Stalinist indoctrination, the children there have been re-Islamicized. I tell her I don't know, that I've only been to Romania, that I'm working on a book, that I'm interested in talking to people who've adopted, that I'm gathering anecdotes. "Anecdotes? My daughter has zillions of anecdotes," she says.

"Anita!" she shouts into a crowd. "A-ni-ta!!"

Anita arrives, a carbon copy of her mother accompanied by three female friends, all attorneys. With no prompting whatsoever, I learn she's a contract lawyer married to a doctor from Bombay and has adopted three good-as-gold Indian kiddies. She's gregarious; a good storyteller, who, because she's a professional married to a professional, has had plenty of time to nurture and raise her children. "The most important thing to know," she says, "is that these kids need time and love. Insist upon your reader having lots of time to spend with their kids. They've all been neglected. You shouldn't just take them because you're a successful Yuppie undergoing a profound sense of loss."

I ask her what she thought of the big, sexy, old bear, Dr. D. "A disseminator of half-truths," she says. She recalls Dr. D showing a run-down shack in Calcutta as part of his slide show and referring to it as 'Middle Class Housing'. It was not Middle Class, she insists. He's giving India a bad rap.

"It probably seems Middle Class to an untouchable," I jest.

Anita is not amused. "Look, the main reason I'm here is that we're starting our own adoption agency.'

"So you're here drumming up business?"

"Well, for that and to learn." She gives me her card. "India is an alternative for you to write about. One can adopt a child much cheaper than the ones that come from Eastern Europe. And Indian doctors are of a high, British-type standard. Their diagnoses are reliable. The adoption agencies and lawyers who deal with Eastern Europe are mostly unscrupulous."

Anita actually serves to set a tone. When we go back, Marty tells us another long *auto de fé* anecdote about her son, Petru, mistaken diagnoses, the general callousness of the system in general and the medical insurance companies in particular.

"Love, hugs and kisses followed by a trip to Toys 'R' Us ain't gonna do it, kids," says our cheerleader.

It's one hell of an introduction to the next speaker, Dr. Bond. An expert on treating attachment disorders, flamboyant and cute in a shirt of purple checks accompanied by a brown and yellow dream o' Jerry Garcia tie, he cuts straight to the chase of just what a pain-in-the-posterior these kids can be, tells us about his bumper sticker: *'My kid beat up your honor student!'*. He swivels and throws out another one, "I didn't take my Ritalin today!" There's no punchline but those in the know laugh. It's a show he's put on before.

He draws a diamond shape on the blackboard, writes 'Trust', 'Need', 'Arousal/Rage', and 'Gratification' in each corner. It's the cycle that's essential to all human development

What's better, he wants to know, neglect or abuse? Who thinks neglect? Who thinks abuse? There's a ghoulish show of well-manicured hands after each choice. I think of *Monty Python's Flying Circus:* Graham Chapman entering a maze of civil service bureaucracy, knocking on a door labeled 'Abuse'. "Neglect is profound removal. If arousal goes down and there's no communication or stimulation, the child only learns to trust itself. And psychological self-reliance equals *trouble*." Dr. Bond runs a hand through his full head of jet-black hair then gestures animatedly. "Abuse is bad, but there's all kinds of gratification—looks, touch, screaming, violence—and it, nevertheless arouses the child." The harsh images in Dr. D's orphanage slides come right back at you as Bond discusses 'rockers'—kids who stimulate themselves, looking within for comfort, banging their heads against walls, wiggling knees, rocking back and forth.

The kids rock physically and metaphorically as does Bond's show. Boom! He cleverly shifts gears. "Why do people adopt? Because women especially have been waiting all their lives... Infertility, or being unmarried is a case of severe personal loss." So, he adjusts his tone, gets closer to the microphone, lowering the volume. "...It's a profound personal *loss* for mothers (not having a child) and the adopted child, who has *lost* its natural mother." He steps away, his head bobbing, upping the timbre of his voice again. "Kids are better off in orphanages than in foster homes where they're moved from place to place. Thus, more detachment takes place, and the more breaks in the cycle of attachment, the more problems you have." He becomes louder, shriller. "Despite the old arguments of early detachment as a panacea, cognitive memories and sense memories remain, even if they're not specific. These detachments, before two years of age, are *disastrous*. You are not born a *tabula rasa* !"

A very effective speaker, Dr. Bond, in between bouts of levity, balances scaring the crap out of the audience with tales of success. In the end, after many anecdotes about detached, angry and semi-sociopathic kids—all cured save for one, he insists—he leads us to *his* cure: authoritarianism and holding therapy. Hug them and squeeze them, no matter how filled with rage they are and how much they struggle. If they misbehave, don't send them to their room because that kind of isolationism is what Ceausescu's orphanages taught them to crave; and don't be democratic because authority (also running in a direct logical line from the orphanages) is *also* what they crave.

A part of the crowd hits upon this contradiction while I'm noting it . One angry lady points out the difficulty of attempting to hold on to a kicking, screaming seven-year -old and Bond can't, or won't, answer in any specific terms. Instead, he speaks of pillows and mattresses as tools, hugging techniques. When the thing ends, as we break for lunch, I sense a buzz of dissatisfaction in the air. I'm no expert, I think, indeed I may well be wrong, but the idea of hugs being enough of a panacea/paradigm sounds a lot too simplistic and New Agey, especially after the good doctor has gone out of his way to weave a very convincing but tangled web of reasoning involving D.N.A., attachment and detachment, the psychiatric triad, conscience development, and entitlement as a buildup. Still, the force of his personality is such that no one has the will to lock horns with him. Whoever is next had better be good, I think as I run to the street, craving fatty food, beer and cigarettes as if I have a hangover (which I don't).

Daniela has disappeared. I think she sees Bond as a bit of a charlatan. I walk the streets alone. I join the crowd and follow them into a deli/restaurant. Marty invites me to sit with her group but I need some down time. I take a stool by the bar, chain-smoke and think.

The chit-chatty bartender looks at my research team badge and asks what I'm doing. I tell him something vague about Romanian orphans and he recalls seeing the infamous *20/20* episode. The guy next to me looks up from reading *The Hot Zone* to inform us that he's half-Bulgarian; that his mama told him most of those kids in orphanages are Gypsies. That, "You know, you dunno what you're getting when you adopt a Gypsy. 'S like, logically, you know, you might as well stay home and adopt a black kid. Save money." I turn away from him and sip my beer.

As my patty-melt and fries arrive, so does Dr. Dominion along with a huge entourage which queues up, filling the space behind me with talk. I hear two people talk about a child adopted in Timosoara. "Doctors said he was retarded, wouldn't eat anything but soup and apple sauce. Anything with lumps in it and he'd spit it at you. All day he'd jump up and down on a trampoline, sca-reeeming. And then one day, like abracadabra, he was fine. A-student. No kidding! I mean, I still always am kind of anxiety ridden, waiting for the other shoe to drop but...Hey!"

Next to me, two very handsome, forty-something ladies take off their raincoats revealing splendid gym-hard torsos encased in matching Angora sweaters. They speak of Guatemalan orphans as bargains. "They're usually short, though, aren't they?" someone else adds.

It's really easy to discount these people, to feel intellectually superior. In so many cases, the people I'd dealt with between speakers had built their own virtual, mostly suburban world. American problems—ghettos, crack, AIDS, etc.—were out of sight, out of mind. Yet here they are, comfy fatcats living in a country which abhors study and discussion of incoherent European (especially East European) history, considering an illogical reflex reaction to an untenable conundrum. Communism, having failed, has left behind the *detritus* of disaster: ethnic hatred, civil war, pollution, mass alcoholism, an incomprehensible level of corruption and babies, lots and lots of babies. Energy and can-do, the American way, decided to meet a need, the desperate need of tens of thousands, often infertile, lonely or plain old do-gooders moved by the horrors of Romanian orphanages shown on *20/20*. They came, they saw, they bought babies.

Only, some of the babies they bought were bad bargains. They were gorgeous and desirable, but in many cases they couldn't bear to be touched, or were violent, or had eating disorders, wouldn't learn or speak, and had no motor coordination. In the worst of worst-case scenarios, they brought with them cases of Meningitis, Hepatitis B and C, HIV, TB—which they passed on to the families who'd taken them in. More commonly, however, there were the less obvious disasters. Referred to in the broadest sense as Sensory Integrative/Deprivation, a huge number of these adopting parents had a difficult time coping with the reality of parenting children whose problems often couldn't be instantaneously evaluated.

There was little or no help available because there was no paradigmatic model (unless one looked back upon the research of the Victorian years). Doctors were often stumped. Medical insurance companies were, naturally, less than sympathetic. The government, often sympathetic but bureaucratized, in most cases categorized the children under the umbrella of good ol' Special Ed. They didn't reckon on the appearance of a handful of interested professionals and citizens with the fanatical, elephant-hide determination of Marty and her cohorts, however.

A PEACOCK OR A CROW

So what I find out between breaks and over lunch is that there are more than a few heroic people on hand. Sure, most of them talked about these kids in blithely venal terms. They were in Cleveland to whine, hold hands, share stories, and, in most cases, to vent into a sympathetic ear. I was reminded of Bob and Frank who always sit next to me to watch *Monday Night Football* at the Bridgeport Inn in Chicago. They are survivors of the Chosin Reservoir Retreat. Beyond the 'Semper Fi!' gung-ho bullshit that I listen to in my voyeuristic, bloodsucking writer's way is the unspoken camaraderie of having marched home in sixty below weather after one of the greatest defeats in Marine Corps history: Survival. There's no real comparison, of course, but, even though men, archetypally at least, have a reputation for not talking about their worst experiences—at least with strangers, I think it has a lot to do with deciding to be mute rather than attempt to describe the indescribable. Masked amidst all this rhetoric I've heard about what it costs financially to adopt, the perceived betrayal of our government, adoption agencies, lawyers, doctors, social workers, and those dreadful dreadful White Orientals, the Romanians, is a deep sense of embarrassment. They just weren't ready for these kids, but who could have been?

Back in the hall, Marty sets the crowd up for the next speaker. Ms. Pupil, a master candidate, is an assistant to one of the foremost Sociologist/Occupational Therapist experts in the world, who can't be here because it's Yom Kippur, a Jewish high holiday. Ms. Pupil is very, very nervous. As Marty regales us with another anecdote about Petru's sensory defensiveness, Ms. Pupil truly has that deer-caught-in-headlights look about her. When she actually begins things go wrong from the start. She explains exactly what Sensory Deprivation is. To whit: 'The ability to organize and interpret information received from our senses.' Kids shut down when it comes to stimulation. They often can't cope with normal motor learning, gravity, or any of the normal means of stimulation. It's all rather dry and abstract. Unfortunately, both the V.C.R. and the slide projector malfunction as she attempts to exemplify problems.

By the time things work properly she seems to have lost the crowd. Doctors Dominion and Bond may have discussed the same problems—head banging, rocking, etc.—but its been shown via still slides accompanied by pie charts, graphs and surveys. Now we have it on videotape. Tiny babes who don't respond to any kind of stimulation. Toddlers who incessantly rock back and forth; toddlers deliberately banging their heads against the walls of their crib as they grip the bars; toddlers pulling away from human contact; toddlers who don't even bother to react to noise, touch or oral stimulation; tiny tots with a 10,000 mile stare. The crowd moans repeatedly as Ms. Pupil reiterates the fact that these kids make no attempt whatsoever to control or manipulate their environment. One child who might, for all intents and purposes, be dead, is lifted up into a sitting position by a pair of adult arms. "This child is two (it's so tiny it might well be nine months) and look!" The poor, tiny mite obviously has no sense of gravity whatsoever and falls like a felled tree, its head crashing against the crib wall.

A lady in front of me starts to weep. Thank God, there is no audio. A blonde woman in the audience puts her hand up after another example of a kid who won't play with the toy that's been placed in front of him. "Is it reversible? I've decided to adopt and I need to know, is it reversible?"

"I don't know," says Ms. Pupil.

"What can we do about it?" the woman says, very shrill, her rage right there.

"I don't know."

Ms. Pupil begins to talk about therapy through trampolines and pillows and is interrupted by a woman who makes what I'm told later is a very valid point, that such a condition is rare.

"A lot of it may have to do with lead paint and pesticide exposure," says Ms. Pupil, too frazzled, it seems, to take a helping hand.

"Is it just Romania?"

"I don't know."

I want to defend her here. Those council housing projects I grew up in, in England, had that sweet-tasting lead paint on their walls. It peels off the walls in kid-size flakes and, believe it or not, it tastes good, sweet in its own weird way. How could these people possibly understand that?

"Were there any kids who were okay?" another lady barks sarcastically.

"Many of them were okay."

"Thank God for that."

Later, she shows us a series of charts, the surveyed odds of adopted children:

81% don't have problems.

19% do have problems.

50% have initial motor problems.

20% exhibit means of 'risky play.'

40% are rockers.

It's a shame that she's lost the crowd at this point. Eight out of ten seems like good odds to me. Still of the 19% who are left out, 9% of whom have profound problems, there's 10% in limbo. A lot of the problems she discussed are, it seems to me, a father, to be common among *all* children. The 20% who engage in 'reckless play,' although I may be underestimating the degree of recklessness and consequent danger, seem like an incredibly low-ball figure when I recall my own lunatic behavior (and that of my crazy friends) growing up in Manchester, England.

A series of therapeutic cures are then recommended. If they move a lot or rock incessantly Ms. Pupil recommends the supervised use of swings. A couple in front of me then talk about how their child's eyes roll back in its head as it swings back and forth. The tension is viable as the couple argue about whether the child is okay. "It's not okay," the lady blurts, "he likes to spin around and around and around and that's *not* normal." Ms. Pupil agrees that its not and starts to discuss the inner ear, gravity, hairs, nerve endings and getting assessments. Assessment is a big word with her.

She's interrupted again then. A very angry lady who wants to know why she's only listening to a litany of horror stories. That lady is interrupted by another one who argues back that a lot of this is "normal or normalish in normal families." Poor Ms. Pupil stands there dumbstruck and dissed. *These* children all need a nap, I think.

Marty takes the mike, points and interrupts the interrupters. "We died for your sins, m'am." Her arms move frenetically, like she's trying to telepathically karate chop us all into a state of concussion. "The other adoption seminars will tell you *lies*. We're telling you the *truth*. YOU CANNOT TRUST YOUR PEDIATRICIAN! I was out there in rural America! I was out there BY MYSELF."

Dr. Bond stands up to be counted. "Marty is right! Marty is right! Please listen up."

All we need is a soundtrack, you know, Piaf, *Je ne Regret Riens*. Dolly back. Fade to black.

Suitably chastened, the audience shuts up. Ms. Pupil gives a final summing up, recommends that they all talk to their medical insurance company before adopting and exhaustedly asks if there are any more questions. There are none.

The large-eared gentleman in front of me has to steady his exhausted wife as she pinches her cheeks to keep from crying. "I need a big drink," he says.

That Evening

I have upset Victor. Dressed, ready to go, the nastiest part of the day left behind in the shower, I'm fairly okay. Yet, having told him about my immediate impressions of the seminar in my own, slightly impressionistic Romanian way, I've truly got him going. Followed by his two Bassett Hounds, Carly and Simon, Victor marches up and down the kitchen, adjusting and readjusting his tie. His agitation ebbs and floes.

"The glass is half-full or half-empty, but if you keep the subject weighed toward the negative, you're just left with a lot of people who are discouraged." He swivels, steps over Carly who is looking at him so pathetically, like a, umm, Bassett Hound. "There's a lot of good to go with the bad."

"Eighty percent is good odds," I put in. "The glass is way more than half full."

"Right," he says. "Yes."

I recognize that look on his face. It's the same one my grandmother wore. I believe she had it on her face when she walked all the way from Bucharest to Hamburg in 1911 with her *gelt* sewn into her corset. I've never met Victor's grandmother but I believe she had it, too. His dark blue eyes are glimmering with determination.

Tomorrow he'll set things right. It's a rainy night. The restaurant is called "That Place" and when we enter I have to lift up my feet and pluck the dead leaves off the soles of my shoes. We have a private room upstairs and I join thirty-odd guests at a long rectangular table. On my way in, I crouch by Marty and ask her if she'll help me with the names of some adoption agency people. She nods. I sit with Victor, other professionals and Margaret. The food is good. The wine is good and plentiful. The conversation is interesting.

Victor and I discuss Romanian roots. The importance of training social workers to be sensitive. The Bucharest Metro. Margaret is a Southern lady who speaks quietly and thoughtfully. Above and beyond adopting her child, I gather she didn't see much of Romania and is reticent about discussing her experience. She wants to know my favorite tourist place. I mention the pristine little German villages in the Carpathians and the Roman remains in Drobeta-Turnu Severin on the Danube, by the Serbian border. Again, I attempt to shift the conversation to her. She smiles genuinely, but her eyes squeeze out grief. She has to fly back and forth to Detroit from her home in Florida to get treatment for her daughter. She's the first person I've dealt with so far who seems reticent to discuss her experiences.

Susan, on the other hand, is particularly perky and garrulous. She's Wonder Woman: Finishing up her doctorate, bringing up three kids, and working on a daily basis with kids suffering from cerebral palsy, head trauma, neurological problems, and behavioral disorders. A ball of positive energy, as she chats away her blonde pageboy rolls along with her bobbing head, moving from side to side like Ringo in the early days of the Beatles. She's very interested in the *idea* of the book because she met these children knowing nothing. Along with the damaged children come damaged parents, Susan tells me. Forewarned is forearmed. The more information they can get, the better prepared parents are by the time they see her.

I ask her if she knows anything about adoption agencies in her city, if any of them have shown any interest in what she does.

"Agencies aren't interested in people, *period*!" a barking voice interrupts. I don't even have to look up to know it's Marty. She offers up a number of expletives vis-a-vis an adoption agency and barks out an order for more wine. "A bunch of liars. If the attorney was Pinnochio, her nose would be in Cincinnati."

The *Turning Point* producer, a suave man of Pierce Brosnany good looks, pours us some more wine and asks me about England. Did I go to boarding school? He wants to know. No, I say, grateful for the change of subject, and crack a few jokes about the regatta in *Another Country*, English public school, buggery, Blunt, Burgess, McLean, Philby and the Queen Mother's bad teeth. Did he go to boarding school in England? Yes. Did the regatta bit and everything and it has served him well; he takes his boat out on the Chesapeake still. Consequently, Susan warbles with glee. Her family too has a boat they take out to the Chesapeake.

A PEACOCK OR A CROW

The rain washes the roof above us making ping-pong noises. We discuss writers. Barbara Kingsolver. Ann Rice. Al Franken's huge best seller about Rush Limbaugh. Justice Borke's opinion that the decline of American civilization began with the transistor radio.

There just aren't that many good books about Romania, we agree. Tour books. Vampire books. History books. Andrei Codrescu's *The Hole in the Flag*, Ed Behr's *Biting the Hand That Feeds You*, and, of course, *Red Horizons*, written by Ion Mihai Pacepa, formerly the head of Securitaté. All of them are useful for information's sake, but there's not much out there for the kind of people who are thinking of adopting.

After dessert, Marty arises and walks tipsy-slow toward our end of the table. "Adoption agencies are liars," she says.

Victor hasn't had a drink all night. I'm glad because outside it's really coming down. Cats and dogs. Romanians and Hungarians. He gives Marty a really sad once-over. "Yes," I say, "the empirical evidence seems to be in. I'd like to talk to anyone who's here anyway."

"I'll take care of it tomorrow," Marty says, flexing her neck. "I'll look after you."

The ABC producer gets up to leave and we say our goodbyes and follow him out. Outside it's raining so hard that it's like the foreshadowing of doom in the most predictable movie you've ever seen. I'm exhausted, sucked dry by a giant magnet of desperate energy. Victor is quiet at the steering wheel. The windshield wiper wars with the rain. I drift, walk the length of my mind into the flash of expensive jewelry accompanied by the paper flutter of *mituire ("bribery")*; failed in-vitro at ten thousand a shot; broken hearts and hysterectomies; Disney characters on the walls of empty kiddie bedrooms. All the plaster saints, crucifixes, hug therapy and trampolines can't prepare you for just how strong Stalin's medicine was. You can't just eat, pay and go home. You say you'll bear any burden to have a child of your own. You saw them on TV, but those cute saucer eyes sometimes turned into huge black islands on the neurological CAT scans. Meanwhile, back at the orphanages, they stand stone still in their cots— 80% good; 20% irrecuperable—waiting.

Day Two

Victor and Sandy are much more 'Up' as speakers than their predecessors. The issue of affection is brought up every which way by both of them. Yet, again and again, when the issue is raised, somebody pops up like a Jack-in-a-box and tells us a story of overt parental affection being denied. You hug and they won't hug back. Their bodies go limp. They pull away. Their cute little saucer eyes are vacant. Or else, they love too much and desperately need constant reassurance and kisses and hugs and squeezes at inconvenient, 'inappropriate' moments. They love too little or they love too much, and, sometimes, I gather, they do both: a relentless war of the mind. The ghost in the machine. The essence of Cartesian ego and dualism. Little people who are only aware of their own thoughts, capable of functioning in a state of disembodied existence, neither situated in a space nor surrounded by others. This is the pure self, the state of *I* posited by Réné Déscartes in 1641, that which we are seduced into imagining is the unique thing that creates our identity. Most of us, whether we're children or adults, have those ghost moments, but our communal society sucks us out of such stasis. An old lover of mine, Patricia, a manic depression sufferer partial to Prozac, had a huge Hallmark sticker on her refrigerator door picturing a wide-eyed young woman in Annie Hall-type regalia with *'Snap out of it!'* in a bubble over her head. I would catch her staring at it. It was an amulet calling for normalcy. *Fin-de-siécle* juju. Well, simply put, these kids aren't conditioned that way. There's no witch doctor in hand with an amulet, unless you go for Dr. Bond's hug therapy.

"I've tried everything to get my kid to show me something," says a woman in front of me. "I've got two of my own and two others we adopted. I've never experienced anything like it and neither has anyone I know."

Victor plays with the starched collar of his shirt and then runs his fingers forward over his suit lapels. "Look, in the U.S.A.," he says, "affection is usual in the family—no matter how abusive. Institutionalized care in Eastern Europe is about separation: Institutionalism. Child to caregiver ratio ranges between 35 to 1 and 8 to 1. Institutional emphasis is on the group, never the individual child. Family relationships are stimulating: Adults for kids, kids for kids. In Romania there was no stimulation."

After saying this, however, he reiterates that the research shows that only a maximum of 25% of these kids have real, honest-to-God problems. Thus, the glass is three-quarters full or one-quarter empty. And still there's the Why? Why? Why? from so many out there. Why the delay in language skills? Why is she so small? And Victor does his best to be patient and clear. He explains how, generally, the other kids researched in this era, mostly from Korea, Vietnam and China, spent far less time in institutions.

The lady in front of me is still not happy. He's not giving her the answer she *wants*. "I went to my international adoption agency because it had a reputation for straight shooting. I got references, I spent a lot of money and…"

"International adoption is a big free-market business and agencies want to keep it deregulated. Children become part of a free market economy. There has been a lot of state to state resistance when it comes to international adoption regulation." The crowd literally buzzes with indignation. "Processes of adoption should be consistently regulated throughout the U.S. vis-a-vis cost, information, risks, and standardized information provided by trained counselors. Training should be mandated by the federal government. For every one agency that's regulated and accountable, there's another one that isn't—no regulations whatsoever. I think we're one step away from the days of slavery when children become the commodities in a market."

A PEACOCK OR A CROW

Victor has *me* all pumped up. Sure, he's just a college professor who trains social workers, but once there was a lowly assistant professor named Newt who dreamed out loud about putting a contract on us all. The nasty little nihilist in me—that which I inherited from my Romanian anarcho-syndicalist grandmother—says: "You know, there are so many well-heeled people in this room. We can start our own lobby in the State Houses. We can buy our own share of lobbyist whores in D.C. to compete with those in the deep pockets of the adoption lawyers and agencies. We can practice the same winning-through-intimidation tactics utilized by the anti-abortion lobby."

Jeez, talk about a Cartesian ego. And then somebody up front makes me snap out of it and get a grip like lightning. "It's not just our people," some lady expostulates, "the Ukrainians and the Romanians are corrupt and they don't stand for criticism." Ah, the patriotic knee-jerk. *Sure, we've got problems, but they're ba-ad.*

"I understand what you're saying, but they see foreigners adopting as Romanian cultural genocide. They're sensitive to criticism; even if pride means hurting their own kids."

A little ra-ra goes a long way with this crowd. As he ends it, post Q and A, repeating the fact that the 20% who are 'special needs' do not supersede the 80% who aren't. Victor shakes a fist. "As a social worker, I believe we must teach parents advocacy skills. Teach 'em to be hellraisers."

I work the crowd again during the break. A couple I spoke to yesterday seem a lot more relaxed. They somehow manage to simultaneously carry all the books and pamphlets that have been made available at the Parent Network table and hold hands. "I went to bed confused and miserable," the woman says. "Now I'm just confused, but less so."

Actually, I see a lot of hand-holding going on. It may not be scientific, but I'll hazard an empirical guess that the hand-holders are adoption possible/probables and, as useful as their education has been, that they're more bamboozled than they've ever been. I attempt conversation with a dourer-than-usual Marty about Victor's lecture but she avoids the subject twice. One of the producer's crew approaches and she smiles, swivels and flirts, instant chameleon. When he's gone, she turns back around and I'm still in her face, low rent Seymour Hirsch. Ouch! What a look.

"I think Victor was a lot more positive than the previous speakers, don't you?"

Of course, what I really want to say is: 'Wine hangover? Or, did you just chug a glass of lemon juice?' Let's play a game. I'll be Marty and you'll be Diane Sawyer.'

"Umm, y'know, Marty, I understand your point of view is out of a far different place to mine." Those blue blue eyes of hers just drill me. "Everybody is relentlessly rough on the agencies and lawyers, but I have to believe there are *some* reasonably decent ones."

"Not a one of them," she barks. "It's just a matter of degree."

I want to talk to her some more but she signals over my shoulder and we're joined by a flock of folk who just seem to want to bask in her presence. "Thank you," says a handsome blonde lady with a leathery tan. "Really, I have to thank you. I've been through a lot with my kids. My own kids, if you know what I mean. I had a pretty rough time of it. But then I think of all that you've been through and it turns out to be a benefit for us. I really really feel so grateful."

"Thank you."

"No. Thank *you*. You're great." Joan of Arc always called for Saint Barbara as I recall. Auto-martyrdom, and it's spreading like a disease.

I collar the tanned woman on the way back in to hear Susan. She's got lots of kids already. Four of her own plus three foster kids. I want to know if she'll take on more after this. "I'd have to be crazy after what we've heard, wouldn't I?"

Susan is way cool and perky. All shiny apple cheeks and enthusiasm. A speech language pathologist, she's not selling a book or offering any form of gimmick therapy. What she has to say is scarily significant, though. In the most recent studies, out of 133 kids, 85 had speech and language problems. Still, once that fact is out of the way and the problems of apraxia, lateral lisping, sound additions, distortions and omissions, et al, are scientifically defined and quantified, she takes the time to explain neglect in a more concrete, less abstract way.

"Bird research—'cos obviously you can't do this with kids— shows that if you tape a bird's eyes and ears shut they do not learn bird songs and do not or cannot catch up. The same with cats. Brain scans and the questioning of Romanian orphans seem to show the first researched evidence that these children suffer profoundly from neglect."

Kids have often been physically abused either at home by their parents or in the institution. Tissue damage to the throat can be from strangulation, choking on food, or, even more common, crying out for help to institutional workers. Its common that their mouths are hypersensitive. Lumpy foods like oatmeal often drive them into a state of temporary dementia. So you've got to grind melting solids like cheese puffs and pretzels into stuff like apple sauce. There's even the possibility of hypersensitivity to tooth brushing, clothing and music.

Then there are the hearing problems: problems with C.A.P. (Central Auditory Processing) where there's no cohesion to the language they hear, and conductive processing, which are inner-ear liquid and nerve problems. These problems can obviously be caused by infection, but, again, are often the result of children having to shout. As a result of their not being picked up and the accompanying lack of exercise and stimulation, the kids may not develop any sense of gravity, which, of course, affects hearing and speaking.

At the end of all this bad news, however, is good news. People share recipes. You can put mashed potatoes in a food processor, it seems. You can learn to massage their little faces. There are special toothbrushes available for such hypersensitive teeth and gums. "The fact is," Susan says, "They all get better. Sometimes it's a degree at a time but they get better. Kids are plastic. You know, really, kids are plastic."

After the Conference

"Orphanages are an evil concept," Victor barks. He is gripping the steering wheel very tight. "Institutions don't fix anything."

"But…" I say, "but somebody's got to do something."

On the way to the airport Victor and I have our umpteenth conversation about Newt Gingrich and his stated longing that there be more orphanages available for the foundling youth of our nation. *Boys Town*, I make a note, I must remember to rent it again. Men were men then. Spencer Tracy in a dog collar. Father Flanagan practiced tough love without resorting to buggery. Irish love that, in retrospect, seemed more Manischean than Roman Catholic. If boys had a problem, they put on boxing gloves and slugged it out with the holy father as referee. Fresh country air, exercise and the love of Jesus Christ. My favorite orphans are Dave Thomas, Clark Kent, Cosette Valjean, Oliver Twist, Heathcliff and my grandfather on my dad's side, Charlie.

Brought up in my grandmother's house, I had to suffer her rules and curfews. That tough old Romanian, she had a soft spot for all those Warner Brothers movies of the thirties. George Raft, Paul Muni, Joan Blondell, Humphrey Bogart, Pat O'Brien; and grandma's main squeeze, Julie Garfinkel, aka John Garfield: *'Julie, Julie, Julie, Do You Love Me?'* I mention this out of a sort of guilt. She passed on a long time ago, but I recall being entranced by all those happy little hard-nosed Hell's Kitchen kids and all that Man Love. I wanted to run away and live in Boy's Town with the good father. Nobody made you join a gang *there*. Nobody came at you with a switchblade or a brick.

Orphans are a sort of mythic archetype of western culture. Raised right, despite the wicked world, they become better, stronger, more disciplined citizens than the average kid. Yet my grandfather was eternally embarrassed by the stigma of it: His mother had *abandoned* him. My friend, Tommy O'Shea, a well known boxing coach schooled in fisticuffs by the Christian Brothers in North Dublin, still becomes apoplectic at the very mention of it. Beatings, beatings, more beatings and relentless abuse.

So what's happening here? The myth seems to clash with the reality of it. Yet the myth looks good to a political technocrat like Uncle Newty. He seems to genuinely believe he knows what's best for us. Crack mothers, crack babies, baby Clockers, nine-year-old Crip hit men, YoYo rappin' on the pleasures of teen fellatio in the high school boy's bathroom, D.C.F.S. horror stories in the *New York Times*: Our world is a sewer and somebody should pay. What we need are more prisons and brand spanking new orphanages. Somebody ought to pay.

"So we're back to Neglect-versus-Abuse, ey Vic?"

"Even an alcoholic mother is sober some of the time."

"That's a hard sell."

I think of my friend Eileen, who owns that ten thousand mile stare from twelve years working for the Department of Children and Family services. She's got a million horror stories: The gatekeeper of hell.

"No matter how bad they are. There's still love there."

"At least our orphanages are better than theirs," I argue. "There's no comparison."

"You don't know anything."

And I really don't, I guess. Government cuts in the U.S. have made our own institutions bad, too. There's a better ratio of workers to orphans but the abuses are massive. The Foster Care industry is a trough at which corrupt venal people feed on government money. This prompts a logical question on my part: "So if we can't help our own, how can we help the Romanian children?"

"Different, distinctly different problems," Victor says.

Here it's about central government changing its laws to let more people, especially older and single people adopt. But we've got plenty of relatively wealthy Americans dying to adopt internationally.

"There are more instutionalized children in Romania now than there were after the revolution. We must help them."

As he drops me off at the airport, we shake hands and talk about next time. I grab my bag and make for the American airlines counter. I recognize the woman in front of me from the conference. She's a flirtatious lady in her mid-forties with a sinuous workout hard body on her way back to Philadelphia. Come to think of it, I've seen a lot of gym bodies this weekend.

"So after all you've heard. Will you still adopt?" she asks.

I shrug. "I'm not sure." Sure, I *should* tell her I'm a writer but I decide to be naughty.

"You know, you can learn from everything you've heard but don't take any of it to heart."

She opens her purse, pulls out her wallet and shows me the picture of a beautiful little girl. "She's four now."

"She okay?"

"Listen, I brought her back from Timisoara." She pulls out another one in which the child is running with a balloon, her pigtails blowing out behind her. "She was tiny. She had scabies and a massive ear infection. She's been a little slow in learning to read but, my God, she's a treasure." It's corny, I know, but the lady looks so damned happy that I want to give her a hug. I've needed to meet her for two days and here we are at Cleveland airport. As she asks me what I do for a living, she carefully puts the photos back in her wallet. I tell her that I write and teach. Do I like it? She wants to know. I tell her I love teaching.

"You know, I'm a lawyer with my own practice. Done very well, thank you. Been married three times. *That* I'm not good at." She pulls a fold-up phone out of her blazer pocket and punches in a number. "Being a mommy I like. In March I'm going back to the same orphanage to get another one, a boy."

The timbre of her voice changes as she starts to speak into the phone. After a minute she gives me the phone. "Say hello to Ana."

I have one of those silly conversations with this little stranger I've only seen in a photograph. 'Hi!', 'How big are you?' Bla! Bla! Bla!' I hand the phone back, and mommy says she'll be home soon. "You got any kids?" she wants to know.

I tell her yes, my son lives with his mother in Santo Domingo. That my girlfriend and I talk a lot about having one. "If you *can't* make your own, go get one," she says, stepping off toward the ticket counter. "If you *can* make one, go there and get another one anyway. It's the right thing to do."

Plots, Deceit or Just Another Media Feeding Frenzy?

Months Later

There's a stress and strain that goes with submerging oneself in the subject of Attachment Disorder Syndrome and involving oneself, albeit peripherally, in the lives of parents, children, social workers, lawyers, therapists, sociologists, journalists. The phone rings.

"Is this Professor Ee-vorr Irwin?"

Woops! It's that Rachel lady from the *Tribune*. She calls a lot. I met her last year at a reading I did. I'm the one who made Attachment Disorder Syndrome funny. I'm good for quips, quotables and epigraphs over the telephone, I guess. I remember her because she looks exactly like the Bulgarian striker, Hirsute Stoichkov.

"Do you believe kids are capable of committing violent suicide?"

Ah, the Denver case and the media feeding frenzy which has accompanied it. These bottom-feeders are forever looking for a new angle. A little Russian boy is beaten to death by a wooden spoon. Either his adoptive mother committed murder, or, according to the tenets of 'Reactive Detachment Disorder', as posited by a small-town psychologist, two-year-old David beat himself to death.

"I don't have either the training or the expertise, Rebecca."

"Rachel."

I apologize and bite into my bagel. Mmm, just the way I like it: Hard on the outside, chewy within. I am kind of an expert on bagels.

"I need help on this. What's your instinct?"

"I've got a terminal degree in writing. I know German Romantic poetry, okay? Kleist. Goethe. Heine. Dead, morbid writer dudes." There's a long silence. "Look, umm, call Victor, my partner in Cleveland. Call Cook County Emergency Room."

"You have inclinations and opinions."

I look out the window. The sky is a flat gray. It hasn't rained in a couple of weeks. Moving around in this kind of humidity is like swimming in spittle. "Sure, I do. It's just…"

"Eee-vorr, if I say the word 'Denver' what comes to mind?"

I correct the incorrect way she says my name again, and tell her she certainly knows more than I do about the case. Friends and other writers have called me about things they've seen on cable: demonstrations outside the Denver courthouse; folks in "I Believe the Mother" T-shirts; others who talk about all East European orphans being the delayed-action, demon seed of communism. Somebody who used to be a famous football coach, now a "Motivational Speaker," says he believes that it's impossible for the mother to get a fair trial in Colorado. And, of course, adding a sort of psychotic self-promoting spin to the thing, there's Marty. In every article, on every show, or so it seems, is Marty.

"Rachel, I can conjecture that the mother probably just snapped. Kids push buttons, you know what I mean? Even your own kid." I swallow. "How about this for a quote? This kid was probably a spunky little manipulator raised in a *Lord of the Flies* atmosphere in a Stalinist orphanage in Minsk or Pinsk. I heard he was bullying the other adopted brother."

According to the television news-byte I saw the other night concerning the trial, the pathologist had located part of the little boy's nose cartilage at the back of his skull. I tell her that I doubt, no matter how much a of masochistic head-banger this kid could have been, whether he could have displaced his own anatomy in such a two-hundred pounds-per-square-inch way. His poor little body has been covered in bruises. "But, look, hey! You know, like, who am I to give an opinion? I'm not a doctor and many people don't even consider me a writer."

"It didn't stop Marty", she says.

I moan audibly. I've got twenty-five, single-spaced, ten-point pages worth of interview with Marty that I'm working on, right at this very moment, between phone calls. My instinct, more and more, is to jettison the chapter I've been writing about her.

"She thinks the kid killed himself." I love it. The Russian child as mini-Mishima. "Don't you think that's possible?"

The other morning, one of those talk show hostesses nodded her head as the lawyer for the family explained how the harsh environment in the Russian orphanage caused the little boy to lash out, flying into violent rages, and to ultimately beat himself to death. Perhaps this "Blame the victim" thing has finally reached its apotheosis, and, if we but had eyes to see, Nicole Brown Simpson may have actually almost decapitated herself.

"Do you think a clever defense lawyer could use Attachment Disorder as a means of getting the mother off?"

"Sure."

"Do you believe a child could beat itself to death with a wooden spoon?"

"No."

"Do you believe there is such a thing as Attachment Disorder"

"Yes."

"Its not some kind of medicine show hokum?" she probes. "A means of defining the indefinable?"

I shrug. What am I, from Minsk or Pinsk? "As a lay person, from the outside, I'd say that it's really a broad rubric. Call Victor in Cleveland. Call Dr. Bond. Call the brain scanner in Detroit. There's a really interesting man in Alexandria, Virginia—a neuropsychologist. They'll all say 'yeah, its not some medicine show hokum' in a more specific way than me. And, you know, I went to the effort of giving you their names and phone numbers already."

"I tried getting the one you said was negative, the guy at Harvard."

"I didn't say he doesn't believe in Attachment Disorders. He just thinks that parents…"

"His secretary was a total…"

"Well, I don't know. Next time you say you're with the *New York Times* or *60 Minutes*."

"These are all very arrogant people, Ee-vorr."

"Did you bother to call Victor at Case Western Reserve University?"

"Umm, as I recall, he never got back to me."

"Try him again. He's easy to talk to."

The true depth of her lack of interest strikes me then. Why isn't she being thorough? Is the *Tribune* really that cheap? All joking aside, can you really be that exploitative of a dead child for the sake of a cheesy headline? Victor's words have proven to be true: in every society on earth, without exception, children are seen as a commodity to be economically exploited.

"Umm," she says, "umm, you've got Harvey's home phone number, right?"

"No."

Harvey is the mother's lawyer. Actually, I *do* have his number because someone I know from grad school freelances for the *Denver Post*. Anyway, I don't think that either Harvey or the mother need any more publicity than they're already getting. At this point, my journalist friend seems to resign herself to my not playing ball and says goodbye. I put the phone down.

The vicissitudes of fate are strange. Think of Ovid, paying for the sin of composing *The Art of Love* and seducing the Emperor's wife, forced to spend his last days in exile from Rome, ebbing away in Romania. Ovid, at least, copped a plea, and kinda/sorta deserved what he got. I think of Marty, adoptive mother of what she refers to as "the Romanian Gypsy sock-monkey eggplant baby," and the concept of her as an 'expert.' The media really are a wicked bunch. She's been quoted as a source in every realm of media, from the *New York Times* to cheesy, sleazy daytime talk shows. The telephone rings again.

I'm okay in that kind of ninety-plus humidity unless I'm forced to move and obsess on the likes of Marty. My sinuses can't cope with air conditioning, and, at a certain point, the fan just moves warm air up and down. I move out of my office chair, take four steps to pick up the telephone, and already my body is weeping.

"She's done it again," says another female voice I don't recognize.

"I'm sorry. Who's done what again?"

"Marty. Have you not read the article in the national news?"

"No."

It's Margaret. We met at the Conference also. She was warm, witty, well-dressed and wealthy. Margaret and I did a long interview about her travails as an adoptive mother and soon-to-be-divorced wife. She adopted her daughter after buying the family a VCR. After the fact, however, having made up with her husband, she had changed her mind. Having spent three days transcribing and editing her words, I was rather irritated about the amount of time I'd wasted, but, as the cliché says: it goes with the territory. A true Marty groupie at the Conference, she's been far more ambivalent the last time we talked.

I charge toward the refrigerator. The soles of my bare feet adhere to the tile floor as I crouch, squeeze the remote phone between my chin and shoulder, take a pair of ice cubes in each hand and make fists. Meanwhile Margaret begins crying. She is a weary warrior. Taking her daughter for a CAT Scan every other week in Detroit is exhausting when you have to travel two-thirds of the way across America. The main thing, I think, is that she just needs someone to talk to. I have entered a sort of inner sanctum of trust. Very few people understand her difficulties. Additionally, it seems, the more her situation is publicized, the more it gets trivialized. *That* she wasn't ready for.

Margaret clears her throat and then asks, in an embarrassed sort of way. "Do you see it all as a plot?"

"Plot?"

"The Romanians, the Ukrainians, the Beerorussians, or whatever they're called. Marty thinks they're dumping kids on us."

"A conspiracy?"

"Yes, a conspiracy. Read the article, you'll see. That woman's agenda is to stop all Romanian adoptions. I heard she told someone very recently not to keep her kid." Then, in a raspy voice, something out of a thriller movie, she says. "We've got to stop her."

My dubious silence says all. I shouldn't doubt. There's an article on it, I'm told. I write down the details. Margaret insists that she has to go. "I've got to find Chinese eggplant." Her husband has to have dinner on the table when he gets home.

We close with a chat about the poor dead baby in Denver. She starts to cry. There's a long silence before we put the phone down. I place my cold, damp palms against the insides of my thighs. It feels wonderful. The truth is, I am already exhausted. I'm supposed to jump in my car and visit the Sensory Integration Day camp at Camp Cheerful the day after tomorrow (Really, Camp Cheerful!).

On my desk is an official document from Constantinescu's government, which, theoretically, at least, explains the new adoption policies. Next to it is a translation executed by a reliable source. The trouble is, no one understands either document. It might as well be written in Cuneiform. Nothing is clear within the bureaucratic post-Stalinist language; except it gives you the opportunity to attempt to interpret the subtext and imagine yourself breaking the Enigma code. The president, I've been told again and again since his election, has committed himself to streamlining the international adoption process and ordered his federal and municipal judges to speed things up. After all the bobbing and weaving, probing and teasing that goes with dealing with bureaucratic shills, I wonder if I'll have anything left for the kiddies at Camp Cheerful. I'm getting punchy.

I make coffee, go through my daily check-mark rigmarole, and start getting my ducks in line. The Brain-Scan doctor's secretary says he's busy when I try to get through to him. Nobody answers when I call the Romanian embassy. A Bulgarian journalist who knows another Bulgarian journalist who interviewed me for a paper in Sofia calls. We make an appointment; she seems to think I really know something authoritative about the current political situation in Bucharest and that I'm plugged-in on the Denver case.

Every day, as I sip my coffee and do my phone stuff, I browse the Adoption page on the Worldwide Web. The number of adoption agencies grows like something malignant. Marty and the media may well be doing their damnedest to discourage the American public from adopting, but nobody seems to be listening anyway.

Outside, the weather has still not broken. There's a thick, stagnant humidity in the air. It's very hot.

Later that afternoon, after a welcome drop or two of rain, Sebastian, my Romanian friend, arrives in town for a convention, and proceeds to eat and drink me out of house and home. I have not vacuumed. He drinks my good Grolsch beer with mayonnaise sandwiches and Ben and Jerry's Chunky Monkey, alternating mouthfuls with puffs from a chain of Malboros.

In spite of the heat of the Summer, he is bound and determined to look like a Home Boy in a hip-hop video when he returns to Bucharest. Having shopped in New York City, he's wearing the appropriate Hugo Boss baggy jeans, Joe Boxer boxer-shorts, and black fleece-lined sweatshirt with the hood up over his head. And what a physiognomy—dark brown football button eyes and eyebrows that look like they've been stitched over his nose by a blind man, guessing. Sweltering, with beads of tzuica sweat popping out of his fish-belly white forehead, Sebby looks like a real-life Romanian Ninja turtle. The owner of a graduate degree in engineering, a fellow lover of Goethe and Nabokov, witty, xenophobic and funny; he is a Romanian spin doctor on a par with Carville and Matalin.

I show him videos of the children adopted from Romania. He reacts accordingly:

"This man looks like a man who sells women at the Athenee Palace," he says of the aging pretty-boy and former journalists with a talk show, as he hugs some poor ravaged blonde who has told a tale of an adopted child trying to push her down the stairs. "Even as a small child," Sebastian sneers, gesturing the height of a four or five-year old with the blade of his hand, "I would have been quite able to push this blonde-from-a-bottle down the stairs."

Anyway, I have been shopping. I give him the article to read from a national magazine that I had in my hot little hand. The writer has taken the high road in an article entitled, "A Dead Child, A troubling Defense." I am no longer capable of objectivity. So, I think: *When in doubt, ask a Romanian.*

Sebby chugs his third beer and eats really fast. "What stupid idiot this man is," Sebastian screams. He reads a section out loud where Marty accuses the former Soviet nations of collectively conspiring to dump their duff children on gullible America. Two-year-old Soviet Moles?

He roles his eyes and makes a crude gesture. I think about mentioning that Marty, the international adoption "expert" in question, is Hungarian-American, but I let it go. "Why do you insult us so? How can we sell you, umm…gunoiu?"

"Rubbish?"

"You Americans are so smart. By law you have to come to our country, see the baby before you take it, and then go see a judge. How can we sell you filthy Romanian rubbish you do not want?"

I try to explain that I'm getting past my despair, despite the sheer amount of paperwork I'm drowning in. I tell him about the negativity perpetuated by the media. The way so many people, disgusted by what they've read and seen, have tried to dissuade me, or worse, laughed and sneered. No matter what, I still feel the urgent need to help these children and attempt to present a reasonably balanced, non-scientific view of what's been going on. The sheer number of desperate children motivate me—more now, I tell him, than after the "revolution."

A PEACOCK OR A CROW

He is dubious. I show him the long letter I received in both English and Romanian from the new prime minister. It's the same ol' *limba de lemn*—the dead wooden language of the party—but it does *clearly* speak of a six-month period for parental reclamation of their institutionalized children. There's a new collective sheriff in town and it is dubbed *The Commission for Child Protection*. This, I've been led to believe by various reliable American adoption sources, is finally, at last, the bona fide real thing.

"I trusted Constantinescu," Sebby says, "But he is just like the rest."

It seems to me that Romanians somehow naively believe that democracy runs on a parallel track with materialism. One of the major crimes perpetuated on pre-millennium Bucharest is the number of American-franchised, fast-food operations owned by securitaté alumni. For Constantinescu, a charming former professor of geology of the University of Bucharest, the road to genuine change is a long, complex, dangerous maze. Sebastian is a mellow, reasonable fellow, still willing to remember how bad the dictator Ceausescu really was; some of his friends, however, long for strong leadership. Before the Ceausescu bully, there was the Gheorgiou-Dej bully, the King Carol bully, and the General Antonescu bully. The bully most longed for, like our own General George Armstrong Custer, is the bully who never fulfilled his full bully potential.

"Pestele de la cap se impute," Sebastian says disgustedly.

I know this one from my grandma: *The fish rots from the head.* Romania is a nation obsessed with creating original proverbs.

"Ah, but…" I laugh because there's something extremely fishy about such a proverb. "Dar de la coada se curata." Yes. *You clean it from the tail.* Think about Constantinescu in positive terms and perhaps you recognize that its the caca at the bottom that needs to be wiped away first.

Early the following morning I go with Sebastian to the airport. While shopping, we found him a police leather jacket and a pair of red patent leather Doc Martin's. For some reason, second-hand leather jackets, once the property of the Chicago police department, are big business in Prague, Berlin and Budapest. I am very impressed by the sight of my distorted self in his boots. "Beware of giving positive publicity to the power (*puterea*)," he warns me for about the fiftieth time. "Constantinescu will bring back Mihai, the former King," he insists, "and then all history will start over again. Perhaps you learned something worthwhile yesterday."

The idea of the King returning to Romania seems to be one of the hot topics of discussion. Yesterday, at the Little Bucharest restaurant, Sebby and I ran into various Peasant Party fund-raisers allied with some humorless men who represent themselves as the "Romanian Freedom Forum." They, too, are hot to trot, to return to what a lip-less man named Liviu referred to as a monarchical republic.

The orphans, when I brought them up, proved to be a taboo subject. A man with azure blue eyes and a Z Z Top beard—a Romanian Orthodox priest in civilian garb, Sebastian suggested after the fact—asked why I cared about the fate of a few dirty Gypsies.

We hug and kiss when the plane begins boarding. "Tell the truth for the sake of the children of Romania."

Off he goes. His hand-held luggage is loaded down with multiple copies of used books, CDs and scores of denims purchased from the Salvation Army. As he walks toward the plane, Sebastian lists ever so slightly to the left as if he's a dinghy with a pinhole, very slowly sinking. On the train back to downtown, I find I have tears in my eyes.

Notes from Chapter 9

---

[1] John Balabar (1991). <u>Remembering heaven's face</u>. New York: Poseidon.

Chapter 10

Adopting a Child from Overseas

The Basic How-To of International Adoption

Adoption is a life long process; the logistics can be a nuisance. There's a fair amount of tedious, time-consuming paperwork to do. A social worker will come into your home. Personal questions will be asked. Your finances will be looked over. The fact is that the adoption agencies, the state, the U.S. government and the country you adopt from all want to be sure that you're a good person capable of raising a child and offering him or her a good life. You really want to think the thing through very thoroughly.

In previous chapters you've read some of the heart-rending, moving anecdotes from parents who adopted after the coup in Romania, either as an altruistic reaction to the news stories, or simply because they wanted a baby fast. The fluid situation of the 1990-1991 period led them to believe Romania had become a sort-of giant supermarket for white babies. For awhile it was. In the chaos following the coup, for example, various vile creatures, mostly poverty-ravaged Gypsies and Securitaté people, were out for a fast buck, selling children they'd bought, kidnapped, or sired in the lobby and the dining rooms of the Inter-Continental hotel. *Those days are over!* There have been many changes since and it would be an unfair slander against the Romanian people and their current government to believe otherwise. The only reason any of the anecdotes from parents who adopted during this time are useful is that they serve as a reminder of how things were historically, the risks and responsibilities in international adoption, and also because they are from the first batch of adopted children upon whom the initial research was done. Also, what we learn from Romania adoptions has implications for parents adopting from other developing countries from around the world.

These are some of the things you'll need to do to begin your adoption. First and foremost, you must search your heart to see if you can parent a child—for better or for worse. If the answer is yes, then you should move to the next step. If not, then international adoption (and maybe parenting) are not for you. Second, you must have the approval of the United States government through the Immigration and Naturalization Service, which will, hereafter, be referred to as the INS. A good source for adopting internationally are two guides published by the U.S. Department of State's Bureau of Consular Affairs, *International Adoptions* (Publication # 10300); and, *The Immigration of Adopted & Prospective Adoptive Children* (Publication # M-249Y). They'll give you a fair idea of how to work with the INS. Write to:

Office of Children's Issues

CA/OCS/CI

Room 4811

Department of State

Washington DC 20520-4818

Phone: 202/647-2688

Fax: 202/647-2835

Or go to these web sites:

<http://travel.state.gov/children's_issues.html#adoption>

<http://www.ins.usdoj.gov/>

For information about Romania (and other countries), there's a 24-hour hotline at 202-736-7000. Make sure you have your phone set to tone; the system is computerized. Messages are long and very specific. It's an expensive phone call but may be well worth it, because issues and bureaucracies change continually. The telephone system is more up-to-date than the web sites. If you're bad at taking notes, purchase a telephone recording device to connect to a cassette recorder from your local electronics store. If you own a fax machine with its own telephone receiver, or are connected to a modem you can call 202-647-3000 to receive the guide or specific country-by-country information. Another way to receive international information is to send a stamped, self-addressed 8 1/2" x 11" envelope requesting information on your country of choice to the above address.

You must operate within the legal confines of the country where you want to adopt; one abuse of the law can shut down adoption for many months.[1] If you are working with an adoption agency, they will help you with the process. *This is actually the best way to proceed.* In fact, many countries will not permit independent or attorney-arranged adoptions. They will also have specific adoption agencies that they licensed for adoption. As one parent commented on her independent adoption (that is, without an agency):

> The independent adoptions were not aided or counseled in any way. We all just went to Romania, found a child, and came home and figured it out for ourselves. I think this is a disservice to children. (All of this is in retrospect of course.)

Besides being a disservice, it is very difficult to navigate the bureaucracies in the U. S. and in other countries. As part of navigating the maze in the U. S., the INS wants you to do five things if you wish to adopt internationally:

1. Purchase an INS brochure, # M-249-Y, entitled *The Immigration of Adopted & Prospective Adopted Children.*
2. Schedule what is referred to as a 'Home Study.'
3. File for child-abuse clearance with the police.
4. Open an adoption file with the INS.
5. Collect all relevant documentation in a file.

The first two pieces of documentation you need are the Application for Advanced Processing of Orphan Adoption Petition: the *I-600A orange form*; then there's the Petition to Classify Orphan as an Immediate Relative: *the I-600 blue form.* The I-600A in 1997 was $155. The I-600A form indicates your desire to adopt abroad and prompts INS to begin a file of its own on you; copies of it are sent to the National Visa Center and the consulate of the country of adoption. Once a child has been picked and the adoption paperwork has been completed, the I-600 is filed at the appropriate consulate.

To go with your I-600A you need: a certified copy of your birth certificate; three letters of reference; a set of fingerprints; and, a completed Home Study Form. Fingerprints can be a quick formality. For many people, you just head down to your local police station and get one of the officers to help you out. However, each state has a different process—some require that you go to a site where you can obtain a copy of your fingerprints and secure clearance from the FBI while others can fingerprint and clear you through the local police department. And, don't be surprised if the process changes while you are trying to secure fingerprint clearance. Consider the fingerprinting process and clearance as just one of the necessary hassles.

The Home Study

Home studies are usually done by a certified social worker picked by the adoption agency or adoption lawyer you've chosen, and vary in cost. They range from about $400 to over $1500, depending on the agency or individual as well as geography (the coasts and major cities are more costly then the midwest and small towns). The more expensive facilitators usually offer both a shoulder to cry on while you go through the bureaucratic *auto-de-fé* and serious post-adoption advice. Be sure to ask for references. Common sense says find someone you like and are confident will support you if there are problems, not the cheapest person.

The home study worker will visit your home and advise you as to its appropriateness as a living space. Size is not necessarily an issue. Still, if you live in a studio apartment or a tiny one-bedroom, they are likely to advise you to move to bigger quarters. At a minimum, the home must be safe for raising a child. What defines a stable lifestyle, anyway? Theoretically, at least, it's not a money issue. If you've had multiple marriages, a substance abuse problem, a non-traditional lifestyle, a variety of jobs or many residences, these may be issues that you'll have to talk through. Still, gay couples, single people (gay and straight) and former drug and alcohol abusers have adopted. The toughest issue with many adoption agencies is age. It's not uncommon to find couples where there is an age gap between partners or where an older couple desires to adopt. Some private agencies tend to be prejudiced against older couples, but countries like Romania, Bulgaria, and the Ukraine tend to be amenable to the idea of older people (50+) adopting. Remember, the Home Study worker is just doing his or her job. Even if the state in which you reside discourages such adoptions, this does not necessarily mean you will be rejected. You simply need to hang tough and establish a good relationship with your worker. He or she will additionally begin collecting biographical information about you, your current and original family background, and employment history. She or he will discuss the ins and outs of adopting. You will be subjected to personalized questioning about your fitness as a prospective parent. Make it easy on your facilitator; let them do their job. Of course, the exact information they collect will depend on the state in which you live as well as with the guidelines developed by the agency. Every state and every agency is different.

As part of the home study and adoption preparation process, parents should either receive training, attend seminars, or read books in the following areas[2]:

- details on the legal and social process of adoption in both the United States and abroad;
- issues of abandonment, separation, grief, loss, and mourning for the adopted child;
- the adoptive family life cycle and unique issues in family formation;
- unique issues of identity and attachment in adoption;
- outcomes and risks in international adoptions;
- dealing with unresolved infertility issues; and,
- if appropriate, resources about being a single adoptive parent.

Parents need to be well informed about neglect, abuse, and trauma that children experience so they can be prepared to meet the challenges ahead of them.[3] As one parent reflected on her own lack of preparation for adoption, she wrote:

> I needed more information on what to expect and why [our daughter] displayed some of the strange behaviors. We were terrified because we did not know where to begin to help the child who had been totally neglected. I also needed someone to explain the mixture of feelings I had for the child so I wouldn't feel guilty for not totally accepting her into our family. [We needed to] know what to expect our family to go through.

Another parent wrote:

> When we adopted [our son] was 2 years old. He understood no language, was resistant to touch, had never eaten solid foods, could not chew, had never drank water, looked at peers as competitors in survival, was frightened, often terrified...I feel that if we had known exactly what we were getting [the problems] we would have been better prepared to help him...and then his and our first year wouldn't have been so traumatic.

Obviously, they also want to know that you are financially stable. Understanding both your own finances and the financial issues in adoption requires some work. Adoptive families should:

- make sure they understand the fees they are being charged and how the fees were calculated;

- determine whether they are responsible for traveling costs and arrangements in a host country, plus any additional fees they might be required to pay once they leave the United States;

- develop a plan if the country from which the agency adopts closes its adoption program while you are in the process of adopting or while you are in-country;

- assess if their adoption agencies will pay for needed services after the children are placed in their homes and the adoptions are legalized;

- discern what expenses they will be responsible for if they are not approved to adopt children, or expenses they will be responsible for in the event they change their minds about adopting.

If all is well, they will then help or advise you on how to obtain a Child Abuse Clearance Form. These vary from state to state; it is a basic form on which you answer a series of simple questions about your background and your fingerprints are processed through the state criminal justice computer system. Obviously, if you have no record, you have nothing to fear. If you have a record, you need to discuss it with your worker and see if it disqualifies you from the agency or the country.

You'll also need a certified copy of your birth certificate, marriage documents, divorce decrees, name changes, and documents pertaining to home ownership or your rental lease. Additionally, you need three or more letters of reference, a copy of last year's tax return, financial statements (the easiest thing is to request a statement in which your bank or other relevant financial institutions itemize your holdings), a physician's report attesting to your health, and, proof of employment (usually a pay stub accompanied by a letter from your employer acknowledging your salary, years of employment, etc.). If you're self-employed, get your accountant to write you a letter.

When the Home Study has been drafted by your facilitator, it should be given to you for comments and corrections. Remember, addendums cost money; beyond the expected correcting of a few mistakes, it will probably begin to cost you more money if changes are required. Getting it right the first time is the main thing. The worker, depending on initial arrangements you make, will either give you the INS form to file or process it through the agency who arranged things. A reminder: file the I-600A right away because the INS is going to run a thorough FBI check on you and that takes time.

A good idea is to purchase extra legal documents and make multiple copies of everything, especially documents like your birth certificate and fingerprints. When using the mail system, realize that unregistered, uncertified packages may go the way of socks in your laundry. Pay the extra at the post office for services you can trace. Federal Express, UPS, or certified mail costs a little extra but is well worth it. If your destination address is a P.O. Box number, be sure to call and find out the alternative address because most specialized delivery services don't use P.O. boxes and require personal signatures.

Another good idea is to make and keep a notebook. In the notebook, besides keeping a duplicate of all the documents, you can make notes about when you completed each task, people you talked to, possible sources of help or guidance after the adoption, and notes that reflect issues that arise.

The Home Study is a process—it is not something you can do in one weekend. It is completed in chunks of time. This is helpful to keep in mind because you can protect yourself from being overwhelmed. Also, having time lets you reflect on things you might not have thought about or considered. Finally, remember that if the process takes *too* long (i.e., over a year, or there is a significant change in your life circumstances such as marriage, divorce, moving, etc.), you will have to update and renew your information. Updating and renewing information will delay the process and add costs.

Finally, even if your home study worker doesn't require you to do this, create a Family Life Book. The Family Life Book is a scrapbook that contains photos as well as other mementos, drawings, and memories about your family. You can take it with you to parent support meetings before adoption and to the country where you are adopting; it provides others with more insight and information about your family. For the parent, it is a reminder about how you planned for this event in your life. It is also a memento you can give your child when he or she is old enough to appreciate it and understand the adoption.

Having sent in all the relevant paperwork to INS, you wait. Once you have passed your FBI check, your file is complete. You will then receive form I-171H, which will inform you of your current status, making official note of when your I-600A was sent to the American Embassy in Bucharest (or the designated city from which you are adopting).

Reminder: No passport? Get one as fast as possible. Be sure to not wait until the last minute to make arrangements for a visa, either. Some agencies or countries require you to provide proof of a passport before your materials leave the U. S.

Finding Your Child

Now that you've taken the plunge, you should be ready for anything. Having found a reputable agency, filed the appropriate paperwork, been through your Home Study Assessment, and received approval from the INS, you'll have to be patient and wait.

After your home study is completed and you begin the search process of matching a child's needs with your strengths, desires and capabilities, at some point you will receive information about the child identified for your family. *Read carefully. Ask questions. Be prepared that all too very little of the information is going to be accurate.* If you understand some of the social, economic, and political history of the country, you are better armed to cope with the frustrations associated with intercountry adoption.[4] You will be asked to make a decision on adopting based on the information given to you. Some parents feel compelled to accept the child, even if they have some concerns. Discuss any concerns you have with the agency or social worker before you commit. Talk to your pediatrician and other adoptive parents. Before you take the next step, reflect about the decision to parent the identified child. Ask the agency about the consequences if you decide that the child identified for you is not a good match. For some agencies, you will go to the end of the list. For other agencies, they will understand your strengths and concerns better and will look for a different match. For a few agencies, refusal ends the adoption process with that agency. Find out how your agency handles these issues and make your decision. If you make the next step, you will probably travel to the country in which your child is located, from 30 to 90 days after you accept the child (although in some countries it can be 6 months or longer). Take a copy of all your documents with you, including any identifiable information you have on the child. You never know if this information could be needed.

Traveling Abroad To Receive Your Child

Some countries allow children to be escorted to their new adoptive families but most do not. You should be prepared to travel. If you understand the current social, economic, and political conditions of the country, you are better armed to cope. Your agency should be able to help you here. What baby clothes and foods will you need? What types of medications should you bring? How should you dress? Who will help you in-country? How will difficulties in-country be handled?

Talk to other families who have traveled to the same country. They are great sources of information. But also be prepared—in the scope of a few months conditions may have changed, for better or worse, in the place to which you are traveling. Make sure you have an international calling card and access to extra cash.

Once you are in-country, take photos of everything! You never know when or if you will come back, so take advantage of the opportunity. It is better to throw away photos than to regret that you don't have them. Many families regret not having taken more photos. Also, within 48 hours, stop at the American Embassy to let them know you are in the country.

Finally, if the child you are picking up is extremely different than the child identified for you (different gender, much older, more severely handicapped), contact your agency. Proceed with caution. *Please note, this is a rare occurrence!* However, if you find yourself in this situation, do not proceed until you have something in writing that clears up any mistakes. Again, take photos and collect any information you can about the child—you can always get things translated.

At this stage, the agency you are working with should be able to get you successfully through this process. *Remember, most families navigate this phase successfully.* Use your good judgment, be careful, and record your experience. Journals are wonderful tools for helping to keep facts straight, sorting out your experiences, and reflecting on this facet of the experience when you read it at a later date.

After the Child Arrives

For the first month, aside from a medical exam, the best plan is to stay home and get to know your child as well as figure out your new life as an adoptive family. The medical exam is the most important activity because medical information received about children from developing countries is often inaccurate.

In the months after arrival, parents should obtain a complete assessment in order to get accurate information about their child's development. This information is necessary in order to make informed decisions and pursue early intervention programs. Early intervention may not help a child with severe problems become normal, but the techniques can prevent the worsening of any difficulties and enhance the child's ability to develop to the fullest extent of her or his potential.[5]

Since most international adoptees come from institutional settings where their needs were not consistently met, one of the first tasks is for the children to know that they can trust the adults in their lives to respond to their needs upon demand. These children should not be placed in day care immediately after placement. Although having a stay-at-home parent may be an additional burden for many families who have two adults working outside the home, it may be in the best interest of the children to be consistently cared for by specific attachment and family figures as they adjust to family settings initially after placement.

Adoptive parents need to provide structure, consistency, nurturance and love. Most children respond favorably to this type of environment. Any interruption or inconsistency in day-to-day routines may be disruptive to the child.

Parents also need to recognize what they can and cannot change. Children are born with certain characteristics—physical genetic make-up, intellectual capacity, and temperamental make-up. While parents are limited in their ability to change basic personality traits, they do have a major influence on the way children express themselves. Parents need to begin the process of understanding their children and the influence they have on their children. For some parents, this means asking themselves what they expect from their children. When children do not meet their parents' expectations, the parents have several choices. One, the parent can reject the child. Two, the parent can attempt to make the child fit the parent's expectations, which can be frustrating for both the parent and the child as well as put the adoptive placement at risk. Three, the parent can accept the fact that the child will not meet the parent's expectations and change the expectations to match what the child can accomplish. This is a very difficult process, but successful adoptive families are able to temper their expectations.

The addition of a new child to any family is a stressful time. Family members need to find support and guidance from extended family, friends, neighbors, other adoptive parents, and colleagues from their work, church or synagogue.

Adopting a Child from Romania

The following information was obtained from the website on international adoption <http://travel.state.gov/children's_issues.html#adoption>. It is only accurate since the latest update (which was December of 1996, at the time this chapter was written). As such, the following information is subject to change.

The government office responsible for adoptions in Romania is the Romanian Adoption Committee (RAC). The Romanian adoption law that went into effect on June 27, 1995, stipulates the following:

- Adoptions directly from families will no longer be allowed in Romania except in cases of close family relationships. (Children who meet this criteria may not meet the "orphan" definition under U.S. immigration law.)

- All adoptions must be approved by the Romanian Adoption Committee (RAC) and are required to be processed through adoption agencies approved by the RAC.

- The Romanian child must have a certificate from the RAC stating that he or she is adoptable by a foreigner. This means that the child has been in an orphanage for at least six months with no contact from his or her biological parents, and that the orphanage has been unsuccessful in placing the child with a Romanian family. It will be one of the tasks of your adoption agency to obtain this certificate.

- The prospective adoptive parents may not go to an orphanage to select a child. Generally, the RAC will propose a child to be adopted, which the couple may accept if it wishes.

A PEACOCK OR A CROW

In general, prospective adoptive parents must have been married for at least three years, although exceptions may be made, including adoption by single persons. The age difference between child and prospective adoptive parent cannot exceed 35 years for mothers and 40 years for fathers. The adopting couple usually may not already have more than two biological or adopted children. Although in general these rules will be adhered to, occasional exceptions are made, especially to facilitate the adoption of a handicapped child, an older child, or to enable a child to join his or her sibling.

Most courts in Romania ask for the following documents; however, prospective adoptive parents are advised to consult closely with their adoption agency to determine whether to expect additional documentary requirements.

- Birth certificates of the prospective adoptive parents
- Marriage certificate (if applicable)
- Police certificate (same as that used for fulfillment of the U.S. I-600A requirement)
- Home study

The U.S. Embassy maintains current lists of doctors and sources for medicines, should either you or your child experience health problems while in Romania.

Before the adopted child can be issued a visa to enter the U.S., you must provide the following documents:

1. Child's Romanian Passport
2. Photographs of the child
3. Immigrant Visa Application (Form OF-230 I&II)
4. Approved I-600A petition or visa cable
5. I-600 signed by both parents after the child has been identified or by one parent who has seen the child and the other who indicates s/he will readopt the child in the U.S. One U.S. citizen parent must be present in Romania unless the I-600 is approved by INS.
6. Original or certified copies and certified English translations of the following:
   a. final adoption decree, which must state that the natural parent(s) have relinquished all parental rights, and the relinquishment statement signed by the child's natural parent(s) or the abandonment decree
   b. homestudy done by the Romanian authorities regarding the child and its natural parents
   c. birth certificate showing the name(s) of the child's natural parent(s)
   d. new Romanian birth certificate issued to the adopting parent(s)

7. Completed medical form from "Colentina" Hospital. Please note: The medical examination takes three days to complete.

The Embassy recommends that you do not make definite travel arrangements until you have all the required documents, have allowed sufficient time for the medical examination results, and are scheduled for the visa interview. The best advice is to work with an agency that you can trust and that has a good reputation. They will help you through the process.

Final Thoughts

Adoption works for children and families. It can be anxiety-producing, there are many trials and tribulations, there are risks, but there are also many rewards. If there were not more positives then negatives, then there wouldn't be over 10,000 children each year who enter the U. S. through adoption. The best thing you can do is be informed, be prepared, and be ready physically, emotionally, and spiritually to be an adoptive parent.

Recommended Books on International Adoption

Alperson, M. (1997). The international adoption handbook: How to make an overseas adoption work for you. Henry Holt.

Bascom, B. B., & McKelvey, C. A. (1997). The complete guide to foreign adoptions. Pocket Books.

Conroy, M. F. (1998). International adoption sourcebook: What you should know about agencies, countries, policies and more. Birch Lane Press.

Sweet, R. O., & Bryan, P. (1996). Adopt international: Everything you need to know to adopt a child from abroad. Noonday Press.

Tepper, T., & Hannon, L. (Eds.). International adoption: Challenges and opportunities. Pittsburgh: Parent Support Network for the Post Institutionalized Child.

Notes from Chapter 10

[1] Bascom, B. B., & McKelvey, C. A. (1997). The complete guide to foreign adoption: What to expect and how to prepare for your new child. New York: Pocket Books.

[2] Adapted from Groza, V. (1997). International adoption. In R .L. Edwards (Ed.). Encyclopedia of Social Work, 19th Edition, 1997 Supplement (pp.1-14). Washington, DC: NASW press.

[3] Bascom, B. B., & McKelvey, C. A. (1997). <u>The complete guide to foreign adoption: What to expect and how to prepare for your new child</u>. New York: Pocket Books.

[4] See Bascom, B. B., & McKelvey, C. A. (1997). <u>The complete guide to foreign adoption: What to expect and how to prepare for your new child</u>. New York: Pocket Books.

[5] Kenny, T. J., & Culberston, J. L. (1993). Developmental screening for preschoolers. In J. L. Culberston & D. J. Willis (Eds.), <u>Testing young children: A reference guide for developmental, psychoeducational, and psychosocial assessments</u>. (pp. 73-100). Austin, TX: Pro-Ed.

Groza, V. (1997). International adoption. In R .L. Edwards (Ed.). <u>Encyclopedia of Social Work, 19th Edition, 1997 Supplement</u> (pp.1-14). Washington, DC: NASW press.

Chapter 11

Lessons Learned

The following questions and brief answers summarize much of what we learned. These questions are the ones we are most frequently asked.

What happened in Romania that so many children were in institutions?

Keep in mind that most Romanian children were not in institutions—less than 1% of the children ended up in institutions. However, about 100,000 children were institutionalized when the world became aware of these children. The problem started with short-sighted family policies designed to increase the population by restricting access to birth control and abortions, as well as by increasing rewards for having many children. These policies included a propaganda campaign about the citizen's obligation to the state and a denial of problems by the communist political machine. It resulted in too many children, too few supports for families, and the building of warehouses for children who were abandoned by families.

Were the images of institutions in Romania accurate?

There was a three-level system of institutions. The media showed the worse tier—and those images were accurate. They were horrible. However, there were other institutions that were better, although by no means would they be considered acceptable by most Western standards.

Are the institutions still as bad as they were?

Institutions are no place to grow up. Even when they are well-staffed and supplied, they can never substitute for a family. In Romania, the institutions have improved physically—most have running water and are in better physical shape. However, there are still too few staff. This staff still does not have the training and skills it needs to help the children grow and develop. Remember, better doesn't mean good—the institutions are now more similar to other developing countries (for example, in many countries of South America) but would not meet the standards of most developed countries (for example, the United States or Western Europe).

What has the United States done to help Romania?

The United States Agency for International Development (USAID) has provided grants and funded projects in Romania since 1990. Most of the effort has gone towards economic development. Between 1994 and 1997, few projects focusing on children, health or other areas of social development were funded because it did not seem that the Romania government was making an effort to change. In 1996, a new president was elected, and, in 1997, USAID expressed confidence in this new government by funding projects or developing plans for projects in the areas of children's issues, health, domestic violence, and other social issues. Aside from this federal funding, many private organizations and individuals donated money, time and material resources to help Romania improve its child welfare system. While few of these start-up organizations are still active, they have, nevertheless, done a lot to help a very poor country move forward in its development.

What is the view of the Romanian people towards out of country adoption?

Many Romanians clearly recognize that a family is better than an institution. Consequently, until they can have enough families to care for their own children, intercountry adoption can help children who need families. Still, a large group of Romanians see international adoption as cultural genocide—they believe they are losing a generation of children, who, as adults, will have no identification or close ties to Romania. There are some who believe the institutions are more than adequate for children. Fortunately, these are becoming fewer in number.

If I adopt from overseas, how do I prepare for the trip home?

Take plenty of juice, butter crackers, diapers, formula, bottles, books, toys, etc. Do not assume that you can purchase these items abroad. The object is to keep the child as occupied and happy as possible. Don't try to be corrective. Nonetheless, it will still be an arduous trip for you both. Be as well rested as possible.

What behaviors could we expect our child to exhibit in our home?

Parents report a range of behaviors—from shock where children seem introvertive and lethargic, to children being too outgoing and over-friendly, to aggressive behavior such as hitting and biting. Some children are very clingy while others seem aloof and disengaged. Many parents report self-stimulating behaviors such as rocking, which decrease over time and only re-appear when there are changes in the daily routine or the child is under stress. Understanding your child's daily routine before placement, and trying to replicate it during the first weeks or months after placement, may help in the transition and help you understand what the child is expecting from you. Children exhibit a range of behaviors—it is important to get both support and guidance during this transition as well as early assessment and intervention for your child.

Overall, how are the adoptees doing?

Contrary to all the negative media hype, most of the adoptees are doing well. They are making developmental progress, many are catching up, and families are very positive about their experiences. About 20%

of the children have profound or continual difficulties, requiring a great deal of help from many different service systems (education, health, occupational therapy, etc.). These children place many strains on the families who are caring for them.

Are the Romanian children making adjustments to their new families?

Most children are doing very well. For the children who were obviously delayed at placement, most are progressing well—catching up in some areas and excelling in other areas.

Are the families making adjustments to their demands?

Most families are able to make the changes necessary to meet their children's needs. Any time a child enters into a family, there is an adjustment period. For some families, this is the first opportunity to parent. They are anxious because they want to be perfect parents. Like all parents, they will make some mistakes but overall can adjust to the demands on parents. For other families, they have expanded their families through adoption. Adoption is different than having a child born into the family—some demands are the same and others are different. Families who can accept and deal with the differences seem to fare the best.

What happens to the kids who have severe problems?

Many families who adopted children with severe problems had little preparation before adopting special needs children. Most families have managed to care for these children, although it has been very stressful for them. Some families disrupted the adoption—that is, they went to court and gave legal custody to the state in which they live. We have no official estimates, but disruption rates for adoption of older and special needs children born in the U. S. are low—less that 15%. It is reasonable to expect that the disruption in international adoption was even less, since these children were much younger at placement and we have ample research to show that rates of disruption increase with age. The least disruptions are for children placed as infants and toddlers (less than 1%). The children with severe problems posed many challenges for families—finding the appropriate types of services and finding help that worked. Parent support groups have been formed as a result of parents struggling alone to help families find services or service providers. These children require a great deal of time, commitment, and perseverance.

A PEACOCK OR A CROW

What kinds of treatments are being offered for these families and kids who experience severe problems and what are the families' perceptions of these treatments?

One treatment that many families reported to be helpful came from occupational therapists specially trained to work with sensory disorders. Children with problems in sensory integration have difficulties involving the way information from the senses is processed by the brain. Many families reported that sensory integration treatment was helpful to their children.

Families who were well-prepared for their adoptions also obtained early intervention services. Early intervention may not help a child with severe problems become normal, but there are many positive effects from early intervention. This includes supporting families as they try to understand their children, helping families provide the appropriate environment for their children's level of functioning, preventing the worsening of difficulties, and enhancing their children's ability to develop to the fullest extent of their potential.

Families have also tried other types of treatment—medication, psychological counseling, attachment therapy—all with varying degrees of success. Sometimes the treatment helps, sometimes it does not. Often, it will help for a short time and then not help—so they look for other services. Trying to find services and understanding what services are effective remains a challenge to parents and professionals.

Would these families do it again if they had a choice?

Clearly, yes! Most families evaluate the impact of the adoption positively on their family and most never think of ending the adoption. These are very stable and successful adoptions.

Can I believe the medical information they give me about my child?

Often, the information is not accurate. Information about your child may not have been gathered properly, or else information about health, development, and living conditions may have been ignored in order to facilitate an overseas placement. Thus, the information received about children from developing countries can be inaccurate. The training of professionals in modern child development assessment, disabilities, and diagnosis is woefully lacking and substandard in many parts of the world. Medical testing information, although better in U.S. embassies, is still problematic.

As much information as possible from the country of origin should be obtained before placement. However, families should get a complete medical assessment by qualified U.S. medical personnel once the child is placed in the United States. Accurate and comprehensive information at the time of placement can be used to plan medical follow-ups in the future. At the very least, it gives parents peace of mind about the health of their children.

At what age is it no longer reasonable to expect that a child will do well in an adoptive family?

The length of time the child has been institutionalized and the age of the child when institutionalized have significant effects on behavior, health, and development. In particular, institutionalization between the ages 7-12 months is particularly problematic. Children seem to do better if they spent the first year of life in a family. Children institutionalized continuously from birth and adopted after the age of three seem to have the most difficulties, although most children are negatively affected by early institutionalization. However, most children adopted before the age of three seem to fare well and recover from the trauma.

What kind of support systems are available to me and my family after our return?

Families get most of their support from other family members and friends. It is a good idea to carefully review with your adoption agency what help they will give you after you return. Make sure that the understanding is explicit and clear—having it in writing helps. The best support for families are adoptive parent support groups and adoption support groups for children. If you do not have one in your community, start one. More than any agency or professional, support groups are the best assistance an adoptive family can have in their life.

We have no other children, are we getting in "over our heads" because we have no experience as parents?

Parenting is difficult, whether you have a typical child or a child with special needs. Examine your heart, and think about dreams and desires—*if* you can make a commitment to a child, regardless of what a child brings to your family, then adoption may be for you. After commitment comes patience. Finally, there are parenting skills. If you don't have them, you can learn them. Parenting a child with special needs requires special skills and talents. Your adoption agency and other parents who have special needs children in their homes may help you gain and improve these skills.

We have other children, what kind of adjustment challenges can we anticipate?

Most children seem to adjust with the addition of other children in the family. Parenting a child who is adopted has some differences from parenting a child born into your family. The child's life began before you knew him or her, and there may be many gaps in understanding for you when it comes to learning the history and truth of your child's early experiences. Learning to deal with differences is a major struggle of any parent. What has worked for one child, may not work for another child. Dealing with differences is one of the biggest adjustments that families must make. It requires patience, creativity, and fortitude.

A PEACOCK OR A CROW

What, if any, characteristics do families have who are coping well with their children have in common?

Success in adoption depends on several factors. First, families who develop informal networks of family, neighbors, friends, other adoptive families, and associates who give them consistent, positive support for the adoption are almost always successful. Two, having access to appropriate, easily accessible and affordable social services positively affects the adoption, also. Three, parents need to be flexible in their expectations of their child—the ability to change your expectations to match the capabilities of the child you adopt is critically important. Finally, creativity and flexibility in family functioning is important. Parents who are patient can wait for rewards from parenting, can let the child develop and change within the child's own time frame, and can alter the way they discipline the child strengthen the adoptive family.

What can/should agencies do to avoid disruption or decrease difficulties in placements?

First, parents need to have pre-adoption training and access to complete information so they can make the best decision. No attempt should be made to dilute the information available—a family must be able to evaluate the risks as well as the benefits in international adoption. Second, families need support after placement. Adoption is a life-long process. Issues will emerge for children and families at different points in the children's development and in the life of the families. If the families have a place to turn to for help when they are having difficulties, and if they can get the assistance they need—whether it is medical evaluation, educational testing, or behavior management techniques—we can decrease disruptions and difficulties in placements.

What efforts are being made to encourage adoption by Romanian citizens?

For many Romanians, there are real economic barriers to adoption. There are families who might give an abandoned child a home, and families who would like to keep their children, but the transition to a market economy is very hard on families. As Romania develops a middle class, which may take a generation or more, you will see increases in domestic adoption. There are adoptions occurring in Romania, but relatively few compared to the number of children needing families. Most of the adoptive placements of Romanian children in Romanian families are the result of efforts from private nonprofit agencies working in-country.

Any other advice?

We would be remiss if we did not mention that there are thousands of children in the United States also waiting for permanent families. These children are not healthy babies—they are older, have histories of abuse and neglect, are members of sibling groups—children with special medical, emotional and behavioral needs. Unlike adopting from overseas, most of these children have adoption subsidies to help families provide for their special needs. If you or someone you know can open up their hearts and homes to one of these children, please contact your local Department of Human Services or Child Welfare Agency. Adoption, even with the many trials and tribulations, works and offers many children the opportunity to heal from the past and to have a future.

Epilogue: The Road to Hell Is...

Paved with Good Intentions

As the book goes to press, there are other changes in Romania that offer hope as well as cause for concern. In June, 1997, the Romanian Parliament passed ordinances related to the protection of children and adoption. These laws provide the base for a major reform in child welfare. In particular, the laws promote decentralization of decision-making from the various ministries to the 41 county councils (judets) in Romania and the six sector councils in Bucharest. The responsibility, authority and funding for the protection of children has been transferred to these councils. Child institutions are now under the administration of local councils, instead of under various national ministries.

The reaction is mixed about the changes, which have yet to be realized and be moved from policy to implementation. Some child welfare experts believe that the decentralization will allow more community involvement in child welfare, better collaboration between the councils and the growing nonprofit (nongovernmental) sector, as well as local solutions and initiatives concerning child welfare. Other experts fear that this will lead to more inequity and inefficiency in services, inconsistency of standards, and competition rather than collaboration. Quite frankly, though, it is difficult to imagine a more inefficient system than the one which existed under communism and immediately afterwards.

As part of this new initiative, this legislation recommends the transformation of institutions into group homes, day care centers, and shelters for mothers and children. However, the laws don't close these facilities or restrict the admission of children to them—in essence, there is no mandate to stop them from continuing as the dumping ground for abandoned children. The new legislation also does not specify how to begin the transformation of the old institutions, although progress starts with having a vision for an alternative to institutionalizing children. At this point, Romania has neither the expertise nor the resources to make this transition. To be successful in this endeavor, Romania needs to develop the community services needed to strengthen and support families. They also need to develop foster care. However, as Social Work Consultant William Saur[1] points out in his report to the United States Agency for International Development in Romania, the presence of community services will not assure a decrease in institutionalization given the current mindset and structure of the system. He clearly suggests that to decrease the number of children entering institutions, you must close them. There must also be credentialed or licensed, professional, and paraprofessional staff who are trained and hired to work as child welfare workers in family preservation, family support, foster care, adoption, and as child care providers for children in group care.

There are still many other issues that need to be addressed. It is not clear how the institutions not involved in child protection—the "special schools" for handicapped children, long-term medical care facilities, or juvenile detention and residential programs—are to be affected by the intent of the child welfare changes. Given the fact that up to one-third of the children are probably misdiagnosed as handicapped, a significant proportion of this group could live in communities with good family and individual support. It is not clear what will happen to these children or institutions.

Lined with Gold

While it is clear that international adoption has a role to play as Romania develops its child welfare system, the role is not clearly defined. As part of this issue, we also should be concerned about the costs in international adoptions. International adoptions range from $8,000 to $25,000. This is a pretty wide variation in costs for different agencies in the same country. While the exact reason for this discrepancy is not known, it should be of concern that it exists. There are several possible reasons. It seems that the more desperate the family (which often means the individual adopting is single, the couple adopting is older, or there has been a long waiting period), the higher the costs. Also, international adoptions are profitable. This has allowed unscrupulous individuals and agencies to prey on naive or unsuspecting potential adoptive parents. For example, some families have paid fees and acquired children through medical visas. The stipulation for this type of arrangement is that once a child's medical needs are met, he or she is to be returned to the country of origin. Some families have been traumatized because they did not understand the agreement, and, having spent a great deal of money for the placement and medical care for their children, they thought they had legal and clear adoptions. In other instances, families continue to pay fees to agencies or individuals who have no legal authority to conduct international adoptions to keep their cases "pending."

When a family pays a fee for adoption, the emphasis is on finding a child for a family (parent-centered) and not a family for a child (child-centered). Contemporary adoption practice has moved to a child-centered model because it is in the best interest of the child. The fee-for-service arrangement undermines this philosophy and often results in compromised adoption practices. A worldwide plan for oversight into costs and regulation of fees and practices in international adoptions, perhaps overseen by the United Nations, is overdue.

Similar to the inner city neighborhoods in the United States, Romania needs economic development. Simply put, if people have jobs, they are more likely to keep their children. It also decreases their risk for many of the social ills that come with poverty—crime, substance abuse, violence, hopelessness. However, economic development must be tied to social development and a social conscience if it is going to have the effects desired— strengthening families and offering abandoned children a permanent home. This is a complicated issue that developed countries have not figured out, but must be part of the social agenda if Romania is going to be a better place for many at-risk children.

Notes from Epilogue

---

[1] Saur, W. G. (1997, September). <u>An appendum to the proposed strategy for a child welfare initiative in Romania</u>. Presented to USAID, Romania.

Afterwards: When Three Paths Crossed

The Journey by Victor Groza

My father's parents emigrated from Romania in the early 1900's, separately. While they both came from Transylvania, my grandfather came from a town near Cluj and my grandmother came from a village near Oradea. They met and were married in the U.S., finally settling in a village of about 3000 people in New Jersey named Roebling. I was raised in this little town with many others who had similar backgrounds—children and grandchildren of immigrants from Eastern Europe. While I was baptized Romanian Orthodox, I was raised in a Methodist Church. The Orthodox Church in my town conducted services in Romanian, a language my mother didn't understand. Nevertheless, from growing up in this community and being so close to my Dad's family, I always had something of an identity as a Romanian-American—an identity which has developed more strongly since my first experience in Romania in 1991.

Growing up, I didn't think much about being Romanian, although if anyone ever asked about my name I would tell them it was Romanian, that it was changed, that I was named after my uncle, etc. My mother wasn't Romanian, but was "adopted" by my father's family. In my village, the Romanian ties were so strong that we had both Romanian Orthodox and Romanian Byzatine Churches as well as a Romanian Social Hall. I grew up knowing the cuss words, the names of foods, the major orthodox holidays, stories from the countryside of my ancestors—I didn't know that my life would take me down a path that would lead to working in Romania and result in a personal search.

I saw the images of Romanian children in the fall of 1990 on a national news program. I can still remember those images so clearly—children herded into cages, sitting naked on little toilets, splashing urine which was all around their feet, and eating some type of mashed food from bowls and from remnants that were splashed on each other's head and bodies. I wanted to go to help. I called the National Resource Center for Special Needs Adoption and talked to the Director, telling her I was willing to go to Romania if anyone called her and wanted to know of any professionals willing to help. I told the Director that I could conduct child assessments, give advice on programming, conduct training—whatever was needed to help. The next week I got a call from the Rocky Mountain Adoption Exchange, which was trying to provide technical assistance to the Ministry for the Handicapped. They were *not* an adoption agency trying to place children from Romania into American families. They were, and continue to be, a resource and information agency. After meeting with them in Denver and providing some training, I was asked to work with them as a volunteer the following summer.

A PEACOCK OR A CROW

I called my grandmother to tell her. She was happy that I was going to the Motherland. As I think back to this first conversation with her, those words touched something in me that is hard to explain. In some way I felt like I was heading forth into what was more than just an adventure and an attempt to be helpful.

I went to Romania for the first time in the summer of 1991. I started writing, at least in my head, about my experiences working in Romania on a plane returning to the United States from Bucharest in July of 1991. If this was my motherland, then children were being ripped away from their mothers. To my left was a couple from Virginia, who had finished the adoption process in Romania at 4 p.m. the day before the flight. They had a three-month-old daughter. To my right sat another couple. I heard them say this was their second child from Romania. Throughout the cabin were four other babies and several couples who had adoptable children identified but who had had to leave the babies behind. I had just finished my first project. I had led a team of social workers to Romania for about five weeks, assessing orphaned and abandoned children. This assessment was done at one of the many "Institutions for the Irrecoverable." At the end of the project, we reported to the Ministry for the Handicapped and our sponsors (the Rocky Mountain Adoption Exchange) that the children we had examined (all of the three to six year olds at this institute) were below the appropriate weight and height and were grossly developmentally delayed. These problems were the result of years of neglect, poor nutrition, and lack of stimulation—altogether the features were what I learned was termed "institutional dwarfism."

While these children were behind in their development, they showed a great potential for learning—they needed to be stimulated and taught. We made recommendations about how to help the children develop. We recognized that few new resources (money, materials, or staff) would come to the institution, and we had to focus on something that would bring some immediate results. We built on strengths and skills already present in the employees—they all knew how to sing. We encouraged the administration to set aside one hour each day when all the children and staff would get together to sing nursery rhymes. It was a simple change, but we knew that it could help children develop language skills. Children need to hear sounds repeated again and again to start mimicking the sounds. Indeed, when we returned the next year, they still had an hour a day set aside for singing but also had other help from Irish volunteers who were there.

During the first year, we saw hundreds of people pursuing or possessing Romanian "orphans" for adoption. It wasn't unusual to enter the Inter-Continental Romanian Hotel or the restaurants frequented by foreigners in Bucharest and see foreigners "parading" their children. The longer I stayed, the more I heard, and the more I saw, the more upset I became. Some of the families were better off purchasing a pet—they didn't want a child and the trials, tribulations, hopes, fears, joys, and anxieties of parenting. They wanted a trophy—something they could be proud of and show off to their friends.

Don't get me wrong. Of course I believe a child should live and grow in a family rather than in an institution. But some of these "nice" people were essentially racist and exploiting the poverty and chaos of Romania. They were not running to Africa—they came to Romania for the white or near-white babies. These babies and toddlers brought the image of Gerber babies to their minds. I heard families say that they first looked at the skin tone of the child offered to them to make sure he or she wasn't too dark. Once the child had passed the race-litmus test, families would gather more information about their backgrounds and make a decision as to whether they wanted to pursue the child for adoption. In many ways, this process made me ashamed that families were so shallow. I had to remind myself that most families really cared about the children and were not only (or solely) motivated by race or cheap adoptions. Nevertheless, when you listened to the stories, you could not help but think there was an inconsistency in what they said and what they did.

Perhaps I am too harsh, but others are too naive. There is no mistaking that the child welfare "system" and child institutions in Romania were horrible. Who could not be moved by the media portrayal of the inhumane conditions of Romania's orphaned and abandoned children? But, the media and the common perception blurred two distinct issues. One issue was the plight of children in institutions and orphanages. The other was the issue of adopting infants and toddlers, a substantial number that were neither orphaned or abandoned because they still had parents—they were children coming from families that were too poor to care for them or were children who needed special care. Over time, as more families came to Romania, instead of the children in institutions, who needed families, being adopted, some adoptive families went to poor families and villages in order to procure children.

Let me be clear, this was not the majority of families. Many good-hearted families were moved by their emotions and the images from television, newspapers, and magazines. They had no idea about the effects of poverty and malnutrition, or how institutionalization and the lack of stimulation affected growth and development in children. They would look at a baby or toddler, perhaps from an institution or a poor family, and sometimes be forced to make a decision on the spot without knowledge or careful consideration. My experiences during this first year left me with many mixed emotions about Americans in general, the process of international adoption, what I could do or should do to help, and about hindering Romanians who were profiting from this market in children.

During this first trip, I lived in one of the bottom-tiered institutions. While I was there, a moratorium was placed on adoptions. Starting in July, 1991, and through the next few years, Romanian adoptions all but stopped. While adoption ceased, I continued to work in child welfare in Romania, concentrating my efforts during the summer when I was free from my nine-month academic job. Every year since 1991 I have returned for a project, taking graduate students with me.

A PEACOCK OR A CROW

Back in the United States, around 1993, I began to hear reports that the children from Romania were not doing well and that some families had given up their children to the U. S. public child welfare system. Having seen the conditions from which children were adopted, it was believable that there would be problems. On the other hand, I know about both the healing power of adoptive families and the parallel powers of the media, rumors and exaggerations of problems. I also had previous work and research experience with older and special needs children in the U. S.. These experiences led me to believe that most of the Romanian adoptions were probably progressing well. To try to understand what, if anything, was happening, I initiated the study, which resulted in the foundation for this book. I was joined in this endeavor by one of my graduate students at that time, Daniela Ileana. Daniela became the co-leader for several teams of social work students who traveled with me to Romania in 1994 and 1995. As a Romanian-American, emigrating at the age of 14 and having the advantage of speaking Romanian, her assistance was extremely valuable.

Subsequent to working on a book about the results, a woman that I had met on the plane to Bucharest in 1992, Tina Leto, read a draft of the book and said it needed a writer, not an academic. Tina said I should talk to Ivor Irwin—a Romanian Jew who was a writer. So, I did. He read the manuscript. I think he or Tina said it "read like oatmeal." I hate oatmeal! So, in 1996 Ivor, after the first draft of the book was completed but a contract was unsigned, began the process of rewriting and adding to the study by conducting interviews with families and with Romanians who knew about child welfare.

My experiences in Romania and writing the book changed me. I have searched for the villages of my grandparents and for family members who are still there. I haven't had much luck, but I continue looking. I took back the original spelling of my name—Groza (you'll read references with the old spelling, Groze). I have taken language lessons since 1992. When I have time, I try to write to my friends in Romanian. I have read most of the books published in English about Romania and Romanian figures. I have surrounded my office with Romanian artifacts and books. My desire to help led me to a personal transformation. It was more than just wanting to help, which is a transforming experience in and of itself. Something spiritual, almost mystical happened to me. It is hard to describe now as I write this afterward, but in some ways I feel that I have found another place to call home. Maybe it is the same for any person—all of us want to belong—and Romania, for me, has made me feel that I am part of a community. Traveling to Romania has made me understand better the concept of male privilege. It has made me deal with my strengths and deficits. Going to Romania every year for a few weeks renews me. So, it is as my grandmother said—I have gone back to the motherland. And it is here that I am refreshed and challenged to think differently about my life and the lives of others, particularly the children.

Personal and Professional Reflections by Daniela Ileana

It was the spring of 1981 and my twin brother, Dan, and I were enjoying an afternoon of play when my mother called us into her bedroom to ask us a question. I'm not sure where Stely, my older brother, was—chances are that he was out somewhere playing soccer. It was a Sunday afternoon and strangely enough we were at home. We were never home on Sunday afternoons. We were always at church. I thought my parents had asked us to come because we did something wrong, broke something or stayed out too late, which we did often. Dan and I loved playing outside with all the neighborhood kids. It turned out that we didn't do anything wrong that day; my parents had asked us in to ask us a very important question: "How would you like it if we moved to America?" Wow! What a question for a regular Sunday afternoon! I remember asking my mom if I could have a new bike and plenty of chewing gum once we moved there and she said yes; at the time that's all I cared about. I was 12 years old. The events that happened in the next few months and two years thereafter were more dramatic and have affected my entire life.

I remember distinctly that Stely did not want to be a part of our decision to leave the country. He had just turned 18 years old in April of that year, was a senior in high school, and had a very active social life. He had many friends and lacked very little. He was very adamant about not leaving, but my parents applied for permanent family immigration anyway. My grandmother, Maica (Elisabeta), joined Stely in his decision. She was in her early 70's and was not about to leave the country where she was born, grew up, raised her family, and was now helping raise her grandchildren. She had another son living in Romania who had two sons, plus, with Romania being communist then, she never did believe that we would actually be allowed to leave. It took years for someone to be approved to leave. She probably figured that's all she had left to live for anyway.

My family was of middle-upper-class status. We lived in our own house, which my parents built themselves when Dan and I were born. Stely was six years old by then and was happy to have two new siblings to play with. We were as happy as we could be living in a communist country where freedom did not exist and people got by on pretending most of the time. There were secret police agents everywhere. Their uniforms were a dark navy color and they wore berets; they were also civilians, making up probably nearly half of the population. Trust was not a value known about or taught to us. Instead, we were taught not to trust anyone, to be suspicious and paranoid—don't tell anyone anything! My parents both worked full-time and they tried to alternate shifts at work so that one of them was always home with us. My grandmother also lived with us and helped out. Maica was my father's mother. She was absolutely wonderful, loving and funny. I will love and miss her always! We took vacations every summer; we owned a car and we used to drive all over the country, always ending up at the Black Sea resorts. We used to camp and visit all sorts of historical sights and monasteries, castles, and then spend days by the sea. How I loved those vacations. They were long and so much fun!

A PEACOCK OR A CROW

My life was very busy growing up in Romania. We went to church every Sunday and Friday. Dan and I were in the orchestra, so that took two evenings of our week as well. We were also enrolled in the Arts and Music school, which meant piano lessons after class at least twice a week. I almost forgot, we did not have the so-called "weekend" in Romania, so school and work was Monday through Saturday, six days a week. We seldom visited with our relatives—there wasn't much time for that. My mother's mom, Onita, lived one block away so we visited her more frequently than anybody else in our extended family. So this was basically my life there. The one thing that was wonderful was the freedom to play without being worried about being shot down by a gang member or kidnapped. These things just did not happen. Growing up, I spent very little time watching television.

When we went back to school in the fall of 1981, I had a hard time with my math class, such a hard time in fact that I failed that quarter. The next quarter, which started in the winter, was just as hard and I was struggling with the same subject. I knew if I failed that quarter too, I had to repeat the whole year, even though I would have only failed in one subject out of twelve. The stress was unbearable. I couldn't put my family through that embarrassment—only poor people failed. All the rich kids had private tutors; we weren't poor, therefore I couldn't fail. What was I going to do? This whole time I did not tell my parents what was going on. They thought everything was fine. My point average was always high since I got great grades in everything else. Well, then came the day for the big exam of the quarter, Teza. This exam was the determining factor in passing the math class if all my grades were poor the rest of the semester. I tried to study so hard for it but I just didn't get it! The night before, I tossed and tossed and could not sleep at all due to worry—worry that I would fail and worry that I would embarrass my family. I finally fell asleep close to the time I had to get up.

My parents were both at work that morning and my grandmother was helping to get us up and out the door. I don't remember much of that morning except waking up, and then waking up again but this time crying and feeling a lot of pain. My brothers and my grandmother were standing over me with panic, shock and confusion on their faces. I had suffered my first epileptic seizure. All other seizures that I have had in my life thereafter followed the same pattern, occurring in the early morning, following a sleepless night caused by worry due to an important event coming up the next day. My parents took me to see an old friend of my father's. She was a neuropsychiatrist. I remember going to her office, which was on the other side of town, Aradul Nou. My mother cried the entire way and when we got there we listened and listened. None of it made sense to me, and she couldn't really give us a cause for this illness. She prescribed some medication for me, which was supposed to keep me from having any more seizures. She recommended that I refrain from any physical activity since becoming too tired might trigger a seizure. This was awful. I had taken gymnastics since I was four years old. I used to ride my bike all the time. I was constantly running around and climbing trees, rooftops, playing—and now she tells me this? Well, like with everything else in a communist country, I had no choice but to accept it. The medication made me really tired and depressed. I lost most of the interest in things I used to like to do.

It was sometime during the spring of 1983 that the doctor recommended to my parents that I go to a psychiatric hospital in Bucharest. My parents agreed to it. They were going to agree with anything that was going to make me better, plus it was in Bucharest, Romania's capital; it had to be the best! I remember when I first got there, the old hospital was surrounded by black iron gates. It had many beautiful gardens but there was no one walking around. My parents dropped me off and left. They couldn't really stay and visit. Besides, they had to take the train back to Arad, our hometown, about 400 miles away. My room was on the second floor. The whole floor housed teenage females. There were ten young girls in my room, all suffering from some sort of seizure disorder. The first day I got there, the nurse administered the Rorschach test. I don't remember much else from my stay there. I don't remember where I ate, bathed, or did anything else. I remember my room but not much of what we did during the day. I do remember one room, larger than the one I slept in, where we used to meet with the doctor, a psychiatrist.

I remember one morning, one of the girls had a seizure and she became incontinent. The doctor became furious with her as she soiled the bed sheets and he ordered two of the orderlies to put her in a straitjacket and shave her head bald to teach her a lesson. We all had the straitjacket on at one point for one reason or another.

The institution had dark cement floors. The windows were covered with heavy drapes. There were iron rods put in each window, probably to prevent us from running away. I wish I could remember more of our daily routine. I only remember pieces. I remember my first doctor's visit. It was in his office, located on the same floor as my room. He was an older guy, all wrinkled up. I still don't know what was the purpose of that visit. I know that he asked me to take off all of my clothes because he had to give me a physical exam. He never did give me a physical exam. He asked me to walk all round the room and around his desk. The floor was made up of cement—my feet were so cold and my whole body was shivering with cold, fear, and a feeling of shame. I didn't say anything. What could I have said? Who would have believed me? When my parents came to visit me a week later, they were not allowed to come into the hospital. We stayed outside and ate fried chicken that they had brought from home. They didn't ask me any questions and I didn't tell them anything. They told me that they missed me and loved me and that I was going to get better soon. This was so hard for me to understand because I didn't know what was wrong with me. No one sat down and explained it to me. Everybody was working hard at covering it up—having epilepsy was a stigma for the family.

I remember one afternoon I went to the restroom. On my way there, I felt like I was going to have a seizure and I remember calling for help. The nurses at the nurses' station were laughing at me. The next thing that happened, I fell down the staircase all the way to the first floor. It was the longest fall down an old spiral staircase. When I came to, I was all bruised and my tongue was severely bitten from the seizure and the fall. I went back upstairs without saying anything, pretending nothing happened. The next day I had a spinal tap, the first of many during my short stay there. That's about all I remember from my entire stay.

My parents came and took me home one day. We got the visa from the American government and had passports now instead of Romanian legal papers. I was no longer entitled to receive treatment from the Romanian government. When I got home, every morning when I woke up and tried to walk, I would collapse, having no feeling in my legs. The feeling and strength would always come back in about 15 minutes, though. I'll never know what caused that—maybe too many experimental drugs? My mom had a friend who worked at a pharmacy, and she gave my mom some of the medications I used to take before. Apparently the ones I was taking now were making me sick and causing the weird effect of me losing feeling in my legs. I remember my dad collecting me from the floor every morning and taking me to the bathroom and back to bed. I was 14-years-old, so it was embarrassing, humbling. Once I quit taking those medications and went back to my old ones, I began feeling better, although I still had occasional seizures.

In January 1982, my brother, Stely didn't come home one night. Nor did he call. This was not like him. I mean, he was always running around doing things, playing soccer, but he always called. My parents were trying not to think of the worst case scenario, but the inevitable letter came the next day. My uncle came over late in the evening and delivered a letter to my parents. In the letter Stely (who was about 21 at this time) explained that he had to leave for many reasons—the lack of freedom but most of all, he said: "if I have to wash toilets for the rest of my life, I don't mind, I need to get Dana (Short for Daniela) out of this country so she can get better treatment." This was a shock for my parents who considered him dead immediately. Stely and my cousin Nelu had decided to try to escape across the Romanian and Yugoslavian borders. This was a risk of a lifetime; most times, if caught, the person was shot to death. If not shot, the person would be imprisoned and tortured so much that one would have almost been better off shot. You see, this was the ultimate crime in Romania—the betrayal of one's country. We heard nothing from Stely or my cousin for two weeks. Then, we got word through a friend of the family that both Stely and Nelu were in refugee camps in Yugoslavia. This was not a comforting thought, but at least we knew they were alive. Stely ended up going to Germany and living there for almost two years. In fact, he arrived in the United States in November, 1983, two months later than us, even though he left the country a year and a half before us. Dan, my parents, and myself, arrived in Cleveland, Ohio, on September 23rd, 1983, after spending nine days in Rome, Italy for further medical examinations and waiting for our turn to take the plane to America. The day we were reunited with Stely was the most glorious one and the saddest one. We all knew that from that day forward, it would be just the five of us—no more extended family, no more loving grandmothers, no more close friends like we'd had growing up. We would have to develop new friendships here with other Romanians and could only hope.

When we moved to our first apartment, two weeks after our arrival, the first thing that my dad said was: "I want to go back." Unfortunately, that was not a choice for him anymore. We all came here with passports that read, "Stateless"—meaning without a citizenship. The Romanians took that right of ours when we left. It was one more way for them to punish us for leaving the country. Upon our arrival we stayed with some friends of ours, the family that sponsored us. When we moved to our first apartment, we suffered a culture shock. The apartment building was located on West 64th and Detroit. On the entrance door, there was a sign reading: "Beware of criminals." The glass making up the door had a few bullet holes in it to reinforce the sign. We lived on the third floor. We had no furniture, so we started hunting for mattresses and other household goods in the suburbs on garbage days. The Romanians already living here were helpful enough to tell us when these great events took place. Some people from church were kind enough to donate some of their old furniture. We made a home with what we had. For the first time in our lives, we were so poor! When we woke up in the morning there were roaches in the cereal boxes, in the linen closet, everywhere. I'd never seen roaches before. Soon, we bought a house and this helped change things a little bit. We had a beautiful house, not far from the apartment building, but at least it was clean, safe, and *ours*! We got some new furniture and we all got our own rooms. My parents were working very hard then. My dad was working 70 hours per week in a factory and my mom had two jobs, a full-time job in a sweatshop and a part-time job cleaning offices.

In 1987, both Dan and I started college. We attended Cleveland State University. Dan was majoring in psychology and I was studying social work. This was hard for my parents as they had to come up with tuition for two of us. They never regretted it. As I was saying, I was studying social work. Why that? Well, when I was 14 years old and we came to America, as soon as we had health insurance, I went to see a neurologist, not a psychiatrist. The first thing that the doctor did was take me off Haldol, which should have never been prescribed to me in the first place as it is an anti-psychotic medication. He also reduced my Phenobarbital by 30 mg. My mind cleared a lot then. I felt like I had spent the past year in a deep sleep.

At my six-month follow-up appointment, my doctor introduced me to a young woman, a social work intern. He referred me to her. I had no clue as to what he was talking about—social work? Her name was Debbie and, apparently, she was doing her clinical placement at Metro Hospital in Cleveland. My doctor recommended that I see Debbie on a regular basis to help me with my adjustment to this country and other issues. Once again, I had no idea what he was talking about—therapy? Adjustment problems? I was so used to going along with everything in Romania that I never stopped and questioned him. All I know is that the more I saw Debbie, the more I loved social work. I used to listen to her explain to me client's rights, the principle of confidentiality, the right to refuse treatment, the right to an advocate—oh, how I loved those sessions! Social work became my love, my passion. This was back in 1984 and to this day I still feel the same way about my profession. This was everything Romania didn't have anywhere, most especially in hospitals and other institutions. I never knew anything about self-worth and positive regard. I never knew any other feelings than sad or happy. Debbie was only in my life for six months and then she went back home, but her kindness and her kindred spirit will be with me always. She was my inspiration.

In January, 1994, after completing my Bachelor's degree in 1992, I did the unthinkable and went back to school. This was something I never thought I would do since I was still nurturing a lot of low self-esteem. Going back to school is one of the best things that ever happened to me. It helped me grow as a person and as a professional and it gave me the confidence I never thought possible. After years of depression and fighting bad memories of the psychiatric institution, I was alive again and I was happy. My epilepsy became irrelevant to the meaning of my life, whereas before it was everything; it had been the center of my life, thus allowing me to indulge in a lot of self-pity for years. It was in the program at Mandel School of Applied Social Sciences, Case Western Reserve University, Cleveland, Ohio, that I met and was befriended by Victor. His was a friendship that would turn into a treasure and lifetime bank account of support, love, affection, and laughter. Victor pushed me and challenged me. He believed in me when I doubted myself. I never knew what I was capable of until then. Together with other students from school, we took two trips to Romania over the course of two years. We trained students and then went to Romania to teach social work as well as work in the children's institutions in order to help revive the social work system, which has not existed since the beginning of communism. Our former dictators believed that Romania did not have any social problems. Following those trips, and based on research we did on Romanian adoptions, Victor and I decided to write a book, incorporating our experiences and stories.

One problem was that neither Victor nor I were writers for a general, non-academic audience. Victor is great at research and talking about his findings. For me, it was more of a language problem. Although I feel my English is good after 13 years of living here, I didn't feel like it was publishing quality. It was after the first draft was completed that we decided to look for a third party: a narrator, an editor. Somehow, Victor met Ivor Irwin, who lived in Chicago, Illinois. After numerous phone conversations with Victor and myself, I was chosen to go meet with Ivor in Chicago so we could talk more about the book, about my experience growing up in Romania, etc. When I got to Chicago, I met Ivor, who was a bundle of energy and asked a million questions. Ivor, too, had an interest in the book, as he too is part Romanian. However, he was born and raised in England. Ivor pushed and asked me questions I didn't have answers to. He kept saying I was in denial or I chose not to know certain things, just like the Germans denied knowing of the Nazi's concentration camps. Ivor is a good writer and I respect him a lot; however, he does not know Romania, having gone there only once or twice for a few weeks doesn't cut it. I disagreed with Ivor's portrayal of Romania. A few Romanians are guilty of many things, such as forming a bad government and the secret police. Perhaps many are guilty of letting these institutions develop. Nevertheless, Romanians, in general, are warm people, who love to play, party, and have a good time. They love their families and take care of their own, unless the government interferes. I tried to talk more about another side of Romania, but I don't think I did it justice. It is a beautiful country, very spiritual, and, yes, about 30 years behind the western world. Such is life. Who's to blame or is anyone to blame? Is it necessarily a bad thing that Romanians don't have credit cards, microwaves, air conditioning, two-ply toilet paper, and sports cars?

I hope you enjoy reading this book and the stories of some families that chose to go to Romania and adopt. Keep an open mind and, if you become interested, read other books. If something is true, there will be a consistency in all the other literature. Truth is not easily distorted.

On My Crusty Old Romanian Grandmother by Ivor Irwin

When I was a kid growing up in Manchester, England, my friends from primary school would like to come by my house after hours of playing football on the street. My grandmother would stuff them with dishes like chopped liver and *sarmale* (stuffed cabbage) and *balmus* and *kreplach* soup and *tocana de miel* and *mamaliga* (corn meal): Her own weird mix of Yiddish/Romanian cooking. Exotic food for bland old England. If she wanted to speak ill of one or more of the kids, she'd speak to me in Yiddish. If she didn't want *me* to understand any of her vindictive gossip, she'd talk to my grandfather in Romanian.

It was weird that she was Romanian. The few other Jews I knew were Galician in background; their food was different; their Yiddish dialect different. "Tell me about Romania," I'd say to the old lady. She usually wouldn't be drawn. I knew bad things had happened there. Still, now and again, after a few glasses of home-made booze—sweet cherry wine or harsh *tzuică*—she'd become either lugubrious or gregariously chatty, in extremis. Names were thrown out—Vlad Tepes, Eugene Ionesco, Magda Lupescu, Ion Antonescu, King Carol, Constantin Brancusi, Octavian Gaga, Mirja Trada, Stephen the Great, Gheorghe Gheorghiu-Dej—and, at least in the case of two of the dictators, they would be preceded by the appellation 'that bastard.' Thus: 'That bastard Antonescu' or '*ca doua bastard Gheorgiou-Dej!*'" (I liked the idea of a 'double bastard.') She told awful World War II atrocity stories about the thousands of Jews the Iron Guard hung alive on meat hooks at the slaughterhouse on Calea Mosilor; the signs around the corpses necks saying 'Kosher meat.'

On other days she'd say Bucharest was the Paris of the east, an island oasis of sensitive civility surrounded on all sides by a vast sea of Slavs, the Teutonic monster race, and 'white Asiatic rubbish' (Hungarians). "Never mind your bloody Picasso," she'd say, "without Brancusi there is no art of value in this century." Years later, I realized that she carried the old country on her back like Quasimodo's hump: You might cut it off, but it would still *feel* like it was there. Strange prejudices and preferences.

I even remember the day the Gypsies, brown people with black patent leather hair, covered in layer after layer of bright-colored clothing, came knocking at the door offering to lay asphalt on our driveway cheap. She cursed them in Romanian. An old lady in a babushka gave her the evil eye and she gave it back.

Everything Romanian was 'the best.' Sculptors, playwrights, architects, poets, dull-witted dictators, secret policemen, brisket: Romania produced them in abundance, then they left. Indeed, the succulent product the brisket makers at the Romanian Kosher Deli in Chicago manufacture seems to be unavailable in the old country. And perhaps it was so. Poor Romania, caught between the hammer and anvil of the Nazis, the Communists, and Islam. Was the Black Sea really black, I wanted to know. Did Vlad Tepes drink blood like Dracula? "No!" she laughed. "But he *would* take big wooden stakes and stuff them up the *tuchises* of Turks and bad little boys." The *real* blood-drinking, it seems, was done by Countess Elizabeth Bathory—Hungarian royalty, of course. Indeed, my grandmother, like a good, typical Romanian, knew well how to hate, and she hated Hungarians with a vengeance.

Years later, 1972, I did my tour of Eastern Europe on the way to Turkey. I stayed with a French-Romanian kid named Sergiu in one of those beautiful luxury flats for foreigners in the Uranus district that later got knocked down in order that the dictator's wife might have her palace. Like Warsaw, it looked like a whole city of dirty, drab, boxy council housing. I met a pretty girl named Violeta at a discotheque with a horrible sound system. Tenacious as a limpet, she came back to Sergiu's with me.

We had a lot of joyless sex for three days and nights and in between our communications in pitiful French she taught me some Romanian. Then, while I was taking a bath, she escaped with all my jeans and t-shirts.

By the time I left Bucharest, my little pseudo-hippie self was happy to go. In the spirit of deténte, Sergiu ended up giving me his ugliest pair of trousers. My embarrassment at wearing polyester as I passed through Bulgaria was sublimely ridiculous. It was all like something out of *Absolutely Fabulous*.

I wasn't really much concerned with any kind of Romanianness until years later at grad school when I became friends with a teacher, Peter Schneeman, who had taught in Bucharest for a year as a Fulbright scholar and had been married to a beautiful Transylvanian German. Ceausescu was the good guy of communism, wasn't he? I asked. The Snowman, a very reserved fellow of great rectitude and laid-backness, was definitely offended. He told me stories about a country where people (artists) were never introduced to each other over a mutual fear of that person being in Securitaté. A lot of grand-guignol anecdotes about a country where there was no heat, no meat, little electricity, etc. At that point, I realized that the whole Western press apparatus was involved in a sort of silent conspiracy to cover up the crimes of Nicolae and Elena Ceausescu.

One gorgeous night in New York City in 1994 I was introduced by a writer friend, Chuck Wachtel, to another writer, Richard Ellman. A pair of crazy Romanians, we drank more than a few—*'Noroc! Noroc! Noroc!'*—and sang *'Romania! Romania!'* Cheers for the splendid Georghe Hagi and Florian Radarescu and the rest of a hugely talented and tenacious Romanian soccer team that could have taken the World Cup back to Bucharest if their defense obsessed coach hadn't been such a gutless worm. Better yet, we compared his mother and my grandmother. They matched anecdotaly, foible for foible, meal for meal. And the way Galicians just don't get it. Drunk, temporarily fanatic, I even called Romania's great poet-in-exile Nina Cassian out on Roosevelt Island. Thank God, she was as lit as I was, and let me have it for making mincemeat of her native language. "You're not Romanian!" she barked. "You don't know *anything* about Romania."

"I've been *in* Romania."

"You may have been *in* many women, dohling. I doubt if you knew many of them."

Anyway, enough with my rambling. What we wrote is information, analysis, stories, and opinion—opinion you can take or leave. Nina Cassian is right; however, compared to some of the 'experts', sociologists and travel writers I've been exposed to over the last few months in my search for the heart of the matter and a 'true' view of Romania, I'm doing okay.

Three Paths Crossed

So, you have three paths which crossed and the product is the book—from the perspectives of an American-Romanian, a Romanian-American, and an English-Romanian-Jew living in the United States. Writing this book, like traveling to Romania, was a difficult task—at times painful, at times frustrating, always taking longer then you'd expect. It's been both fun and exhausting, sometimes making you feel you wanted to get drunk at the first chance, sad, and ever wondering why and about the direction of life. We hope that reading this book will help you understand the many complicated issues in Romania and in Romanian adoptions. It is a collage of information and perspectives woven into stories told in several ways. We hope you found it interesting.

APPENDICES

List of Some U. S. Adoption Agencies Operating in Romania

(Revised December 13, 1996 from State Department Web Site)

ADOPT INTERNATIONAL
121 Springdale Way
Redwood City, CA 94062
Tel: (415) 369-7400
Fax: (415) 369-7300

ADOPTION ASSOCIATES SERVICES
8703 WURZBACH ROAD
San Antonio, TX 78240
Tel: (210) 699-6094

ALASKA INTERNATIONAL ADOPTION
3605 Arctic Blvd., Suite 1177
Anchorage, AK 99503
Tel: (907) 276-8018
Fax: (907) 258-5410

BAL JAGAT
Children's World
9311 Farralone Ave.
Chatsworth, CA 91311
Tel/Fax: (818) 709-4737

BETHANY CHRISTIAN SERVICES
901 Eastern Ave., NE
Grand Rapids, MI 49503-1295
Tel: (616) 459-6273
Fax: (616) 459-0343

CARING CHOICES, INC.
1438 Campbell Road, 104
Houston, TX 77055
Tel: (713) 722-8100

CATHOLIC CHARITIES OF
RICHMOND, INC.
P. O. Box 6565
1512 Willow Lawn Drive
Richmond, VA 23230
Tel: (804) 285-5990

CHILDREN'S FOUNDATION
ADOPTION AND COUNSELING
P. O. Box 338
602 West Amity
Louisburg, KS 66053
Tel: (913) 837-4303
Fax: (913) 837-4309

CHILDREN HOME SOCIETY
OF MINNESOTA
2230 Como Avenue
St. Paul, MN 55108
Tel: (612) 646-6393
Fax: (612) 646-0436

FAMILIES ARE FOREVER
4114 NE Fremont, Suite 1
Portland, OR 97212
Tel: (503) 282-7650
Fax: (503) 282-2852

HOLT INTERNATIONAL CHILDREN'S
SERVICES
P. O. Box 2880
Eugene, OR 97402
Tel: (503) 687-2202
Fax: (503) 683-6175

HOMESTUDIES, INC.
Licensed N. J. Adoption Agency
1182 Teaneck Road
Teaneck, NJ 07666
Tel: (201) 833-9030
Fax: (201) 833-1714

INTERNATIONAL FAMILIES
Licensed Adoption Agency
518 South 12th Street
Philadelphia, PA 19147
Tel: (215) 735-7171
Fax: (215) 545-3563

LIFE ADOPTION SERVICES, INC.
440 West Main Street
Tustin, CA 92680
Tel: (714) 838-5433
Fax: (714) 838-1160

LOS NINOS INTERNATIONAL
ADOPTION CENTER
1600 Lake Front Circle, Suite 130
The Woodlands, TX 77380-2189
Tel: (713) 363-2892

MAINE ADOPTION PLACEMENT
SERVICE MAPS - INTERNATIONAL
One Forest Ave.
Portland, ME 04101
Tel: (207) 775-4101
Fax: (207) 775-1019

M. C. INTERNATIONAL
ADOPTION AGENCY
P. O. Box 7712
Bloomfield Hills, MI 48302-7712
Tel: (810) 258-7167
Fax: (810) 646-6660

NEW HOPE CHILD AND
FAMILY AGENCY
2611 NE 125th St., Suite 146
Seattle, WA 98125
Tel: (206) 363-1800
Fax: (206) 363-0318

RAINBOW HOUSE INTERNATIONAL
19676 Highway 85
Belen, NM 87002-8235
Tel: (505) 861-1234
Fax: (505) 864-8420

SMALL WORLD MINISTRIES
401 Bonnaspring Drive
Hermitage, TN 37076
Tel: (615) 883-4372
Fax: (615) 885-7582

THE ALLIANCE FOR CHILDREN, INC.
40 Williams St., Suite G 80
Wellesley, MA 02181-3902
Tel: (617) 431-7148
Fax: (617) 431-7474

UNIVERSAL AID FOR CHILDREN, INC.
First Union Bank Bldg., 2nd Fl.
1600 S Federal Hwy.
Hollywood, FL 33020
Tel: (954) 925-7550
Fax: (954) 925-6303

VAN DYKE, INC.
ROMANIAN ADOPTION ASSISTANCE
1727 A Stahl Rd., County Trunk KK
Sheboygan, WI 53081
Tel: (414) 452-5358
Fax: (414) 452-5515

WELCOME HOUSE SOCIAL SERVICES
The Pearl S. Buck Foundation
P. O. Box 181
Green Hills Farm
Perkasie, PA 18944-0181
Tel: (215) 249-1516
Fax: (215) 249-9657

WILLIAMS-ILLIEN ADOPTIONS, INC.
3439 Venson Drive
Memphis, TN 38135
Tel: (901) 373-6003
Fax: (901) 373-0130

WORLD ASSOCIATION FOR CHILDREN
AND PARENTS
P. O. Box 88948
Seattle, WA 98138
Tel: (206) 575-4550
Fax: (206) 575-4148

Adoption Resources for Families

Adoption Therapist
House of Tomorrow Productions
4209 McKinney Avenue, Suite 200
Dallas, TX 75205

Child Welfare League of America
440 First Street, NW, Suite 310
Washington, D C 20001-2085

Adoption Quarterly: Innovations in Community and Clinical Practice, Theory and Research
The Haworth Press Inc.
10 Alice Street
Binghamton, NY 13904-7981

Adoption Network
291 East 222 Street
Cleveland, Ohio 44123
216 261-1511

Council for Equal Rights in Adoption
401 East 74th St . Suite 17 D
New York, NY 10021-3919
212 988-0110

National Committee for Adoption
2025 M Street NW Suite 512
Washington, DC 20036
202 463-7559

Evan B Donaldson Adoption Institute
6 East 94th Street
New York, NY 10128
212 360-0283

Adoption Roundtable,
Journal of the National Resource Center for Special Needs Adoption
16250 Northland Dr. Suite 120
Southfield, MI 48075
810 443-7080

American Adoption Congress (AAC)
1000 Connecticut Avenue, NW, #9
Washington, DC 20002
202 483-3399

House of Tomorrow Book Catalogue
4209 McKinney Ave, #200
Dallas, TX 75205
800 944-4460

Tapestry Book Catalogue
PO Box 359
Ringoes, NJ 08551-0359

Adoptee Liberty Movement Association (ALMA)
PO Box 154
Washington Bridge Station
New York, NY 10033
212 581-1568

Adoptive Families of America, Inc.
2309 Como Ave.
St. Paul, MN 55108
651 645-9955

North American Council on Adoptable Children (NACAC)
1821 University Avenue
Suite N 498
St. Paul, MN 55104
612 644-3036

The Adoptive Parents Committee
80 Eighth Avenue
Ste 303
New York, NY 10011

Attach
2775 Willa Creek, #240
Dallas, TX 75234

Parent Support Network for the Post-Institutionalized Child
217 North Wade Avenue
Washington, PA 15301

Selected Books for Children and Families about Romania

Benedek, Dezso, & Spariosu, Mihai I. (1994). <u>Ghosts, vampires, and werewolves: Eerie tales from Transylvania</u>. Illustrated by Laszlo Kubinyi. New York: Orchard Books.

Olson, Arielle North. (1992). <u>Noah's cats and the devil's fire</u>. Illustrated by Barry Moser. New York: Orchard Books.

Matthews, Wendy. (1996). <u>The gift of the traveler</u>. Pictures by Robert Van Nutt. Bridgewater Books.

<u>The enchanted pig, A Romanian fairy tale</u>. (1984). Illustrated by Jacques Tardi. Mankato, Minnesota: Creative Education Inc.

Professional Journals Where the Research Has Been Published

Groza, V., Proctor, C., & Guo, S. (In Press). The relationship of institutionalization to the development of Romanian children adopted internationally. <u>International Journal on Child and Family Welfare.</u>

Groza, V., & Ileana, D. (In Press). International adoption and adoption services. In <u>International Adoption: Challenges and Opportunities</u>. Pittsburg: Parent Support Network for the Post Institutionalized Child.

Groza, V. (1998). Adopted children from Romania: A special focus on Roma (Gypsy) children. <u>International Journal on Child and Family Welfare, 3</u>(1):6-25.

Cermak, S., & Groza, V. (1998). Sensory processing problems in post-institutionalized children: Implications for social work. <u>Child and Adolescent Social Work Journal, 15</u>(1):5-37.

Groza, V. (1997). International adoption. In R.L. Edwards (Ed.). <u>Encyclopedia of Social Work, 19th Edition, 1997 Supplement</u> (pp.1-14). Washington, DC: NASW press.

Groze, V., & Ileana, D. (1996). A follow-up study of adopted children from Romania. <u>Child and Adolescent Social Work Journal, 13</u>(6):541-565.

Johnson, A., & Groze, V. (1993). The orphaned and institutionalized children of Romania. <u>Journal of Emotional and Behavioral Problems, 2</u>(4):49-52.

Organizations Working in Romania that Accept Donations

Most of the adoption agencies listed accept donations. This organization provides other services to Romanian children, not international adoption.

BRIDGES for Children in Romania
P. O. Box 904223
Tulsa, OK 74105

The Peacock

One day, a peacock became restless and decided to go farther away than usual from home and friends. His parents were dismayed. "Why would you want to leave us," cried the mother. "We have such a wonderful life here." "You have no idea how difficult the world can be," boomed the father. His friends thought him odd. "What can be more interesting than our lives here?" questioned his friends. But he was determined. So, he started to fly. Peacocks, by nature, do not fly far at any time—their bodies are so heavy that they only go short distances and then must rest. Many days later, he met a pair of crows. What strange birds they were—so big, so dark, and happily eating some carcass! And they shared the food. The peacock had never seen a bird eat other dead animals. He gazed down sadly at his own skinny body because he hadn't been able to find much food to his liking on the trip. He decided to spread his gorgeous tail, mocking the crows and ridiculing the dark hue of their plumage. He said, "I am robed, like a king, in all the colors of the rainbow; while you have not a bit of color on your wings." "True," replied the crows; "but we soar to the heights of heaven, lift up our voices to the stars, never go without food, and never are alone for very long. Fine feathers don't make fine birds." And with that, the crows flew away, leaving the Peacock to ponder his folly and begin his trip back to his pampered life.

Adapted from an AESOP Fable